CAN I TRUST MY BIBLE?

For additional copies contact:

4459 Highway 17 South
Orange Park, FL 32003
Phone: (904)264-5333
Fax: (904)264-9185
Email: info@thebereanbaptistchurch.com
www.thebereanbaptistchurch.com

CAN I TRUST MY BIBLE?

BY

AL LACY, LITT. D., D.D.

AL LACY PUBLICATIONS
20657 Del Ray Drive
Eckert, CO 81418

Copyright © 1991 by Al Lacy

Second Printing 2008 by Berean Publications

All rights reserved. No part of this book may be reproduced or transmitted in any form or by any means without permission in writing from the publisher.

Published in Orange Park, Florida, by Berean Publications.

Library of Congress Cataloging-in-Publication Data

Lacy, Al
Can I Trust My Bible?/Al Lacy
p. cm.

ISBN 978-0-9771829-3-0

Library of Congress Control Number: 2008927780

Printed and bound in the United States of America.

DEDICATION

This book is humbly and lovingly dedicated to the Almighty triune God (Matt. 28:19) of the universe . . . to my wonderful FATHER who gave us His Words by His Son (Heb. 1:1-2; John 17:8) . . . to my precious SAVIOUR who dictated those Words to the Holy Spirit (John 16:13b) . . . and to the sweet HOLY SPIRIT who moved on the men of old (Heb. 3:7; 4:7; II Pet. 1:21) to speak those Words (Luke 24:25), then write them (Matt. 4:4, 7, 10) in a Book so we could know the Almighty triune God of the universe and spend eternity with Him (John 20:31).

The Author

CONTENTS

FOREWORD ix

I.   CAN I TRUST SATAN? 1

II.   CAN I TRUST THE MODERN JEHOIAKIMS? 29

III. CAN I TRUST MY BIBLE'S TRANSLATION? 107

IV. CAN I TRUST MY BIBLE'S INSPIRATION? 223

V.   CAN I TRUST MY BIBLE'S PRESERVATION? 241

VI. CAN I TRUST MY BIBLE'S AUTHORITY? 263

VII. CAN I TRUST MY BIBLE? 283

FOREWORD

A short time ago, I was preaching a series of meetings on the east coast of the United States. A pastor friend of mine who was starting a new church in a large New Jersey city had asked if I could give him a Sunday morning service when I was in the area. I gladly scheduled him such a service, planning to begin a protracted meeting in another church in a nearby town that evening.

A few days before I was to arrive in New Jersey, my pastor friend called me and said he and his wife had decided to be out of town the Sunday I was to preach for him in the morning service. He had made arrangements for his congregation to meet with a nearby Conservative "Baptist" church for the day, but the pastor of the other church had agreed to have me preach to the combined churches that morning. I am an INDEPENDENT BAPTIST to the very core, and I was quite hesitant about doing so; but my pastor friend pleaded with me to do it, so I told him I would.

When I went to the pulpit that Sunday morning and began to preach, I noticed the people of the Conservative "Baptist" group whispering among themselves while I was reading my text. Fairly soon I began to figure out what the problem was. None of them had the Bible from which I was reading. They all had "bibles" in their hands, but not a one of them had the King James from which I was reading, and from which I was about to preach.

CAN I TRUST MY BIBLE?

Of all things, my sermon that morning was one I call, "The Innocent Bible." The entire message is taken up in showing how the scoffers who despise the AV1611 King James Bible attempt to prove that it is guilty of errors, and I use the Book itself to shoot them down and prove it is innocent of any errors. Needless to say, for about thirty-five minutes, the pastor of the "Conservative" side and all of his people appeared to have the proverbial ants in their "you-know-what"!

When I finished the message and gave the invitation, the pastor and people were glaring at me with blazing, vitriolic eyes. If looks could kill, my wife would have collected on my life insurance that week!

I walked to the vestibule while the pastor was giving a closing prayer. Immediately I had a circle of people around me like red-eyed hounds that had treed a coon. They were waving their various and sundry perverted "bibles" at me, demanding that I apologize for saying the King James was the only real Bible in the English language. I was not about to make such an apology and the debate got hot. The pastor stood aloof, gripping his New International Version while the controversy between his hounds and me proceeded.

While they were shaking seven or eleven different versions in my face and snarling viciously, two big, husky men crowded in, looking even more angry than the rest of the pack. They backed me up against a wall and informed me that I was a troublemaker, and it was men like me that were dividing Christians and hurting the cause of Christ by my bigoted view of the King James Bible. They informed me quite vehemently with their florid faces only inches from mine (Both of them could have used some Scope!) that there was no such thing as a perfect translation and that I was grossly ignorant to make such a bold statement.

While the sweet little pastor stood and watched with a smirk on his puss, I was told by those bad-breathed men that there had

FOREWORD

not been any perfect, infallible Scriptures since the "originals" had disappeared; and that by presuming that I had an infallible Bible in my hands, I was giving evidence that I was both unlearned and uneducated. Both men were quite sure I had purchased my doctor's degrees at K-Mart during a blue-light special. While letting me have it, one of the two men poked his New American Standard in my face repeatedly. The other kept shaking his bible so hard that I could not make out what kind it was.

When they had sufficiently vented out their wrath on me and had given me the tonguelashing that troublemakers like me deserve, they backed off, sucking hard for breath. I smiled sweetly (It's just my nature to be sweet!) and said as I lifted up my double-edged Sword (Heb. 4:12; Eph. 6:17) and held it in front of their faces, "If you boys want to stumble along through life wondering if you or anybody else knows what God said, I'll just stick to this precious old Book and *know* what God said!"

Strange thing. That pastor put me in his car and drove me to the motel where I was staying without hardly a word. The motel did not have a restaurant, and there was not an eating place within reasonable walking distance in any direction. He pulled the car to a stop in front of the motel and gave me a cold look that said, *You can get out, now. So you haven't eaten since yesterday. Tough stuff. That's what you get for being a troublemaker.* I got out. He drove off. I went hungry.

That is just one story. I could go on. I could give you many instances of people actually standing up in services where I was preaching and defending the Book (Whenever I say "the Book," I mean the old fashioned, two-fisted, double-edged, rough, tough, Devil-kicking, Christ-exalting, Heaven-blessed, soul-saving AV 1611 King James Bible!), and screaming at me to shut up. I have been attacked so many times after services that I have lost count of them over the years. Sometimes they won't face me eyeball to eyeball.

CAN I TRUST MY BIBLE?

They will jam a note in my hand as they are leaving the service, or they will write a scathing letter and spend the cost of a stamp to mail it to me.

Let me point out that these are not modernists or Buddhists. These are people who claim to be born again. They will tell you they are saved and on the road to Heaven. And I believe many of them are. But what is happening, here? Why are Bible-believing people like myself coming under such condemnation by those who claim to be born again, Heaven-bound Christians? Why are we who have a Bible in our hands that we know is the very Word of God looked on as troublemakers? Especially when those who shake their perversions in our face do not even claim that what they are shaking is the very Word of God!!!

The answer to these questions is found in three words I just stated . . . *"in our hands."*

As Hamlet said, "Aye, there's the rub!"

In the body of this book, I will be speaking about the modern day Jehoiakims, also known as the Alexandrians. These people will tell you that they believe in a verbally, plenarily, God-inspired, inerrant Bible. They believe in it, but they have never seen it. They believe in it, but they cannot obtain a copy of it. They believe in it, but in no way on God's green earth could they ever hold a copy of it in their hands.

When we who HAVE a perfect, infallible, God-inspired, God-preserved Bible, clasp it between our fingers and say, "I am holding the perfect, infallible, inerrant Word of God IN MY HAND," they look at us like wicked King Ahab of old when he sneered narrowly at Elijah and said, "Art thou he that TROUBLETH Israel?" (I Kings 18:17).

Kinda weird, isn't it? The very people who were troubling Israel were AHAB and those like him! And yet Ahab has the

FOREWORD

unmitigated gall to stand there with his face hanging out and backhandedly accuse Elijah of being a troublemaker! Look at the next verse. You will see that Ahab and his bunch are the REAL troublemakers, and I want you to note WHY they were!

> *And he [Elijah] answered, I have not troubled Israel; but THOU, and thy father's house, in that ye have FORSAKEN THE COMMANDMENTS OF THE LORD, and thou hast followed Baalim* (I Kings 18:18).

As I shall demonstrate in the last chapter of this book, God's *commandments*, when used in a context such as the one above, are the same thing as His WORD . . . the entire sixty-six books of the canon. God's Word is made up of WORDS. According to a recent computer count, the King James Bible has 810,697 words. All of these words put together comprise His *commandments*. The Word of God is called His *commandments* because every word is given with authority, and (as the word signifies) lodged with us as a trust.

Elijah wisely informed wicked old King Ahab that he had FORSAKEN THE COMMANDMENTS OF THE LORD; and that in so doing, he was following Baalim, which was to worship the false god, Baal (I Kings 16:30-31). You may remember that Ahab was married to that vile Jezebel (Shades of Revelation 2:20-23!).

Bring this Ahab thing up to today. There was a time not so many years ago when everyone in the English speaking world except Roman Catholics thought of one Book when anyone mentioned "the Bible"—The AV1611 King James. This was especially so among those who claimed to be born again children of God. There was no question raised about it.

Then . . . at the turn of this century came the American Standard Version, published in 1901. (There had been another in 1884, but it fizzled quicker than a diamondback rattler can move its tongue.)

CAN I TRUST MY BIBLE?

At that time, the Northern Baptists were carrying the blood-stained banner of the cross high. The American Standard Version began to creep into their ranks. They soon sunk into gross modernism. The good old King James was still being preached by those who cared about keeping souls out of Hell while the American Standard Version began to die. The Federal Council of Churches (now known as the National Council) pumped zillions of dollars into the American Standard to save it. The thing rallied for awhile, then finally did us all a favor and expired.

In 1953 the National Council (made up of rank infidels) produced the Revised Standard Version, which blatantly attacked the virgin birth and deity of the Lord Jesus Christ. I can remember that there were independent Baptist churches that bought copies of the Revised Standard Version and burned them publicly in their parking lots to show the world their outrage at the publishing of such a monstrosity that would dare call itself a Bible. While the smoke from the blazing RSVs liked toward the sky, those independent Baptists waved their King James Bibles and sang "Victory in Jesus," "The B-I-B-L-E," and "Get the New Look from the Old Book"!

But something has happened since those good old days. Today among the independent Baptists, (We'll leave the others alone for now.) it's hard to find five out of ten pastors who believe that there exists on earth today an inerrant, infallible Bible that they can hold in their hands. They have linked up with the crowd that believes in an inerrant, infallible, God-breathed "bible" that they have never seen, never will see, can't find a copy of it, and can't hold it in their hand.

It is much safer and popular to belong to that crowd. No one will mock you, call you an uneducated idiot, back you against the wall and shake a book in your face, or stand up in a service and scream at you.

When did this problem start?

FOREWORD

It started exactly twenty years after the National Council of Churches came out with their Revised Standard perversion. In 1973, the Lockman Foundation published their NEW American Standard Version. This so-called "bible" also launched an attack on the virgin birth and the deity of the Lord Jesus Christ, and even went so far as to have Him telling a lie in John chapter seven (Of course since the NASV flat says Joseph fathered Jesus, that makes Him a sinner . . . and sinners DO lie! . . . Rom. 3:4).

But something was different in 1973 than in 1953. Where were the burnings of the New American Standard Version? Aha! The Lockman Foundation had done a clever snow-job on "Christendom." They announced that the translators of their new version were godly, well-respected men in the Christian world (although they never published their names, nor could you find out who they were if you crawled on broken glass and begged!).

Many gullible independent Baptists swallowed the snow-job hook, line and sinker. These "godly" men published their NASV, saying that it was time to bring the Word of God up to date. Christians needed to throw aside the old, worn-out, archaic King James Bible and use a Bible that was written in modern English.

Then . . . along came Kenneth Taylor's "Living Bible." Even the cover is a lie. It is NOT living and it is NOT a Bible! Taylor sold "Christendom" a bill of goods, saying that his "Living Bible" was in modern language and was vastly much easier to understand than that ancient King James Bible. I agree it is in modern language, all right. Some of the language in it is vulgar! But a lot of independent Baptists got caught up in it and are using Taylor's nefarious book.

Then . . . directly on the heels of the New American Standard Version came the New International Version, published by the International Bible society. This one also was produced in order to "put the Word of God in present-day English so people could understand it." Many independent Baptists have been gulled into

CAN I TRUST MY BIBLE?

throwing aside their King James Bibles in preference to the NIV.

Since 1973, I have seen a sharp decline in independent Baptist churches in soulwinning, evangelism, godliness, separation, and zeal for the Word of God. I left the pastorate in 1972 to enter evangelism on a full-time basis and have been at it ever since. I have watched independent Baptist churches deteriorate from vibrant soulwinning lighthouses to dismal social clubs. I could easily list for you seventy-five to a hundred churches where I used to hold meetings on a regular basis, but I am no longer allowed in their pulpits. I have been flat told by many of the pastors, "We don't want your kind of preaching anymore. Our ministry is taking a different direction."

Though I am deeply saddened by this deterioration, I am not surprised by it. God warned us.

> *Now the Spirit speaketh expressly, that in the latter times SOME SHALL DEPART FROM THE FAITH, giving heed to seducing spirits, and doctrines of devils;* (I Tim. 4:1).

And again . . .

> *The time will come when THEY WILL NOT ENDURE SOUND DOCTRINE; but after their own lusts shall they heap to themselves teachers, having itching ears; And they shall turn away their ears from the truth, and shall be turned unto fables* (II Tim. 4:3-4).

And thus we have seen this very thing taking place in front of our eyes among independent Baptist churches. What is it that is causing them to depart from the faith? That question is answered when we realize where our faith comes from:

> *So then FAITH cometh by hearing, and hearing by THE WORD OF GOD* (Rom. 10:17).

The FAITH that saved us and that system of doctrine the

FOREWORD

Bible calls *THE* FAITH has only one source . . . THE WORD OF GOD! When pastors lead their people to "bibles" that are not THE Word of God, or into a position that they "use" the King James Bible but correct it and often quote from perversions, it is not long until they depart from the faith.

When the man in the pulpit confuses the people in the pew by telling them "all the versions are the Word of God, but I prefer the RSV, or the NASV, or the LB, or the NIV" and/or says, "I *use* the King James to preach from, but in my Bible study I also use the other versions," it is not long until the people in the pew will no longer endure sound doctrine. They have been caused by such pastors to turn their ears from the truth (the REAL Word of God) and to turn unto fables (The other versions that are NOT the truth!).

The confusion that is present in the minds of so many men and women in the pews . . . and in the minds of the pastors, themselves, is causing the deterioration I spoke of earlier. I ask you . . . is this confusion of God? Absolutely NOT!

God is NOT the author of CONFUSION! (I Cor. 14:33)

To add to the confusion among independent Baptists (We are still leaving everybody else alone.), the Thomas Nelson Publishing Company came out with the NEW King James Version in 1982. Of course, the reason they gave for producing it was that they had seen the confusion in the churches caused by so many versions on the market (There are about thirty available at the moment.); and in order to clear up the confusion, they wanted everybody to rally around their New King James Version, toss out all the other versions (including the OLD King James), and let their New King James Version become the "standard" bible for "evangelical, fundamental" Christians.

Seems to me if they wanted to remove the confusion, the thing to do is throw away all the versions and get back to the blessed old Book that has been God's infallible, inerrant Word in the English

CAN I TRUST MY BIBLE?

language for nearly four hundred years!

Thomas Nelson's New King James version is no more the New King James than I'm the NEW KING TUT! It has only added to the confusion.

Thank God that all across these United States and in many foreign countries, there are pastors, evangelists, and missionaries who stand for the AV1611 King James Bible. Not only do they use it, but they also BELIEVE it! Within the past few years, many of the pastors for whom I hold meetings on a regular basis have approached me about writing a book in defense of the 1611 Authorized Version in plain, simple language, that they can place in the hands of their people.

One dear pastor called me long distance quite recently and said, "Al, God has given you a gift with words. You can take the most profound truth and make it so the common folks can grasp it. You do it in the pulpit, and you do it when you write. You seem to have a simple mind. How about writing a book, showing in simple terms that God's people have the Word of God in their hands when they hold the precious old King James Bible? Show them that they can trust it implicitly. I need a book like that to place in the hands of my people."

I was not quite sure how to take his statement, "You seem to have a simple mind," but I told him I would make it a matter of earnest prayer. I did, and the Lord has pressed my heart to write this book. I am fully aware that some good books have been written in the defense of the King James Bible, and I thank God for them. Those that I have read, however, are full of technical language concerning the Hebrew and Greek manuscripts as the authors have sought to show that the AV1611 King James Bible was translated from the proper manuscripts and the other versions were not. And this is good . . . *but though preachers and Bible college professors will laboriously wade through hundreds of pages of long and unfamiliar*

FOREWORD

words to glean the facts about manuscripts and all . . . the average "layman" will not.

My purpose, therefore, in setting forth this volume on "Can I Trust My Bible?" is for the common man or woman out there in the pew who is bombarded with all kinds of "bibles" and is wondering which one is the REAL one (if such a Bible exists). We will not delve into the maze of such things as Codex A, B, W; Aleph A, B, D; the Conflate Papers; the Byzantine Readings, or the Complutensian Polyglot of 1514. We will stick with the simpler things such as the fact that we are saved by FAITH (Gal. 3:26), we are sanctified by FAITH (Acts 26:18), our hearts are purified by FAITH (Acts 15:9), we walk through this life by FAITH (II Cor. 5:7), we live by FAITH (Gal. 3:11), Christ dwells in our hearts by FAITH (Eph. 3:17), we obtain God's righteousness by FAITH (Phil. 3:9), we have access into God's grace by FAITH (Rom. 5:2), we are justified by FAITH (Rom. 5:1), we know that God exists by FAITH (Heb. 11:6), we know the universe was created by the Word of God by FAITH (Heb. 11:3), we can only please God by FAITH (Heb. 11:6) . . .therefore we BELIEVE by FAITH that He has given us His written Word in our language so that we can hold it in our hands and READ it (Rev. 1:3), STUDY it (II Tim. 2:15), MEMORIZE it (Psalm 119:11), PREACH it (II Tim. 4:2), DELIGHT in it (Psalm 116:16), MEDITATE in it (Psalm 119:15), REJOICE in it (Psalm 119:14), WALK in it (Psalm 119:1), FOLLOW it (Psalm 119:105), KEEP it (Psalm 119:67), TRUST it, (Psalm 119:42), DEPEND on it (Psalm 119:86), BELIEVE it (John 20:31), and NEVER BE ASHAMED TO HOLD IT UP BEFORE ALL THE SCOFFERS (whoever they are!) AND DECLARE THAT WE ARE HOLDING IN OUR HAND THE INSPIRED, PERFECT, INERRANT, INFALLIBLE, TRUSTWORTHY WORD OF GOD!!!

We know it by FAITH, brethren! By FAITH! And anybody who does NOT believe that God has provided for us in our language

CAN I TRUST MY BIBLE?

the INSPIRED (II Tim. 3:16), PERFECT (Psalm 19:7; James 1:25), INERRANT (Psalm 19:8), INFALLIBLE (Psalm 19:9), and TRUSTWORTHY (Psalm 119:74) *WORD OF GOD* seems to me to have a fairly low opinion of God. The English speaking people have been the *only* people who have been evangelizing this world since the close of the Dark Ages (end of the 16th century). Have they been preaching a false message? Have they not had the very Word of God in their hands as they have gone forth preaching this precious old King James Bible? It is a fact that missionaries have gone into foreign lands all over this globe and translated STRAIGHT OUT OF THE KING JAMES BIBLE to give the people to whom they ministered THE WORD OF GOD in their language. This has been done in over eight hundred languages. Have these missionaries been so foolish as to translate from a Book that is not the very Word of God?

The God I serve is NOT weak and puny, NOR can He lie. By FAITH, I believe that my God is powerful enough to preserve His Word down through the ages (even through translation), and that since He SAID He would preserve it forever (Psalm 12:6-7; Matt. 24:35; I Pet. 1:25), I BELIEVE BY FAITH THAT HE HAS AND WILL!!! For those who do not, that is their problem. *Whatsoever is not of FAITH is SIN* (Rom. 14:23).

So . . . let us proceed. In this volume I will seek to show you what SATAN has done about the Word of God, what unbelieving and confused MEN have done about the Word of God, and what the ALMIGHTY GOD has done about the Word of God. It is my earnest prayer that if my reader has any questions or doubts on the subject at this time, they will all be settled when you have read the last page and closed the book. It is also my earnest prayer that if you already have your faith rock-solid on the AV1611 King James Bible, that this book will strengthen your faith in it even to a greater degree. May the Lord bless you as you read it!

FOREWORD

One word of caution. I have pointed out to you that up until 1973 when the perverted "bibles" began to multiply, those who claimed to be born again, fundamental type Christians were all at least "using" the King James Bible. Things have deteriorated to such a degree today that if you say you BELIEVE it, you are "one who troubleth Israel." You are a cultist and a troublemaker. Just as Elijah pointed out that it was not HE who was the troublemaker, but rather it was Ahab and those who had FORSAKEN the commandments (Word) of the Lord . . . just as it is today.

We who BELIEVE it have not moved. Those who deny it are the ones who have moved, *not us*! So who are the REAL troublemakers? The answer is obvious.

So, dear reader, if you come to the place where you KNOW you can trust your good old King James Bible and are willing to declare it publicly . . . get ready to be scorned as a cultist and a troublemaker. But you are in good company. The Lord Jesus Christ believed He held the very Word of God in His hands when He walked this earth, and yet what He held and preached from was not an "original" piece of parchment, nor was it even in the language in which it had been first written. It was a translation!!! (I will demonstrate this in Chapter 3.) But in spite of the fact that He did not have the "originals" and that He had a translation, He called it "Scripture" and trusted it explicitly. Of course, Jesus was labeled as a troublemaker (Luke 23:2), and a crazy devil-inspired cultist (Matt. 12:24; John 10:20).

Oh, well . . . how does it go? *Sticks and stones may hurt my bones, but words will never harm me.* Let us take our stand on the infallible Word of God and say with David of old:

Thou art my hiding place and my shield: I hope in THY WORD. (Psalm 119:114).

Al Lacy

I
CAN I TRUST SATAN?

It will help us a great deal in our study on the subject of "Can I Trust My Bible?" if we will face the fact that there exists a real, living, wicked, evil, malignant, nefarious, malicious, destructive, pernicious, vile, iniquitous, immoral, rebellious, vicious, corrupt, depraved, perverse, harmful, injurious, malevolent, dirty, God-despising, Christ-loathing, Holy Spirit-abhorring, Bible-hating, Christian-detesting snake-in-the-grass whose name is Satan.

The Lord Jesus said of him:

...He was a murderer from the beginning, and abode not in the truth, because there is no truth in him. When he speaketh a lie, he speaketh of his own; for he is a liar, and the father of it (John 8:44).

You will note that the Lord Jesus said all these things were so of Satan "from the beginning." From *what* beginning? Certainly not from his creation, for God did not create evil, nor did He create the devil (Job 34:10; Psalm 92:15; Rom. 9:14). God created Lucifer and anointed him as a cherub upon the holy mountain of God in Heaven. Lucifer gave birth to sin in his own heart, fell from his exalted position, and *turned himself* into the devil. God said to Satan:

Thou art the anointed cherub that covereth;

CAN I TRUST MY BIBLE?

and I have set thee so: thou wast upon the holy mountain of God; thou hast walked up and down in the midst of the stones of fire. Thou wast perfect in thy ways from the day that thou wast created, TILL INIQUITY WAS FOUND IN THEE . . . thou hast SINNED: therefore I will cast thee as profane out of the mountain of God:" (Ezek. 28:14-16)

And again, God said to Satan:

How art thou fallen from heaven, O Lucifer, son of the morning! . . . For thou hast said IN THINE HEART, I will ascend into heaven, I will exalt my throne above the stars of God: I will sit also upon the mount of the congregation, in the sides of the north: I will ascend above the heights of the clouds; I will be like the most High. Yet thou shalt be brought down to hell, to the sides of the pit, (Isa. 14:12-15).

We learn, then, that when Jesus said, "from the beginning" in John 8:44, He was talking about the day that SIN began in the heart of Lucifer by Lucifer's own will and volition. The creator of sin is the devil!

Let us note that Jesus taught us five things about Satan in John 8:44 that we need to know:

1. Satan was a MURDERER from the beginning.
2. From the beginning, Satan ABODE NOT IN THE TRUTH.
3. From the beginning, THERE HAS BEEN NO TRUTH in Satan.
4. Satan is a LIAR.
5. Satan is the father of a LIE.

I sort of get the idea from the Lord Jesus Christ that the devil

CAN I TRUST SATAN?

is an acid-mouthed LIAR, don't you? Let's look a little further.

> And t*he great dragon was cast out, that old serpent, called the DEVIL, AND SATAN, which DECEIVETH the whole world . . .* (Rev. 12:9).

We are taught five things about Satan, here, that we need to know:

1. He is called the GREAT DRAGON.
2. He is called that OLD SERPENT.
3. He is called the DEVIL.
4. He is called SATAN.
5. He is a DECEIVER.

Let's sum up what we learn here about the great dragon, that old serpent who is called the devil and Satan. It is simple to see that the Lord wants us to get one great big fact straight in our minds. Satan is a deceiving, lying, deviating, underhanded LIAR without one ounce of truth in him!

We can see by Satan's five "I wills" in Isaiah 14:13-14, that he has a burning hatred for the Almighty God. His very desire is to kick God off His throne and become God, himself. Since God IS truth (John 14:6), and since God's Word IS truth (John 17:17) . . . and since Satan is God's enemy, it follows that he is also the enemy of the TRUTH.

Now dear reader, if YOU were the father of a lie, a liar from the beginning, had no truth in you, and were God's avowed enemy, and thus had an unholy hatred for God and His truth . . .wouldn't you launch an attack where it would hurt God the most? Wouldn't you attack His truth? If God spoke to someone His truth, would you not do everything in your power to convince someone that God was lying? Would you not do all you could to get that person to doubt God's veracity and make HIM look like the liar? I mean, if you were

CAN I TRUST MY BIBLE?

the arch-deceiver of the universe and a cold-blood murderer to boot, and you saw an opportunity to murder someone that God loved by deceiving them right into the jaws of death, wouldn't you do it? Hmm? Of course you would! Let's watch!

> *And the LORD God took the man, and put him into the garden of Eden to dress it and to keep it. And the LORD God commanded the man, saying, Of every tree of the garden thou mayest freely eat: But of the tree of the knowledge of good and evil, THOU SHALT NOT EAT OF IT: for in the day that thou eatest thereof THOU SHALT SURELY DIE* (Gen. 2:15-17).

Let us note a couple of facts here. God pronounced both a commandment and a warning. He COMMANDED Adam concerning the tree of the knowledge of good and evil, *"THOU SHALT NOT EAT OF IT!"* He backed up the commandment with a warning. He WARNED Adam that if he defied Him and broke the commandment, *"THOU SHALT SURELY DIE!"*

You can put this down, draw a red circle around it, and put a blue line under it . . . GOD ALWAYS *SAYS* WHAT HE MEANS AND GOD ALWAYS *MEANS* WHAT HE SAYS!!!

After laying out His commandment and His warning to Adam,

> *The LORD God said, It is not good that the man should be alone; I will make an help meet for him* (Gen. 2:18).

Let me point out something here that is really not relevant to what I am discussing, but I think it is important enough to mention. If you will read Genesis chapter one through, you will see in His six days of creating and renovating work, SEVEN times God looked at it and saw that it was good (Gen. 1:4, 10, 12, 18, 21, 25, 31). Has my reader ever noticed the first time God ever said something was NOT good? It is in the verse I just quoted. God said, *"It is NOT good that the man should be alone."*

Do you see how important a WIFE is in the eyes of God? In Proverbs 18:22, He says, *"Whoso findeth a wife findeth a GOOD THING, and obtaineth favour of the LORD."*

It is also notable that God said of the man, *"I will make an HELP meet for him."* I have seen preachers and theologians hyphenate the two words "help" and "meet," making it "help-meet." I have also seen them go to "helpmate," making it one word. You will note that God did not say He would make Adam a "help-meet," nor did He say He would make him a "helpmate." This is why it is so absolutely important that we have a Bible where we know God has preserved EVERY WORD for us (as we shall discuss in later chapters). When we make the Bible something different than God actually said, we miss the truth. God said here, *"I will make an HELP meet for him."*

You don't have to chase down a scholar in the Hebrew language to get the truth of this. All it takes is a good English dictionary. The word "help" in Genesis 2:18 is a noun. The word "meet" is an adjective. I have before me Webster's New World Dictionary of the English language. Looking up the word "help" as a noun, I find the definition: *"one who helps another."* The definition of "meet" as an adjective is "suitable." The definition of "suitable": *"that which fulfills or completes a given purpose."*

Thus we learn that God made Eve for Adam because he needed a helper to complete him! A man is not complete without a WIFE! No wonder God said when a man finds a wife he finds a GOOD thing! The poor guy is incomplete without her!

See what you miss when some "theologian" tampers with God's words? Hyphenate "help meet" or ram them together into

CAN I TRUST MY BIBLE?

"helpmate" and you miss the truth of what God was actually saying! Pooey on the "scholars" and the "theologians"! The only helps you need to understand your good old King James Bible are the Holy Spirit (John 16:13a; I Cor. 2:12-13), a normal brain, some common "horse sense," and a good English dictionary.

Let's see, now . . . where were we? Oh, yes! God has pronounced both a COMMANDMENT and a WARNING to Adam. *"Thou shalt NOT eat of it!" "Thou shalt surely DIE!"*

I would have you notice that God had SPOKEN these words in chapter two. Chapter three opens up with these three words: *"Now the SERPENT . . .* Do you see it? God SPEAKS and the devil shows up! Let's look at the narrative:

> *Now the serpent was more subtil than any beast of the field which the LORD God had made. And he said unto the woman, Yea, HATH GOD SAID, Ye shall not eat of EVERY tree of the garden? And the woman said unto the serpent, We may eat of the fruit of the trees of the garden: But of the fruit of the tree which is in the midst of the garden, God hath said, Ye shall not eat of it, neither shall ye touch it, lest ye die. And the serpent said unto the woman, Ye shall NOT surely die: For God doth know that in the day ye eat thereof, then your eyes shall be opened, and YE SHALL BE AS GODS, knowing good and evil* (Gen. 3:1-5).

Yes, sir! God speaks the truth and the father of a lie sticks up his ugly head! I want my reader to please note that THE VERY FIRST APPROACH SATAN EVER MADE TO THE HUMAN RACE WAS TO THROW A DOUBT ON WHAT GOD HAD SAID!!!!!!!!!!!!!!!

Remember . . . Satan is a DECEIVER! He is a LIAR! From the beginning there has been no truth in him, and he has not abode in the truth!

CAN I TRUST SATAN?

"Now the SERPENT..." Just read those three words and you know something sinister and evil is about to unfold. The plot thickens when the narrative adds, *"Now the serpent was... SUBTIL..."*

When you are the father of a lie and the arch-liar of the universe all wrapped up into one wicked, evil, malignant being, you most definitely are going to be subtil! Webster's definition of subtil (which today is spelled *subtle*) is: "mentally keen:" "delicately skillful;" "crafty;" "not obvious."

The Word of God hit the nail right smack on the head, eh? God's choice of words is always right on target! If you will take exactly what God says in the Bible about the devil, you will know exactly how the old boy works! *"... we are not ignorant of his devices"* (II Cor. 2:11).

God says Satan is *mentally* keen. You better believe it! Don't ever for one minute let yourself think that Satan is dumb! He is plenty smart! He is mentally keen! He is subtle!

God says Satan is *delicately skillful*. He is a furtive, clandestine, sneaky, underhanded liar! He is also a murderer! God tells us that dirty devil is delicately skillful at lying and murdering! Don't ever underestimate him! He is subtle!

God says Satan is *crafty*. Webster says "crafty" means *sly* or *cunningly deceitful*. It just keeps surfacing, doesn't it? The devil is a lowdown sneaky deceiver! He is subtle!

God says Satan is *not obvious*. Webster says when you are obvious, you are "evident; easy to see and understand." When you are subtle, you are NOT obvious. What you really are is NOT EVIDENT . . . you are NOT SEEN AND UNDERSTOOD FOR WHAT YOU REALLY ARE!

What a perfect description of that old lying, deceitful, designing, fraudulent, deceptive, tricky, wily, hypocritical, double-dealing, treacherous, delusive, false-fronted, two-faced murderous

CAN I TRUST MY BIBLE?

roaring lion who appears to gullible human beings as an angel of light (II Cor. 11:14; I Pet. 5:8)!

Satan's very first attack on the human race was to question WHAT GOD SAID! We are not ignorant of his devices. The old snake-in-the-grass is STILL putting a question mark over the Word of God! The sad thing is that so many religious people AND saved people cannot see the devil at work in this controversy over the King James Bible and the false "bibles" today. Satan has so many "scholars," "theologians," college professors, Sunday School teachers, pastors, missionaries, evangelists and "laymen" duped with the idea that there is no perfect Word of God today in any language! He is STILL at it! *"Hath GOD said?"*

God said He would preserve EVERY WORD of His Word FOREVER!

The WORDS of the Lord are pure WORDS: as silver tried in a furnace of earth, purified seven times. Thou shalt KEEP THEM, O Lord, thou shalt PRESERVE THEM from this generation FOR EVER (Psalm 12:6-7).

Yet as we shall see in the next chapter, we have leading "fundamentalist" pastors, professors, evangelists, and educators who are telling us that there has been no perfect, infallible, inerrant, inspired Word of God since the "original manuscripts" got old, cracked, peeled, crumbled, and finally disintegrated with age. They flat say that we DO NOT HAVE God's words today in ANY LANGUAGE.

Yea, *hath* God *said* He would KEEP and PRESERVE His words FOREVER? A blind bat without a seeing-eye dog could catch on to who is behind this false teaching!

Jesus Christ is God. The words that comprise the Word of God are HIS words. Listen to Him:

CAN I TRUST SATAN?

Heaven and earth shall pass away, but MY WORDS SHALL NOT PASS AWAY (Matt 24:35).

Yea, *hath* God *said* heaven and earth would pass away, but HIS WORDS would NOT pass away? When men stand in pulpits, in classrooms, or write in letters and books that there is no Word of God today because the "original autographs" were the only inspired Word of God, a deaf man with his eyes shut could pick up the hiss of the serpent!

Who would want you to believe that God lied when He plainly stated that He would preserve His WORDS forever? Who would want you to believe that Jesus was defrauding us when He said heaven and earth would pass away, but His WORDS would NOT pass away? Huh? Who? C'mon! You KNOW who! That old lying, deceitful snake-in-the-grass!

Many of these "fundamentalist" leaders will tell us that even though God lied and has not preserved and kept His WORDS, we do at least have the "message" or the "content of the message" or the "ideas" that were set forth in the "originals." THERE IS NOT ONE SCRAP OF SCRIPTURE FOR SUCH TOMMYROT! God said His WORDS would be kept and preserved forever. Jesus said His WORDS would not pass away. In fact, He even got more particular than that. Listen to Him:

For verily I say unto you, Till heaven and earth pass, one JOT or one TITTLE shall in no wise pass from the law, till all be fulfilled (Matt. 5:18).

Yea, *hath* God *said* not ONE JOT or ONE TITTLE would pass from His Word? Satan is the liar. Satan is the deceiver. He wants us to believe the mouths of those who tell us we do not have God's WORDS today.

In the passage in Genesis chapter three, did you notice Satan's exact words when he threw the doubts at Eve? Look at it again.

CAN I TRUST MY BIBLE?

> *... Yea, hath God said, Ye shall not eat of EVERY Tree of the garden?* (Gen. 3:1)

It sort of reminds us of the old Dragnet program. I can almost hear Sergeant Joe Friday saying, "Now, just give me the facts, ma'am. There's just one thing that I'm not quite clear on, I want to be sure I have the facts down correct. Did God actually get so persnickety as to tell you that you couldn't eat of EVERY tree in the garden? I mean, are you absolutely positive God is that careful about EVERY word He speaks? What I'm trying to say here, ma'am, is since God's original language is a heavenly language, and you are an earthly being, that when God translated it so you could get it in your language . . . maybe you lost some of what He said in the translation! Couldn't that be a fact, ma'am?"

DUM-TA-DUM-DUM.

Today that old deceitful snake-in-the-grass is saying, "Now, come on! You don't really think God is that particular about EVERY Word He speaks, do you? I mean, you don't really believe that even if He IS that particular, He is wise enough, strong enough, determined enough, and powerful enough to preserve EVERY word and even put it in English and have EVERY word exactly like He wants you to have it! You don't REALLY believe that, do you? Why, think of all the great godly, educated, intelligent, wonderful Christian men who don't believe that! You are wrong, Bible-believer! Wrong, I tell you! Dead wrong!"

Let me ask you something right here, dear reader . . . WHO is the liar? WHO is the deceiver? WHO is the father of a lie? WHO wants you to believe that God storied to you when He said He would preserve and keep every word forever? WHO wants you to think that you cannot get your hands on a real, genuine copy of the perfect, infallible, inerrant Word of God? We are not ignorant of Satan's devices. If he attacked Eve with doubts as to God's veracity, will he not do the same to *you*? If he attempted to make Eve believe

CAN I TRUST SATAN?

that God's Word has flaws in it, don't you think he will do the same to *you*?

How utterly sad that Eve believed the devil instead of believing God! God said, *"Thou shalt surely die!"* The devil said, *"Ye shall NOT surely die!"*

Have you noticed that when the devil put the question to Eve, she did not quote God exactly in her answer? God had told Adam:

> . . . *in the day that thou eatest thereof thou shalt SURELY DIE* (Gen. 2:17).

Eve's answer was:

> . . . *We may eat of the fruit of the trees of the garden: But of the fruit of the tree which is in the midst of the garden, God hath said, Ye shall not eat of it, neither shall ye touch it, lest ye die* (Gen. 3:2-3).

Now, I take exception to some preachers, teachers, professors, and expositors who snarl at Eve here, and say that she deliberately misquoted God. If she had done so, THAT would have been her initial transgression to make her a sinner. But the Scripture says, *"The woman BEING DECEIVED was in the transgression"* (I Tim. 2:14).

When Eve misquoted God, she had not yet been deceived. Eve's misquote is in verse 3. The deceit did not come until verse 4 and verse 5. There was no transgression UNTIL AFTER she had been deceived.

Mother Eve has enough guilt on her. Please don't heap any more on her than she deserves. Eve had not been made yet when God spoke the commandment and the warning to Adam. She had gotten it second-hand from him. Don't slap her face for not getting it quite right.

CAN I TRUST MY BIBLE?

My point in bringing it up is that when Satan answered Eve after her misquote, he used the same phraseology God did. Look at it.

... *thou shalt SURELY DIE* (Gen. 2:17).

... *Ye shall not SURELY DIE* (Gen. 3:4).

See what I mean about that old serpent? He's sneaky! He had been slithering around in the grass eavesdropping on God and Adam's conversation in the garden the day God gave Adam the commandment and the warning.

And don't think he doesn't eavesdrop today when the Bible-doubting "fundamentalists" get together and search out the "mistakes" in the King James Bible, so they can get real Bible believers in a "corner" and hiss at them, "Yea, hath God said?" The devil LOVES to be quoted, and he LOVES to see "fundamental" leaders throw his age-old question in the faces of "poor ignorant, uneducated, backwoodsy" Bible believers. Actually what this is, is *humanism* in its most subtle form. These "fundamentalists" who believe God gave the "originals" then backed off and turned His Word over to MAN, so we have no inerrant, perfect Word of God today . . . are nothing short of HUMANISTS. They will decry my statement and vehemently deny it, but they are still HUMANISTS, no matter how loudly they deny it. Humanism began in the garden of Eden at the mouth of the devil, and those who echo his words are HUMANISTS.

I have heard it said that the religion of humanism began with the ancient philosopher Protagoras who invented the famous saying: *Homo Neusura*—Man, the Measure. Man is the Measure of all things. He is Supreme. He is All. He is the Ultimate. There is none higher.

No, the irony of it all is that humanism did not begin with Protagoras. It began with the serpent in the garden who hissed,

CAN I TRUST SATAN?

"... *hath God said, Ye shall not eat of EVERY tree in the garden?...*" then followed with *"Ye shall NOT surely die: For God doth know that in the day ye eat thereof, then your eyes shall be opened, and YE SHALL BE AS GODS..."* (Gen. 3:1, 4-5).

Satan is subtly trying to counteract a word that God used when He gave the warning and the commandment to Adam. The word: *freely*.

> *And the Lord God commanded the man, saying, Of every tree of the garden thou mayest FREELY eat: But of the tree of the knowledge of good and evil, thou shalt not eat of it: for in the day that thou eatest thereof thou shalt surely die.* (Gen. 2:16-17)

When Satan told Eve she and Adam would become as gods if they ate of the forbidden tree, he was saying in essence, "Listen to me, Eve. God said you could FREELY eat of all the trees in the garden, then He immediately put a restriction on your freedom by denying you ONE tree. Can't you see what God is doing? He's LYING to you, Eve! He uses the word *freely*, then turns around and takes away your freedom. God is lying to you because He doesn't want you to become a god! He knows if you eat of the forbidden tree, YOU will become a god, and you will be FREE like He is! All you have to do is eat the fruit and YOU will be deity!"

Humanists zealously maintain that unless man is utterly and completely autonomous, he is not free. If he has any restrictions placed upon him, or has any higher power to which he is morally responsible, he is not free. Do you see where they got the idea? From their devil daddy!

Satan's humanist children use the "freedom" idea to prove to themselves that there is no God. They say since we have proof that man exists, but no proof that God exists, there is no God. Since man IS, God CANNOT BE because intrinsic to their notion of humanity is the concept of human subjectivity and freedom. They say if there

CAN I TRUST MY BIBLE?

is a Supreme Being to whom man is ultimately responsible and accountable, a Creator who has sovereignty over us, then we do not have autonomy. If we do not have autonomy, we do not have freedom. If we do not have freedom, we do not have subjectivity. If we do not have subjectivity, we do not have humanity. Humanists argue that since they have never laid eyes on some all-powerful figure somewhere in the sky who holds a club in his hand and lays down certain restrictions, man DOES have autonomy, freedom, and subjectivity. Therefore, God does not exist.

Of course, in the garden of Eden, Satan knew he could not convince Eve that God did not exist since she had been made and brought to Adam by God, Himself (Gen. 2:22) . . . so he went to work to implant in Eve's mind the humanist philosophy that unless you are utterly and completely free, you have no freedom at all. Eve, then, is urged to throw off God's restrictions, take the fruit, and become a god, herself. Adam and Eve, as humans, could become gods, themselves, and God would have no authority over them. Thus we have the irony of ironies. The father of humanism was not even human. He is the devil.

When men reject the idea that there exists a perfect, infallible Book on the earth today, saying that only the originals were perfect and infallible, what they really desire is to be gods themselves. Since there is no Book that is the very Word of God today, THEY become the authority. THEY are free to "correct" the Book that they teach and preach from, which gives THEM authority over the Book, rather than the Book having authority over them. They can deny it all they want to, but they are employing the principles of devil-inspired humanism!

The Bible correctors will deny it, but the hiss of the serpent is in their entire approach. *"Yea, hath God said, Ye shall not eat of EVERY tree of the garden? . . . Yea, hath God said He would Preserve EVERY word?"* Yes, Mr. humanist Bible corrector, He DID say He

CAN I TRUST SATAN?

would preserve EVERY word forever!

> *The WORDS of the Lord are pure WORDS: as silver tried in a furnace of earth, purified seven times. Thou shalt KEEP THEM, O Lord, thou shalt PRESERVE THEM from this generation FOR EVER* (Psalm 12:6-7).
>
> *Heaven and earth shall pass away, but MY WORDS SHALL NOT PASS AWAY* (Matt. 24:35).

It is amazing to me that men who claim to be saved and washed in the blood of the Lamb cannot seem to see that Satan is out to put doubts in people's minds as to God's *veracity* when He said He would preserve EVERY WORD forever . . . and to make us wonder as to His *capability* to do so. I have listened to debates on the King James Bible issue, and I have been in countless confrontations with Bible correctors. NEVER have I heard them say or intimate that there is a devil who is out to discredit the Word of God . . . NEVER! NOT ONE TIME have I ever heard a Bible corrector even mention Satan in connection with the confusion that is being caused by all the "versions" on the market. They seem utterly BLIND to the fact that Satan's very first approach to the human race was to discredit the Word of God . . . to put in question what God had said.

Paul told us in II Corinthians 2:11 that we are not ignorant of Satan's devices . . . but I'm afraid the Bible correctors are TOTALLY ignorant of Satan's devices. They cannot see the devil's hand in this conflict over the King James Bible versus all the perversions. They are absolutely oblivious to Satan's devices. The only "devils" they see are those of us who believe that God HAS preserved every word like He said He would do . . . and that He was ABLE to get it into the English language.

It is beyond me why they cannot see that Satan is a deceiver and a liar . . . and that being a deceiver and a liar, he is naturally a COUNTERFEITER. The Bible correctors will readily admit that

CAN I TRUST MY BIBLE?

Satan has a counterfeit CHRIST (II Thes. 2:3-4, 7-9; I John 4:3). They will not deny that Satan has a counterfeit TRINITY (Rev. 20:10). They will agree that Satan has a counterfeit CHURCH (Rev. 13:8a; 17:1-6). They will not argue that Satan has counterfeit MINISTERS (II Cor. 11:13-15) who preach a counterfeit GOSPEL about a counterfeit JESUS, by a counterfeit SPIRIT (II Cor. 11:3-4) . . . but they are stone blind to the fact that the same devil has also used counterfeit scholars to produce counterfeit "BIBLES"!!! Since Satan has most definitely produced all these counterfeits (and many others I have not taken space to mention), why is it so hard to believe that the dirty old devil has done all he could to cloud the truth by producing COUNTERFEIT bibles??? Satan has already clearly demonstrated WAY BACK IN THE BEGINNING that he desires to blind people's minds as to WHAT GOD SAID. Only a blind fool would say he is not still at it!

We find Satan at his trade in the first book of the Old Testament, and we find him at it again in the first book of the New Testament.

> *Then was Jesus led up of the Spirit into the wilderness to be tempted of the devil. And when he had fasted forty days and forty nights, he was afterward an hungred. And when the tempter came to him, he said, If thou be the Son of God, command that these stones be made bread. But he answered and said, It is written, Man shall not live by bread alone, but by every word that proceedeth out of the mouth of God. Then the devil taketh him up into the holy city, and setteth him on a pinnacle of the temple, And saith unto him, If thou be the Son of God, cast thyself down: for it is written, He shall give His angels charge concerning thee: and in their hands they shall bear thee up, lest at any time thou dash thy foot against a stone.*

CAN I TRUST SATAN?

Jesus said unto him, It is written again, Thou shalt not tempt the Lord thy God. Again, the devil taketh him up into an exceeding high mountain, and sheweth him all the kingdoms of the world, and the glory of them; And saith unto him, All these things will I give thee, if thou wilt fall down and worship me. Then saith Jesus unto him, Get thee hence, Satan: for it is written, Thou shalt worship the Lord thy God, and him only shalt thou serve. Then the devil leaveth him, and, behold, angels came and ministered unto him (Matt. 4:1-11).

Now let us learn from the passage of Scripture that we have just read.

You will note that the devil came to Jesus when He was ALONE as he had done with Eve. If Adam had been there when the devil began to tempt Eve, certainly the narrative would have said so, and we would have had some input from Adam. Satan knew the best time to get Eve to fall was when she was alone.

When we are put to a test in public, it is less difficult to compromise. Others will see what we do. But when we are alone, we are more vulnerable to do wrong. So like with Eve, the devil came to Jesus when He was ALONE.

I pointed out earlier that God had just SPOKEN when we read, *"Now the serpent . . ."* (See Genesis 2:16-17 Cf. Genesis 3:1). It happened the same way with Jesus' temptation in the wilderness. The last verse in Matthew chapter three says: *"And lo a voice from heaven, saying, This is My beloved Son, in whom I am well pleased."* Matthew 4:3 says:

And when the tempter came to him, he said, IF thou be the Son of God . . .

Do you see the devil's tactic? God had just spoken and said,

17

CAN I TRUST MY BIBLE?

"THIS IS MY BELOVED SON." The dirty devil hastens to the wilderness and hisses, *"IF* thou be the Son of God . . ."

Immediately Satan casts doubt on what GOD SAID! There's his subtlety again! When will "fundamentalist" wake up to the fact that Satan has never changed his tactics? When will they realize that behind this smoke screen of "only the originals were the inspired Word of God and we don't have a perfect Bible today" . . . is a subtle, conniving, deceitful snake-in-the-grass who is casting doubt on what GOD SAID when He stated that He would preserve His words FOREVER???

Anyone who thinks Satan is not still at it today, and that ALL the versions are the Word of God (which I have been told by people who should know better!) has fallen into the devil's trap! He is producing counterfeit bibles right under your nose, and you are too blind to see it! Wake up! If you are ignorant of Satan's devices, it is because you are WILLINGLY ignorant. Read the real Bible, and see it for yourself!

And so like with Eve in the garden, the devil suggests to Jesus that when God had spoken, what He said was not altogether true. *"IF Thou be the Son of God . . ."*

However . . . Jesus responded differently than Eve. He replied, *"It is WRITTEN, Man shall not live by bread alone, but by EVERY WORD that proceedeth out of the mouth of God"* (Matt. 4:4).

Do you see why the devil has a burr under his saddle about God's EVERY WORD doctrine today? The Lord Jesus flung it in his smuddy face in the wilderness. He has hated the idea ever since. So what does the devil do? He comes in the latter part of the twentieth century and whispers to "fundamental" scholars, teachers, college professors, pastors, evangelists, and missionaries and says, "Hath God said, Man shall not live by EVERY WORD that proceedeth out of the mouth of God?" The sad thing is, they listen to him and

CAN I TRUST SATAN?

proclaim that God has NOT preserved EVERY WORD that has been written from His mouth. He has only preserved the message, or the concepts, or the content, or the thoughts.

The devil is a LIAR and a DECEIVER and a COUNTERFEITER! He has the bulk of present-day "fundamentalists" thinking and talking the same way about the Authorized Version of 1611 that the modernists, liberals and cults were doing twenty, thirty, forty, fifty, and a hundred years ago. They have joined ranks with that ungodly crowd and are too blind to see it!

Does man have EVERY WORD to live by today, or does he not? When Jesus spoke, He was quoting from the book of Deuteronomy, which had been written by Moses about 1600 years previously. Certainly no one is going to tell me that the "originals" were still around. By that time, what they had were copies of copies of copies of copies of copies of copies of copies of copies of copies. Yet Jesus did not say, *"It WAS written."* He said, *"It IS written!"* The originals were long gone, but still the perfect Word of God was available for man to live by!

God had hovered over those scribes and made sure they copied every word, letter jot and tittle correctly (Matt. 5:18). Of course, the devil is a counterfeiter, so he made plans to come up with some manuscripts that were corrupt in order to produce his counterfeit bibles a little later in time. But the modern-day Jehoiakims, also known as the "Alexandrians," which we will deal with in the next chapter, are too blind and intelligent to see the devil at work in these areas. They are suckered in by the devil with his corrupt manuscripts that he kept preserved in Alexandria, Egypt for centuries and then brought into light at just the right time. Since GOD has preserved HIS pure manuscripts, Satan is not to be outdone. HE has preserved his impure manuscripts.

The Alexandrians do not claim the manuscripts Satan has preserved are without error, but they say they are much better than

CAN I TRUST MY BIBLE?

God's manuscripts. From God's pure manuscripts came the AV 1611 King James Bible. All the others come from the devil's impure manuscripts. Since you cannot get a pure thing out of an impure thing (Luke 6:43), the NIV, the NASV, the "Living Bible," the "New" King James, etc., etc., are corrupt because they came from Satan's preserved Alexandrian manuscripts. Hence, the King James Bible is the pure, perfect, infallible, inerrant Word of God in the English language. The Alexandrians (Bible correctors) disagree, of course. Satan has done a snow job on them, and they can't see it. Of course, they don't WANT to see it. If they came to the place where they admitted God had preserved His Word in the English language and that He did it in the year 1611, they couldn't be gods anymore, having authority over the Book.

Recently, I read an article by a Bible-correcting Alexandrian. He said in his article: "Now I suspect that if God, in this day, opened up the heavens and spoke to us directly and said, *'This Book* (the King James Bible) *is the inerrant Word of God,'* the debates would be over, and we would all believe it." And I say BALONEY!!! The debates would NOT be over, and everybody would NOT believe it! The Bible-correctors would not sit still for it. They would have to stand before their classes and congregations and admit they have been wrong . . . and that would split their gall bladders! They could not play god any more and say, "The King James Bible is incorrect here . . ." and "This is a poor rendering, here. The original says . . ." and "A better translation would be . . ." and "This passage right here is a spurious one. It is not in the better manuscripts, etc."

No longer could they be like Catholic priests and lord it over those poor ignoramuses in the classroom and in the pews by showing off their superior intelligence and scholarship because they are adept in the Hebrew and the Greek. Don't you think for a minute that they would give up being gods just because the God of Heaven thundered out in an audible voice and told them the AV1611 King

CAN I TRUST SATAN?

James Bible is His inerrant Word in the English language! Not on your life! They would go right on calling those of us who believe we hold the infallible, inerrant Word of God in our hands troublemakers and uneducated, backwoods stumblebums. They would still refer to the *originals* that none of them have ever laid eyes on and claim that since the *originals* are gone, there is not any infallible, inerrant Word of God on the face of the earth today. They would still insist on having authority over the Book, and bow their necks against the Book having authority over them!

My reader might say, "But Brother Lacy, I don't understand. How can the Alexandrians say that the only infallible, inerrant Word of God was the original manuscripts, but since we don't have them, there is no infallible, inerrant Word of God on earth today . . . then correct my King James Bible by referring to the original Hebrew and Greek? It sounds like a bunch of double talk to me." Hey! You're catching on!

God flat speaks and says of Jesus, *". . . THIS IS MY BELOVED SON . . ."* (Matt. 3:17), and Satan rushes up to Jesus and says, *"IF* thou be the Son of God." The Bible correctors are just like the devil. No matter what God says, they question it.

Let's move on with the narrative of the temptation in the wilderness. When the Lord Jesus hit Satan with "It is written . . ." the devil says in essence, "Okay, Jesus, let's go into Jerusalem and climb up on a pinnacle of the temple. You have come back at me with this 'It is written' stuff. I've got something to say to You."

> *Then the devil taketh him up into the holy city, and setteth him on a pinnacle of the temple, And saith unto him, IF thou be the Son of God cast thyself down: for IT IS WRITTEN, He shall give his angels charge concerning thee: and in their hands they shall bear thee up, lest at any time thou dash thy foot against a stone* (Matt. 4:5-6).

CAN I TRUST MY BIBLE?

Scripture, hence, exposes Satan's manner of dealing with the Word of God. Watch very carefully now, and you will see that the Alexandrians treat Scripture EXACTLY like Satan does. Satan said, "It is written" . . . then quoted Psalm 91:11-12. But something is awry. Look at it.

For he shall give his angels charge over thee, to keep thee in all thy ways. They shall bear thee up in their hands, lest thou dash thy foot against a stone (Psalm 91:11-12).

My reader will note that Satan MISquoted the passage by LEAVING OUT WORDS and ADDING WORDS. In so doing, he TWISTED THE MEANING of the passage.

In MISquoting Psalm 91:11, the devil left out, *"to keep thee in all thy ways."* In MISquoting Psalm 91:12, he added, *"lest at any time."*

By LEAVING OUT "To keep thee in all thy ways," Satan is hoping to make Jesus forget that His ways must coincide with the Father's ways (John 8:29; Heb. 10:7). It was the will of the Father that Jesus die on the cross . . . not on the pavement below the high pinnacle of the temple. If Jesus listened to Satan's MISquotation of the Scripture and took the fatal leap, there would be no Calvary . . . no cross . . . no salvation for sinners. Jesus would be in direct disobedience to the Father by jumping from the pinnacle of the temple. His ways would not coincide with the Father's ways, and the Father would be under no obligation to take care of Him.

By ADDING "lest at any time," Satan is trying to convince Jesus that He would have the angels' protection for any move He made at ANY TIME, no matter what the circumstances . . . even taking a foolish leap off the pinnacle. By TAKING AWAY FROM and ADDING TO the Scripture, the devil TWISTED its meaning saying that Jesus had the full right to tempt His Father by casting

CAN I TRUST SATAN?

Himself toward the pavement below, and that the Father would see to it that He was caught by the angels before He hit bottom.

The Lord came back with, "IT IS WRITTEN again, Thou shalt not tempt the Lord thy God." Now what is Jesus saying, here? Is He thrusting His deity at the devil and telling him he should not tempt Him because He is God? He certainly could do that because He is God, but it seems to me if that is what He meant, He would have hit Satan with this Scripture right off the bat when Satan tempted Him with turning the stones into bread.

What Jesus is saying, here, is something like this: "God has said, as you have pointed out, Satan, that He will give His angels charge over Me. Now at the present time, I can look all around the temple from up here, and I cannot see one angel anywhere. So you want Me to test God and see if He really meant what He said about those angels. You want Me to jump off this pinnacle and see if the angels are suddenly dispatched from Heaven to catch Me in their hands before I hit the pavement below. Well, there is something you don't understand, devil. What is going on here is not a test of God, but a test of ME!

"As the Son of God, I am human, Satan. As the human Son of God, I am being tested to see if I will do right in the face of your subtle temptation while you add to and take away from the Word of God and twist its meaning. I have no right to turn the test around and put it on My Father's shoulders. Why should He be put to the test? HE never violates His covenant. He never breaks His Word. The Scripture cannot be broken. The question of loyalty, here, is not My Father's, but MINE. I am the one who is to be tempted, not My Father. It is written, *Thou shalt not tempt the Lord thy God!*"

As we shall see in chapter 3 of this book, the Alexandrian Bible collectors both TAKE AWAY FROM and ADD TO the Word of God; and by so doing, TWIST its meaning. They copy Satan's tactics to the letter.

CAN I TRUST MY BIBLE?

Let's follow the narrative further.

Again, the devil taketh him up into an exceeding high mountain, and sheweth him all the kingdoms of the world, and the glory of them; And saith unto him, All these things will I give thee, if thou wilt fall down and worship me. Then saith Jesus unto him, Get thee hence, Satan: for IT IS WRITTEN, Thou shalt worship the Lord thy God, and him only shalt thou serve. Then the devil leaveth him, and, behold, angels came and ministered unto him (Matt.4:8-11).

One thing you've got to say for that dirty devil . . . he IS persistent. Not being easily discouraged, he tries another angle. He takes God's only begotten Son up on top of a high mountain. In essence, he says, "Look, Jesus. Do You see all those kingdoms out there in the world? Now, I know Your Father has promised to give them all to You. But in order to get them, You will have to walk the *via dolorosa*. You will have to be crucified and die first. Before You can have the crown by Your Father's plan, You will first have to endure the cross. But, hey, Man, I've got a better way! I'm the god of THIS WORLD, You know (II Cor. 4:4). Those kingdoms out there belong to me! Tell you what, Jesus, I can save You all that pain, suffering, and bleeding. You can take a shortcut, here.

"If You will do one little teensy-weensy thing for me, I'll give You all those kingdoms right now! You won't have to wait, and You won't have to suffer! My way is a whole lot better than Your Father's! All You have to do is drop to Your knees and worship me. That's all You have to do, Man! Now, what would be so difficult about that? How about it?"

Jesus looks at him askance and replies, "You seem to have overlooked something, devil."

"Yeah? What's that?"

CAN I TRUST SATAN?

"The Scripture."

"The Scripture?"

"Yes. It is written. IT IS WRITTEN. IT *IS* WRITTEN! Thou shalt worship the LORD THY GOD and HIM only shalt thou serve!"

Satan retorts, "There's something wrong, here, Jesus."

"Oh? What is that?"

"Well, You keep coming on with this *IT IS WRITTEN* stuff. Weren't You quotin' from Deuteronomy?"

"Yes."

"Well, what do You mean, it IS written? You're not gonna tell me that those original parchments are still in existence, are You?"

"Of course not. They crumbled back to the dust well over a thousand years ago."

"Hah! See there! You're quotin' stuff that is gone! The originals are gone, Man!"

"So what?"

"What do You mean, so what?"

"God's Word is still intact. You seem to have read some Scripture, Satan. Have you read Psalm 12:6-7?"

The devil puts his scaly hand to his forehead. "Well, now let me see . . . uh . . . yeah . . . how does that go?"

"It says that God will preserve His WORDS forever. So, you see, that is what He is doing. Many copies are being made so that when the parchments wear out and crumble, we still have fresh ones."

"Yeah, but there are bound to be errors that will creep in, Jesus. After all, those scribes are only human, you know."

CAN I TRUST MY BIBLE?

"So is Moses, devil, but God can use a human to give His originals, and He can use humans to make copies and keep them free of error because HE is watching over them."

The devil scratches his head. "Yeah, but You've got another problem."

"And that is?"

"Well, You just quoted in the language of today. Aramaic. Deuteronomy was written in Hebrew. Do You realize, Jesus, that You're quoting from a *translation?* Don't You realize that something is always lost in translation? The guys who did the translatin' were only human, You know. I'll bet they botched it up."

"They would have," replies Jesus, "if they had been left to themselves, but you seem to ignore the fact that God said He would preserve His WORDS forever. He can use mortal men to give the original writings. He can use mortal men to make copies and keep the WORDS correct, and He can use mortal men to TRANSLATE and make the WORDS come out EXACTLY as He wants them."

Satan grins wickedly, "Heh, heh. Then I'll tell You what I'm gonna do."

"What is that?"

"I'm gonna get some of my followers to make up some manuscripts and take away words and stick others in. That'll fix things. Then when translations are made, they will be full of error, too. I'll have me some bibles of my own."

"I do not doubt that you will, Satan," says Jesus. "You are a dirty deceiver, a liar, and a counterfeiter. But I will make you this guarantee, devil. No matter how many bad manuscripts and corrupt bibles you produce, God will always keep pure manuscripts; and He will always see to it that there are translations that He has preserved so that His Word remains intact. He WILL preserve His WORDS forever!"

CAN I TRUST SATAN?

Satan knew the truth of those words. He had no more to say.

Then the devil leaveth him, and, behold, angels came and ministered unto him (Matt. 4:11).

Then the very angels that Satan had brought up came to their Master to minister unto Him. Jesus had whipped the socks off the devil, and the Father in Heaven was pleased.

When Eve was tempted *alone* by the devil, she gave in and sinned. Eve believed IN God, but she did not BELIEVE GOD. When the Lord Jesus was tempted *alone* by the devil, he DID NOT GIVE IN. He DID NOT SIN. HE BELIEVED GOD! Jesus believed that God would preserve EVERY WORD of His Scriptures forever. Though He did not have the "originals," He believed He had the pure, written Word of God available in His day . . . even in a *translation*.

How about my reader? Do you believe IN God . . . or do you BELIEVE GOD? Do you believe that TODAY we have EVERY WORD that proceedeth out of the mouth of God . . . even in a translation? If not, you are taking sides with the devil. If you DO . . . which translation in our language is the one that has EVERY WORD that proceedeth from the mouth of God? There can only be ONE, you know. All the translations have *different words*. If ONE translation has EVERY WORD that proceedeth out of the mouth of God, all the others DO NOT.

Thank God, we DO have a perfect translation. We DO have EVERY WORD that proceedeth out of the mouth of God. In spite of the devil and the scoffers who follow him (whether they be "fundamentalists," modernists, liberals, or cults), the Authorized Version of 1611, known as the King James Bible, is that Book!

Let me now return to the title of this chapter. CAN I TRUST THE DEVIL?

I declare unto you that you CAN trust the devil! Yes, you

CAN I TRUST MY BIBLE?

CAN! You can trust him to always be a liar. You can trust him to always be a deceiver. You can trust him to always be a counterfeiter. You can trust him to produce counterfeit manuscripts and counterfeit translations. According to Jude 4, you can trust Satan to send his emissaries creeping into Bible-believing ranks to destroy the old-time Faith. The old-time Faith has but ONE foundation . . . THE WORD OF GOD (Rom. 10:17). Jude tells us to earnestly contend for that old-time Faith (Jude 3), so I plan to obey. The Bible correctors can call me a troublemaker, a nitwit, a nut, a backwoods, uneducated fool, or anything else they want to . . . but by the grace of God, until the day I'm called out of this world, I WILL EARNESTLY CONTEND FOR THE FAITH BY EARNESTLY CONTENDING FOR THE BOOK BY WHICH I GOT MY FAITH!

II

CAN I TRUST THE MODERN JEHOIAKIMS?

Through the pen of David (Acts 4:25; Heb. 4:7), God has declared His attitude toward His WORD.

I will worship toward thy holy temple, and praise thy name for thy lovingkindness and for thy truth: for thou hast MAGNIFIED THY WORD above all thy name (Psalm 138:2).

It has been correctly said that *a man's word is his bond*. A man's character is established by how he stands by his word. If he allows his word to change or if he fails to keep it, his NAME is soiled, his reputation is ruined, and his character is shown to be unsavory. Therefore, if a man cares about his reputation, he will guard his word very, very carefully.

The Almighty God of Heaven feels the same way about HIS Word. His name means nothing if His Word fails.

Anyone who has read the Bible knows that God thinks quite a bit of His name, but we learn here that He thinks EVEN MORE of His Word! He has magnified His Word ABOVE His name! When God speaks, His Word is made up of WORDS. He is so interested in keeping His Word pure and perfect, that He is very touchy about someone messing with His WORDS. He does not want anyone ADDING to His Word or TAKING AWAY from His Word. To do

CAN I TRUST MY BIBLE?

either is to tamper with the WORDS. God has issued three solemn warnings concerning this in His Bible . . . once near the FRONT, one near the MIDDLE, and the third time, ON THE VERY LAST PAGE. Watch:

> *Ye shall not ADD UNTO THE WORD which I command you, neither shall ye DIMINISH OUGHT FROM IT* (Deut. 4:2).

> *EVERY WORD of God is pure: he is a shield unto them that put their trust in him. ADD thou not unto his WORDS, lest he reprove thee, and thou be found a liar* (Prov. 30:5-6).

> *For I testify unto every man that heareth the WORDS of the prophecy of this book, If any man shall ADD unto these things, God shall add unto him the plagues that are written in this book: And if any man shall TAKE AWAY from the WORDS of the book of this prophecy, God shall take away his part out of the book of life, and out of the holy city, and from the things which are written in this book* (Rev. 22:18-19).

Pretty solemn stuff, wouldn't you say? Yet there have been men in the past, and there are men living today who ADD TO and TAKE AWAY from the Word of God by tampering with the WORDS that make up His Word. A classic example in the Bible is the wicked Jehoiakim, king of Judah. We will look at the story of Jehoiakim, then compare some modern day Jehoiakims. From this, we will learn some valuable lessons.

I want us to carefully note some comments God has made about King Jehoiakim in His Word, then we will read the story and see why God found the man to be so wicked.

Jehoiakim has twenty and five years old when he

CAN I TRUST THE MODERN JEHOIAKIMS?

began to reign; and he reigned eleven years in Jerusalem . . . And he did THAT WHICH WAS EVIL in the sight of the Lord (II Kings 23:36-37).

How would you like to have that for your epitaph? Must be something pretty bad that Jehoiakim did for God to say that over his dead body!

Jehoiakim was twenty and five years old when he began to reign, and he reigned eleven years in Jerusalem: and he did THAT WHICH WAS EVIL in the sight of the Lord his God. Now the rest of the acts of Jehoiakim, AND HIS ABOMINATIONS WHICH HE DID, and that which was found in him, behold, they are written in the book of the kings of Israel and Judah . . . (II Chron. 36:5,8).

Whew! God sure was upset about something Jehoiakim did! Not only were his acts EVIL, but God says they were ABOMINATIONS!!! Well, let's read the story and see what Jehoiakim did.

And it came to pass in the fourth year of Jehoiakim the son of Josiah king of Judah, that this word came unto Jeremiah from the Lord, saying, Take thee a roll of a book, and write therein all the WORDS that I have spoken unto thee against Israel, and against Judah, and against all the nations, from the day I spake unto thee, from the days of Josiah, even unto this day. It may be that the house of Judah will hear all the evil which I purpose to do unto them; that they may return every man from his evil way; that I may forgive their iniquity and their sin. Then Jeremiah called Baruch the son of Neriah: and Baruch wrote from the mouth of Jeremiah ALL THE WORDS OF THE LORD, which He had spoken unto him, upon a

CAN I TRUST MY BIBLE?

roll of a book (Jer. 36:1-4).

To conserve space here, let me tell you what happened immediately thereafter; then we'll pick up the narrative when it returns to the story of Jehoiakim's deeds.

Jeremiah sent Baruch with the book, telling him to read it aloud to all the people in the house of the Lord on the fasting day.

Baruch did as he was commanded. Among those in the house of the Lord who heard God's words was a man named Michaiah. The words were sharp, piercing, and full of condemnation against the people of Israel and Judah. Michaiah was shaken to his tennis shoes. He ran to several princes who were close to the king and told them about the words of the Lord in the book. The princes were stunned and sent a man named Jehudi to fetch Baruch, so he could read the words straight from the book into their ears.

Baruch came and did so, and fear gripped the hearts of all the princes. They agreed that King Jehoiakim had to hear the Lord's solemn words. They knew the king was not going to like what he heard, so they left the book in the chamber of Elishama the scribe and went to the king and gave him the words orally. Jehudi was there. All the princes were there, including three named Elnathan, Delaiah, and Gemariah. A number of the king's servants were there also.

When Jehoiakim heard the words, he did not like them one bit. He figured since he did not like them, all he had to do to remove the condemnation from his head was to get his hands on the book and destroy it.

> *So the king sent Jehudi to fetch the roll: and he took it out of Elishama the scribe's chamber. And Jehudi read it in the ears of the king, and in the ears of all the princes which stood beside the king. Now the king sat in the winterhouse in the ninth month: and there*

CAN I TRUST THE MODERN JEHOIAKIMS?

was a fire on the hearth burning before him. And it came to pass, that when Jehudi had read three or four leaves, he [King Jehoiakim] CUT IT WITH THE PENKNIFE, AND CAST IT IN THE FIRE that was on the hearth, until all the roll was consumed in the fire that was on the hearth (Jer. 36:21-23).

Later, I am going to show my reader how the modern day Jehoiakims operate in the same manner as their predecessor. As a basis for this, let us take a good look at the picture.

Jehoiakim had an immediate reaction within him as the words came from Jehudi's mouth. While the princes and the servants watched, the king jumped off his chair, snatched the book from Jehudi's hands, and picked up his penknife. With the sharp blade of the knife, he sliced the book into ribbons. Then he casted it into the fire on the hearth. As I have studied this passage, I have found seven things that stand out. These seven things will help us in our study of the modern day Jehoiakims. They are the following points:

I. DIVINE INSPIRATION
II. DIVINE INTENTION
III. DIVINE CONVICTION
IV. HUMAN INTERVENTION
V. DIVINE PRESERVATION
VI. HUMAN INTERCESSION
VII. DIVINE CONDEMNATION

Let's examine them closely.

I. DIVINE INSPIRATION

Let us notice how the Divine Inspiration took place.

And it came to pass in the fourth year of Jehoiakim the son of Josiah king Judah, that this word came

CAN I TRUST MY BIBLE?

> *unto Jeremiah FROM THE LORD, saying, Take thee a roll of a book, and write therein ALL THE WORDS THAT I HAVE SPOKEN UNTO THEE against Israel and against Judah, and against all the nations, from the day I SPAKE UNTO THEE, from the days of Josiah, even unto this day. It may be that the house of Judah will hear all the evil which I purpose to do unto them; that they may return every man from his evil way; that I may forgive their iniquity and their sin. Then Jeremiah called Baruch the son of Neriah: and Baruch wrote FROM THE MOUTH OF JEREMIAH ALL THE WORDS OF THE LORD WHICH HE HAD SPOKEN UNTO HIM, upon a roll of a book* (Jer. 36:1-4).

Follow the succession here. God, Himself, spoke ALL THE WORDS to Jeremiah. God did not just give Jeremiah the general message, then say, "Okay, Jerry, YOU put it in your own words." NO! NO! NO! God said, "Write therein ALL THE WORDS that I have spoken unto thee."

Jeremiah then turned around and dictated EVERY SINGLE WORD to Baruch, the scribe. Baruch wrote EVERY SINGLE WORD down in the book.

> *Baruch wrote from the mouth of Jeremiah ALL THE WORDS OF THE LORD, which He had spoken unto him, upon a roll of a book* (Jer. 36:4).

We hear so much talk from the Alexandrians about the "originals." Well, let me ask them . . . were the "originals," here, the SPOKEN words, or the WRITTEN words? The answer is simple. I have before me Webster's New World Dictionary of the English Language. The definition of the word "original" on page 423 is as follows:

> *original*: 1. *first; earliest*

CAN I TRUST THE MODERN JEHOIAKIMS?

Other definitions follow, but it is notable that the number ONE definition of *original* is *first* or *earliest!* Which came *first,* the written words or the spoken words? The SPOKEN words!!! Then the actual "originals" were not on the parchments at all! The "originals" were the SPOKEN words!

Some will argue, "Yeah, but this was only the case with Jeremiah when he dictated God's message to King Jehoiakim and the people of Judah. It wasn't Scripture."

Oh, but it WAS Scripture. Take another look at Jeremiah 36:2. God says there that the words Jeremiah must put in a book are the words He had spoken to Jeremiah "from the days of Josiah." God began to give Jeremiah His words as recorded in chapter 25 . . . and He gave him the words intermittently all the way through chapter 35. The basic message was the foretelling of the seventy years of Babylonian captivity that were going to befall God's rebellious earthly people. All the words that were in the book Jehoiakim cut up and burned are found in chapters twenty-five through thirty-five of Jeremiah. The wicked Jehoiakim took his penknife to SCRIPTURE! He threw SCRIPTURE into the fire! God SAYS it was Scripture in Jeremiah 36:29 by quoting Jeremiah 25:9!!!

Now let me come back to my question. Were the "originals" the WRITTEN words or the SPOKEN words? The answer is obvious. So in actuality, the "originals" were NOT the words WRITTEN on the parchments! They were the words SPOKEN by the prophets! Scripture attests to this:

> *For the prophecy came not in old time by the will of man: but holy men of God SPAKE as they were moved by the Holy Ghost* (II Pet. 1:21).

> *That ye maybe mindful of the words which were SPOKEN before by the holy prophets, and of the commandment of us the apostles of the Lord and Saviour* (II Pet. 3:2).

CAN I TRUST MY BIBLE?

> *Then he [Jesus] said unto them, O fools and slow of heart to believe all that the prophets have SPOKEN:* (Luke 24:25).

Thus we conclude that the "originals" were the SPOKEN words, not the written words. Actually, it has been a SPEAKING situation from the very beginning. Follow it.

> *God, who at sundry times and in divers manners SPAKE in time past unto the fathers by the prophets, Hath in these last days SPOKEN unto us by his Son,* (Heb. 1:1-2).

> *All things that I have HEARD of my father I have made known unto you* (John 15:15).

At this point we can see that God SPOKE unto the Hebrew fathers through the mouths of the prophets (Luke 24:25). When the Father sent Jesus, he SPOKE unto Him the words to give to men on earth, and Jesus turned around and SPOKE them to men while He walked this earth. In His prayer of John 17, Jesus said to the Father, "I have given unto them the words WHICH THOU GAVEST ME": (John 17:8).

In John 16, Jesus had the twelve seated before Him. Take note of what He said.

> *Howbeit when he, the Spirit of truth, is come, he will guide you into all truth: for he shall not speak of himself; but whatsoever he shall HEAR, that shall he SPEAK: and he will shew you things to come* (John 16:13).

In that group were five men who were going to write a good part of the New Testament. Matthew was there. He would write the very first book of the New Testament. Peter was there. He would write two books of the New Testament. Jude and James were there. They would each write one book of the New Testament.

CAN I TRUST THE MODERN JEHOIAKIMS?

It is interesting that the Lord Jesus called the WORDS that would make the Word of God HIS words (See John 12:47-48; Matt. 24:35). In John 16:13, He says the Holy Spirit will HEAR a message, then SPEAK that message to men. Jesus (who IS the Word of God ... John 1:1,14; Rev. 19:13) would SPEAK the words to the Holy Spirit. Then the Holy Spirit would SPEAK the words to the men who were to write the New Testament.

When we SPEAK, we BREATHE, do we not? Since that is true, we conclude that when the Holy Spirit SPOKE to the men who wrote the sixty-six books of the Bible, He BREATHED on them. With the BREATH of the Holy Spirit upon them, the men of old SPOKE the words breathed into their minds by the Holy Spirit. I say, again, that the "originals" were the words breathed into the men of old by the Holy Spirit, andthat they then SPOKE. The "originals" were the SPOKEN words.

As we shall see when we study what the Bible-correcting Alexandrians teach . . . they say the only God-inspired, inerrant, infallible Scriptures were the "originals." They say when copies were made that there were errors in the copies. Let me take you back to the dictionary. I said earlier that there were some other definitions of the word "original." I want you to see another one. I am going to give it to you here exactly as it is written in the dictionary. You will actually see FOUR definitions. Pay particular attention to number FOUR.

Webster's New World Dictionary, Second College Edition, printed 1983, page 423 . . .

original: 1. *first; earliest* 2. *never having been before; new; novel* 3. *capable of creating something new; inventive* 4. *being that from which copies are made*

Did you get a good gander at number four? BEING THAT FROM WHICH COPIES ARE MADE!!! As I will document, the

CAN I TRUST MY BIBLE?

Bible-correcting, modern day Jehoiakims say that ONLY the *originals* were perfect, inerrant, and infallible . . . and that ALL COPIES had errors in them. We know from Scripture that what the holy men of old SPAKE, they then dictated or wrote down themselves. Over and over again the Bible refers to that which is WRITTEN, but if the Alexandrians are correct in their claim that ONLY the originals were perfect, inerrant, and infallible and all the COPIES had errors . . . then THERE WERE ERRORS IN WHAT THE MEN OF OLD WROTE WHEN THEY PUT THE WORDS THEY HAD SPOKEN ON PARCHMENT BECAUSE WHAT THEY PUT ON PARCHMENT WITH PEN AND INK WERE *COPIES* OF THE ORIGINALS!!!!!!

So when the Alexandrians so piously refer to the "originals," meaning what was first WRITTEN, they refer to COPIES, and the Alexandrians (as I shall prove) are therefore referring to manuscripts with ERRORS! They have absolutely NOTHING infallible to base anything on because the real originals were the SPOKEN words that died out in the air as they came from the mouths of the men of old.

So we have here in Jeremiah chapter 36 a perfect picture of how INSPIRATION took place. God SPOKE the words to His prophet. Jeremiah SPOKE the words to the scribe, and Baruch WROTE them down in a book. I will guarantee you that GOD stayed right there to make sure Baruch penned them down accurately.

II. DIVINE INTENTION

What was God's intention in giving all these words to Jeremiah? Look at it. God says,

> *It may be that the house of Judah will hear all the evil which I purpose to do unto them; THAT THEY MAY RETURN EVERY MAN FROM HIS EVIL WAY; THAT I MAY FORGIVE THEIR INIQUITY AND THEIR SIN* (Jer. 36:3).

CAN I TRUST THE MODERN JEHOIAKIMS?

Isn't that just like our wonderful Lord? He is not willing that any should perish, but that all should come to repentance (II Pet. 3:9). His greatest desire is to redeem lost, Hell-bound sinners. Just as HE gave divinely inspired words to Jeremiah so the people of Judah would hear them and repent, our great and merciful God has given sixty-six Books of Scripture that ALL men might hear His message of salvation and forgiveness . . . and come to Him in repentance that He might pardon and redeem them. Listen to His voice through Isaiah's pen.

> *Incline your ear, and COME UNTO ME: HEAR and your soul shall live . . . Seek ye the Lord while he may be found, call ye upon him while he is near: Let the wicked forsake his way, and the unrighteous man his thoughts: and let him return unto the Lord, and HE WILL HAVE MERCY ON HIM; and to our God, for HE WILL ABUNDANTLY PARDON* (Isa. 55:3, 6-7).

God has ordained that men be brought to salvation and forgiveness through His inspired, infallible WORD.

> *For by grace are ye saved through FAITH . . . So then faith cometh by HEARING, and hearing BY THE WORD OF GOD* (Eph. 2:8; Rom. 10:17).

> *Of his own will begat he us with the WORD OF TRUTH . . .* (James 1:18).

> *. . . Except a man be BORN AGAIN, he cannot see the kingdom of God. Seeing ye have purified your souls in obeying the TRUTH . . . Being BORN AGAIN, not of corruptible seed, but of incorruptible, by THE WORD OF GOD, which liveth and abideth forever* (John 3:3; I Pet. 1:22-23).

The WORD OF GOD, which is His WORD OF TRUTH is the INCORRUPTIBLE seed by which we come to saving faith and get born again. The Word of God is made up of the *WORDS* of God. If the WORDS are taken away or supplanted by words that are not GOD'S WORDS, then the "word" is no longer HIS Word . . . it is no longer the Word of TRUTH and has become CORRUPTIBLE. Men cannot be saved . . . men cannot be born again by a book that is corruptible! If it is not the WORD OF TRUTH, it cannot bring a person to SAVING FAITH!

As we shall see . . . when Jehoiakim took his penknife and shredded the roll of the book that held God's WORDS and burned them in the fire, GOD WENT RIGHT TO WORK TO REPLACE HIS WORDS AND KEEP THEM INTACT, so His intent toward the people of Judah could be accomplished! Satan has raised up many a Jehoiakim since . . . even down to the day in which we live . . .but just as God took care of His WORDS in Jehoiakim's day, He will do so today. He still is desirous that lost sinners come to Him and be saved, and He is still preserving EVERY WORD of His Word so they CAN be!

III. DIVINE CONVICTION

Let us watch God's WORDS slice, cut, tear, and rip into the sinful hearts of the princes of Judah.

> *When Michaiah the son of Gemariah, the son of Shaphan, had heard out of the book ALL THE WORDS OF THE LORD, Then he went down into the king's house, into the scribe's chamber: and, lo, all the princes sat there, even Elishama the scribe, and Delaiah the son of Shemaiah, and Elnathan the son of Achbor, and Geremiah the son of Shaphan, and Zedekiah the son of Hananiah, and all the princes. Then Michaiah declared unto them ALL THE WORDS that he had heard, when Baruch read the book in the ears of the people.*

CAN I TRUST THE MODERN JEHOIAKIMS?

Therefore all the princes sent Jehudi the son of Nethaniah, the son of Shelemiah, the son of Cushi, unto Baruch, saying, Take in thine hand the roll wherein thou hast read in the ears of the people, and come. So Baruch the son of Neriah took the roll in his hand, and came unto them. And they said unto him, Sit down now, and read it in our ears. So Baruch read it in their ears. Now it came to pass, when they had heard all the words, THEY WERE AFRAID both one and other, and said unto Baruch, We will surely tell the king of ALL THESE WORDS (Jer. 36:11-16).

God's Word has tremendous convicting power. When read or heard correctly, it will produce the fear of the Lord in sinful hearts.

For the word of God is quick and POWERFUL, and sharper than any twoedged sword, PIERCING even to the dividing asunder of soul and spirit, and of the joints and marrow, and is a DISCERNER of the THOUGHTS AND INTENTS OF THE HEART (Heb. 4:12).

The princes of Judah were AFRAID when they heard God's WORDS. They FEARED what God was going to do to them for their sin and iniquity committed against Him. They were not sure how the king was going to take God's scathing words, but they looked upon Baruch and Jeremiah as men of God, and did not want anything to happen to them.

Then said the princes unto Baruch, Go, HIDE thee, thou and Jeremiah; and let no man know where ye be. (Jer. 36:19)

I believe the princes (who now had the fear of God in them) were hoping that by giving the king God's message of pending wrath for their sin, Jehoiakim would lead the people to repent. For the

CAN I TRUST MY BIBLE?

people to repent without being led to do so by the king would bring death upon them. They must follow the leadership of Jehoiakim. Hoping the king would do right about God's message, they went to him with it. "And they went in to the king into the court, but they laid up the roll in the chamber of Elishama the scribe, and TOLD ALL THE WORDS IN THE EARS OF THE KING" (Jer. 36:20).

Apparently Jehoiakim was startled by the words, and he could not believe that such fury could be pending for him and his people at the hand of Almighty God. Let us look at a portion of that message.

> *The word that came to Jeremiah concerning ALL THE PEOPLE OF JUDAH in the fourth year of Jehoiakim the son of Josiah king of Judah, that was the first year of Nebuchadrezzar king of Babylon; The which Jeremiah the prophet spake unto ALL THE PEOPLE OF JUDAH, and to all the inhabitants of Jerusalem, saying . . . the Lord hath sent unto you all his servants the prophets, rising early and sending them; BUT YE HAVE NOT HEARKENED, NOR INCLINED YOUR EAR TO HEAR. They said, Turn ye again now every one from HIS EVIL WAY, and FROM THE EVIL OF YOUR DOINGS, and dwell in the land that the Lord hath given unto you and to your fathers for ever and ever: And GO NOT AFTER OTHER GODS to serve them, and to worship them, and PROVOKE ME NOT TO ANGER with the works of your hands; and I will do you no hurt.*
>
> *Yet ye have not hearkened unto me, saith the Lord; that ye might provoke me to anger with the works of your hands TO YOUR OWN HURT. Therefore thus saith the Lord of hosts; Because ye have not heard MY WORDS, Behold, I will send and take*

CAN I TRUST THE MODERN JEHOIAKIMS?

all the families of the north, saith the Lord, and Nebuchadrezzar the king of Babylon, my servant, and WILL BRING THEM AGAINST THIS LAND, and AGAINST THE INHABITANTS THEREOF, and against all these nations round about, and WILL UTTERLY DESTROY THEM, and MAKE THEM AN ASTONISHMENT, and AN HISSING, and PERPETUAL DESOLATIONS. Moreover I will take from them THE VOICE OF MIRTH, and THE VOICE OF GLADNESS, the voice of the bridegroom, and the voice of the bride, the sound of millstones, and THE LIGHT OF THE CANDLE. And this whole land SHALL BE A DESOLATION...

For thus saith the Lord God of Israel unto me (says Jeremiah); Take the wine cup of this FURY at my hand, and cause all the nations, to whom I send thee, to drink it. And they shall drink, and be moved, and be mad, BECAUSE OF THE SWORD THAT I WILL SEND AMONG THEM (Jer. 25:1-2; 4-11; 15-16).

Under such conviction for his wickedness, King Jehoiakim wanted to see the scroll that held the condemning words for himself.

So the king sent Jehudi to fetch the roll: and he took it out of Elishama the scribe's chamber. And Jehudi read it in the ears of the king, and in the ears of all the princes which stood beside the king. Now the king sat in the winterhouse in the ninth month: and there was a fire on the hearth burning before him (Jer. 36:21-22).

God's pungent words coming right from the scroll lanced into King Jehoiakim's wicked heart. DIVINE CONVICTION burned into his guilty soul. He had indeed been evil in his doings, and he had led the people of Judah to serve other gods and worship them. He had provoked the true and living God to anger, and was now going to reap what he had sowed. God was going to send the Babylonians against Jehoiakim and his people. Their mirth would be taken from them, the voice of gladness in Judah would disappear, their "light" would go out, and the land would become desolate.

This DIVINE CONVICTION was eating Jehoiakim to the very core of his evil being.

IV. HUMAN INTERVENTION

Suddenly, anger boiled up within Jehoiakim against God. He did not like what the roll of the book had to say about him. He decided that he could take authority over the book and do what he wanted to with it. In his fit of temper, he thought that by destroying the roll of the book. He could negate the punishment that the words in the book were promising would come from their Author.

> *And it came to pass, that when Jehudi had read three or four leaves, he [Jehoiakim] CUT IT WITH THE PENKNIFE, AND CAST IT INTO THE FIRE that was on the hearth, until all the roll was consumed in the fire that was on the hearth* (Jer. 36:23).

How utterly ridiculous for a puny little mortal human being to think he could actually stay the judging hand of the Almighty God by using a penknife on the parchment that held the condemning words, then casting the tattered fragments into the fire! Satan was the first to intervene when God had declared a warning to human beings. He approached Eve and attacked God's WORDS by saying, "Yea, HATH GOD SAID?" (Gen. 3:1). The devil has raised up his Jehoiakims down through the ages who would dare intervene when GOD had spoken, and he has attempted to thwart His plan and purpose by destroying the Word of God.

No matter how hard the old snake-in-the-grass works to

CAN I TRUST THE MODERN JEHOIAKIMS?

destroy God's Word through men, he has raised up for that very purpose . . . neither Satan nor his co-workers will ever be able to do it! There will always be . . .

V. DIVINE PRESERVATION

Watch the Lord go to work now to UNDO Jehoiakim's wicked deed.

> *Then the word of the Lord came to Jeremiah, AFTER that the king had burned the roll, and the words which Baruch wrote at the mouth of Jeremiah, saying, Take thee again ANOTHER roll, and write in it ALL THE FORMER WORDS THAT WERE IN THE FIRST ROLL, which Jehoiakim the king of Judah hath burned . . . Then took Jeremiah ANOTHER ROLL, and gave it to Baruch the scribe, the son of Neriah; WHO WROTE THEREIN from the mouth of Jeremiah ALL THE WORDS OF THE BOOK which Jehoiakim king of Judah had burned in the fire: and there were added besides unto them many LIKE WORDS* (Jer. 36:27-28; 32).

As we proceed in this book and I quote many modern Jehoiakims, my reader will hear much about the "originals." The modern day Jehoiakims make a great to-do over the "originals," saying that only the "original autographs" were inspired, so only the "original autographs" were infallible and without error. They will tell us that even the Greek and Hebrew manuscripts that we have today are filled with errors because they were copies by MEN, and MEN make mistakes. Thus, they would leave us with no PRESERVED set of manuscripts, and no PRESERVED Bible in our own English language. In essence, then, they are thinking as did Jehoiakim of old. Since the "original" parchments are gone, there is no perfect, inspired, infallible, inerrant Word of God in the world today.

CAN I TRUST MY BIBLE?

What these "great intellectuals"(?) are saying, then, is that what was inspired was not the WORD of God, but the PARCHMENTS!!! Where in the name of Yogi Bear did they ever read ANYWHERE in the Bible that the PARCHMENTS upon which the words were written were inspired? NO! NO! God did not inspire the fabric and the fiber of the papyrus into which the ink soaked as the writing was done! He inspired the WORDS!!! When Jehoiakim's penknife ripped up the papyrus and the flames of the fire turned the fabric and the fibre into ashes, THE WORDS OF GOD WERE NOT GONE!

All SCRIPTURE is given by inspiration of God . . .
(II Tim. 3:16).

The SCRIPTURE is the written Word of God. You see the very word "script" right in the word. Jesus said,

Heaven and earth shall pass away, but my WORDS shall NOT pass away (Matt 24:35).

Jesus did NOT say, "Heaven and earth will pass away, but my 'ORIGINAL AUTOGRAPHS' will not pass away." By "autographs," the modern day Jehoiakims mean the *parchments*. Jesus did NOT say, "Heaven and earth shall pass away, but my 'ORIGINAL PARCHMENTS' will not pass away." The parchments were not inspired. He said, "My WORDS shall not pass away!"

The truth of this is demonstrated right here in Jeremiah chapter 36. Look at it again.

Then took Jeremiah ANOTHER Roll [it has to be WRITTEN to be SCRIPTure!], and gave it to Baruch the scribe, who WROTE therein from the mouth of Jeremiah ALL THE WORDS of the book which Jehoiakim king of Judah had burned in the fire . . .
(Jer. 36:32).

WHOOEE! HALLELUJAH! PRAISE THE LORD! Though

CAN I TRUST THE MODERN JEHOIAKIMS?

the "original parchments" had been burned, THE WORDS WERE STILL IN EXISTENCE!!! God simply had them written down AGAIN to PRESERVE them, and even added some more words as it pleased Him!

Now let's think about this for a moment. We have already established that the actual "originals" were the SPOKEN words . . . and that the first time they were WRITTEN, they were COPIES of the "originals." So what do we have here in Jeremiah 36? We have Jeremiah getting the words *originally* from God as God SPOKE them to him. Then Jeremiah SPOKE the words to Baruch. Jeremiah's spoken words, then, would actually be COPIES of the words that God spoke to him. So when Jeremiah spoke the words to Baruch, Baruch was getting COPIES, so he could write down COPIES OF THE COPIES. Look at the scripture again, now, and use your noggin. The Lord said to Jeremiah,

> *Take thee a roll of a book, and write therein ALL THE WORDS THAT I HAVE SPOKEN UNTO THEE. Then Jeremiah called Baruch the son of Neriah and Baruch WROTE from the mouth of Jeremiah ALL THE WORDS OF THE LORD, which he had SPOKEN unto him, upon a roll of a book* (Jer. 36:2, 4).

Do you see it? ORIGINAL #1 was when God spoke the words to Jeremiah. ORIGINAL #2 was when Jeremiah spoke the words to Baruch. ORIGINAL #3 was when Baruch wrote the words on the parchment.

But of course, King Jehoiakim cut up ORIGINAL #3 and threw it into the fire. So what do we have in Jeremiah 36:32? We have ORIGINAL #4!!!

The Alexandrians (I'll explain that term shortly.) of today, who are the modern Jehoiakims, tell us that only the "originals" were inspired of God. I would like for them to tell WHICH originals were inspired of God in Jeremiah chapter 36. Seems to me that they

CAN I TRUST MY BIBLE?

were ALL inspired of God! Even when we get down to ORIGINAL #4, WE STILL HAVE *ALL* THE WORDS THAT GOD HAD ORIGINALLY GIVEN TO JEREMIAH IN ORIGINAL #1!!!

Now it seems to me that if the Great and Almighty God could preserve His WORDS in Jeremiah's day even though the "original autographs" got burned up, He could keep on doing it down through the centuries so that we would have reliable and perfect COPIES of the original written words, even though time took its toll on those original parchments and crumbled them back to the dust. The modern Jehoiakims have a pretty puny little god, don't they? Their god is so weak and effeminate that he can't preserve his word. Tch. Tch. Too bad.

My God is ALMIGHTY. HE can keep His words intact down through the ages BECAUSE He is almighty! Would somebody please tell me why in the name of common sense God would go to all the trouble to verbally, plenarily inspire His WORDS in the "originals," then turn them over to mortal men and let them corrupt them, change them, and LOSE them? The god of the Alexandrians works that way, but not the God of the BIBLE!

The Alexandrians garnish the memory of the "originals" to the point of nausea . . . as my reader shall see. Let me show you what God thinks of the "originals." Certainly WE should not put more emphasis on the "originals" than GOD does.

First, let me point out that Jeremiah chapters 45 through 51 give us the full text of the FOURTH ORIGINAL as described in chapter 36 and verse 32. Chapter 45 opens up.

> *The word that Jeremiah the prophet SPAKE unto Baruch the son of Neriah, when he had WRITTEN these words in a book at the mouth of Jeremiah, in the fourth year of Jehoiakim the son of Josiah king of Judah . . .(Jer. 45:1).*

CAN I TRUST THE MODERN JEHOIAKIMS?

If my reader will compare Jeremiah 36:1 with 36:32, you will see that what we have in Jeremiah chapters 45-51 are the words that were written in ORIGINAL #3 (which went into the fire); then they were re-written, along with additional words in ORIGINAL #4.

This is confirmed in chapter 37 and verses 1 and 2. Now follow it to chapter fifty-one where Jeremiah, speaking for God, refers to ORIGINAL #4 and says to a prince named Seraiah.

> ... *When thou comest to Babylon, and shalt see, and shalt read ALL THESE WORDS ... when thou hast made an end of reading THIS BOOK, thou shalt bind a stone to it, and CAST IT INTO THE MIDST OF THE EUPHRATES ...* (Jer. 51:61, 63).

Did you SEE that? Jeremiah told Seraiah to throw ORIGINAL #4 into the river!!! Now, what are you Alexandrians going to do with THAT? It'll probably give you boys a heart attack, a hernia, and gastronomical pains all at the same time! Yep, you saw it right. Jeremiah actually told Seraiah to toss the "originals" in the river!

(Yawn) ... But that's no problem. We have a COPY of the original text in chapters 45 through 51. This COPY came from ORIGINAL #4, which went into the river. So it looks to me like we're still doing all right, wouldn't you say? God let the "original autographs" go into the river. BIG DEAL. God also let ALL the "original autographs" go back to the dust. SO WHAT? We've still got EVERY WORD. Every AV1611 King James Bible has Jeremiah chapters 45 through 51 in it ... so we STILL have *every word,* just as we still have EVERY WORD THAT GOD EVER GAVE IN ALL 66 BOOKS OF HIS BIBLE!!! If He can preserve EVERY WORD once, He can keep on doing it. The god of the Alexandrians can't do that. He is too puny and frail. But the God of the BIBLE not only CAN do it, He HAS done it, and will KEEP ON doing it!!!

"The WORDS of the Lord are pure WORDS: as silver tried

CAN I TRUST MY BIBLE?

in a furnace of earth, purified seven times. Thou shalt KEEP THEM, O LORD, thou shalt PRESERVE THEM from this generation FOR EVER" (Psalm 12:6-7).

Thy word is true from the beginning: and EVERY ONE of thy righteous judgments endureth FOR EVER (Psalm 119:160).

As for me, this is my covenant with them, saith the Lord; My spirit that is upon thee, and my WORDS which I have put in thy mouth, shall not depart out of thy mouth, nor out of the mouth of thy seed, nor out of the mouth of thy seed's seed, saith the Lord, FROM HENCEFORTH AND FOR EVER (Isaiah 59:21).

Man shall not live by bread alone, but by EVERY WORD that proceedeth out of the mouth of God (Matt 4:4).

For verily I say unto you, Till heaven and earth pass, ONE jot or ONE tittle SHALL IN NO WISE PASS FROM THE LAW, till all be fulfilled (Matt. 5:18).

And it is easier for heaven and earth to pass, than ONE TITTLE OF THE LAW TO FAIL (Luke 16:17).

Heaven and earth shall pass away, but MY WORDS SHALL NOT PASS AWAY (Matt. 24:35).

Being born again, not of corruptible seed, but of incorruptible, by the word of God, WHICH LIVETH AND ABIDETH FOR EVER (I Peter 1:23).

But the word of the Lord ENDURETH FOR EVER . . . (I Peter 1:25).

The grass withereth, the flower fadeth: BUT THE WORD OF OUR GOD SHALL STAND FOREVER (Isaiah 40:8).

CAN I TRUST THE MODERN JEHOIAKIMS?

With all the hullabaloo about the "original autographs" that comes from the Alexandrians (who are the modern day Jehoiakims) . . . I ask this simple question: DID GOD'S "ORIGINAL AUTOGRAPHS" GIVEN BY JEREMIAH TO BARUCH LAST FOREVER?

The answer is an obvious *NO*. They went into the Euphrates River. Then is God a liar when He says over and over again that His WORDS which comprise HIS WORD shall stand forever? He WOULD BE if the Alexandrians are right when they say that the only inspired, inerrant Scriptures that ever existed were the "original autographs"!

I declare unto my reader that even though God's "original autographs" given to Jeremiah ended up at the bottom of the Euphrates River and soon disintegrated, HIS INFALLIBLE WORDS REMAIN INTACT IN THE *COPIES!!!*

And so it has been down through the centuries. Even though the "original autographs" have long ago disintegrated and gone to the dust, WE STILL HAVE EVERY WORD GOD EVER PUT IN THE SIXTY-SIX BOOKS OF THE BIBLE IN *PRESERVED* COPIES!!!

You have to be severely retarded in order to overlook the fact that God wasn't nervous at all about what happened to the "originals" once there were COPIES intact and the message itself had been delivered.

Then why should we get all up tight about the "originals" when God isn't? In our King James Bible, we have an EXACT COPY of the book of Jeremiah in OUR language! Not ONE WORD has been lost! God has PRESERVED the WORDS (Psalm 12:6-7; Matt. 24:35, etc.). Besides . . . even if we HAD the "originals" . . . we couldn't READ them! What good would they do us? God, in His divine wisdom and power, has PRESERVED His WORDS for us in ALL SIXTY-SIX BOOKS OF HIS BIBLE! Hallelujah! Praise His

CAN I TRUST MY BIBLE?

wonderful name!

I don't know of anything you Alexandrians can praise *your* god about. Since he couldn't even preserve his words intact down through the centuries, you must not think very much of him. Well, to be honest with you, I DON'T EITHER.

VI. HUMAN INTERCESSION

In our Jeremiah story, it is important to note that there were three princes who spoke up to King Jehoiakim before he destroyed the scroll and pled with him not to do it. After we read of Jehoiakim cutting up the Word of God and throwing it into the fire, we are told,

> *Nevertheless Elnathan and Delaiah and Gemariah had made INTERCESSION to the king THAT HE WOULD NOT BURN THE ROLL: but he would not hear them* (Jer. 36:25).

Elnathan, Delaiah, and Gemariah were sensible men who no doubt held the Word of God in high respect and were aware that God is very particular about His Word. They were right to make intercession on behalf of the Word of God and earnestly plead with King Jehoiakim not to destroy the scroll. They knew that the Lord would severely deal with him if he did it.

All across this country of ours, as I have traveled in my work of evangelism, I have pled with Baptist pastors not to take the penknife of their so-called "education" and "scholarship" and CUT UP the King James Bible by correcting it . . .which is to do the same thing that Jehoiakim did. I have warned them not to "throw the King James Bible in the fire" and turn to perverted "bibles" that are abundantly available today. Many of them have not listened to my intercessions on behalf of the Word of God. They have scoffed at me, ignoring my warnings.

I've seen it happen in fellowship meetings . . . when other

CAN I TRUST THE MODERN JEHOIAKIMS?

preachers who stand for the King James Bible as I do have stood in the pulpit and preached their conviction that the Authorized Version of 1611 is the inspired, infallible Word of God in the English language. They have been booed and hissed at by Baptist preachers in the crowd who belong to the Alexandrian cult. Those King James men have stomped on the god of the Alexandrians; and in response, they boo and hiss.

As I will demonstrate throughout the book, the only pure, perfect Word of God in the English language is the AV1611 King James Bible. To USE it and to CORRECT it, or to cast it aside for one or more of the perversions IS THE SAME THING IN THE EYES OF ALMIGHTY GOD AS WHAT JEHOIAKIM DID TO THE ROLL OF THE BOOK IN THE WINTERHOUSE OF THE PALACE SO LONG AGO! Sooner or later, those preachers (and laymen alike) who "cut up" the King James Bible because they don't like what it says WILL ANSWER TO ITS AUTHOR!!!

Which brings me to . . .

VII. DIVINE CONDEMNATION

Look what God did to the man who cut up His WORD and threw it into the fire.

> *Then the word of the Lord came to Jeremiah, after that the king had burned the roll, and the words which Baruch wrote at the mouth of Jeremiah, saying. . .thou shalt say to Jehoiakim, king of Judah, Thus saith the Lord; THOU HAST BURNED THIS ROLL. . . Therefore thus saith the Lord of Jehoiakim king of Judah; He shall have none to sit upon the throne of David: and HIS DEAD BODY SHALL BE CAST OUT IN THE DAY TO THE HEAT, AND IN THE NIGHT TO THE FROST* (Jer. 36:27, 29-30).

God made it clear that Jehoiakim was going to pay WITH

CAN I TRUST MY BIBLE?

HIS LIFE for cutting up His Word and burning it in the fire! God was so angry about what Jehoiakim did. He would see to it that before Jehoiakim's carcass was finally buried, it would lie around decomposing day and night. Then when his rotting, smelly, worm-infested corpse was finally buried, God would see to it that it was a very repugnant burial. Listen to God.

> *Therefore thus saith the Lord concerning Jehoiakim the son of Josiah king of Judah; They shall not lament for him . . . He shall be buried with the burial of an ASS, drawn and cast forth beyond the gates of Jerusalem* (Jer. 22:18-19).

That's what the Almighty God thinks of a men who would dare tamper with His Word!!! Just because you don't like what God's Word says doesn't give you the right to "cut it up" by CORRECTING it nor to "throw it in the fire" by tossing it aside for a modern-day perversion! In the eyes of God, Jehoiakim made an ASS of himself by daring to tamper with the Word of God . . . and I don't think He looks at today's Alexandrians any differently. The modern-day Alexandrian has made the same thing of himself that Jehoiakim did, and if you don't like my language here, take it up with God. HE'S THE ONE WHO CALLED JEHOIAKIM WHAT HE WAS! ! ! !

Having laid this foundation from the Book of Jeremiah concerning Jehoiakim, we then return to the question . . . CAN I TRUST THE MODERN JEHOIAKIMS?

Let us proceed so that we can give a satisfactory answer to the question. I referred to the modern-day Jehoiakims (those who would cut up and burn my King James Bible) as "Alexandrians." Let me now explain the term.

There are TWO main sources of manuscripts from which the New Testament has been translated. The *first source* is the Traditional Text, which is also known as the Majority Text, or the Received Text, known in Latin as the Textus Receptus. It is this Text

CAN I TRUST THE MODERN JEHOIAKIMS?

which the King James translators used; and properly so, for it is this Text that has its roots in Antioch, Syria.

The *second source* is two-fold: the Vaticanus and Sinaiticus texts. Both of them have their roots in Alexandria, Egypt. These are known as the Minority Texts. The AV1611 King James Bible is the ONLY one we have today that was translated from the Antioch Text. ALL . . . I repeat . . .ALL the other English versions came from the Alexandrian texts. Let us do a little Bible study here and compare the two cities, Antioch and Alexandria.

Strangely enough, the first time either city is found in Scripture, they are found in the same chapter. The New Testament church in Jerusalem was getting so big that the apostles couldn't handle all the work, so they called the church together and explained that they needed seven men to help them . . . and that they wanted men of honest report who had wisdom and were Spirit-filled.

And the saying pleased the whole multitude: and they chose Stephen, a man full of faith and of the Holy Ghost, and Philip, and Prochorus, and Nicanor, and Timon, and Parmenas, and Nicolas a proselyte of ANTIOCH: Whom they set before the apostles: and when they had prayed, they laid their hands on them. And THE WORD OF GOD INCREASED; and THE NUMBER OF THE DISCIPLES MULTIPLIED IN JERUSALEM GREATLY . . . (Acts 6:5-7).

Let me point out that the only man whose city of origin is mentioned is Nicolas of ANTIOCH. We learn quickly that like the other six men, Nicolas was Spirit-filled, was of honest report, and was full of wisdom. You will note that with men like Nicolas working for the Lord in the Jerusalem church, THE WORD OF GOD INCREASED. And, of course, when the Word of God increased, so did the number of saved people. Souls were getting saved!

Question: WHY DID THE HOLY SPIRIT CHOOSE TO

CAN I TRUST MY BIBLE?

LIST ONLY ANTIOCH IN ACTS 6:5 AND NOT THE HOME TOWNS OF THE OTHER SIX MEN?

Answer: BECAUSE THE HOLY SPIRIT WANTED TO LINK ONE CITY IN THIS CONTEXT WITH THE WORD OF GOD IN VERSE 7 . . . *ANTIOCH*. God was going to assemble His perfect, preserved manuscripts in Antioch; and He wanted to draw our attention to Antioch, connecting it with His Word. Nicolas had plenty to do with the Word of God INCREASING in Jerusalem. Now, let's continue.

> *And Stephen, full of faith and power, did great wonders and miracles among the people. Then there arose certain of the synagogue, which is called the synagogue of the Libertines, and Cyrenians, and ALEXANDRIANS, and of them of Cilicia and of Asia, DISPUTING WITH STEPHEN. And they were not able to RESIST the wisdom and the spirit by which he spake.*
>
> *Then they suborned men, which said, We have heard him speak blasphemous words against Moses, and against God. And they stirred up the people, and the elders, and the scribes, and came upon him, and caught him, and brought him to the council. (As in NATIONAL Council, maybe?) And set up FALSE WITNESSES, which said, This man ceaseth not to speak blasphemous words against this holy place, and THE LAW;* (Acts 6:8-13).

Right here, God begins to show us the color of the ALEXANDRIANS. Stephen's "wisdom" no doubt came from his knowledge of the Word of God; for had it been his own wisdom, the Lord could not have given him the power that he had, nor could he have been full of faith. My reader will note that IMMEDIATELY

CAN I TRUST THE MODERN JEHOIAKIMS?

Stephen is *resisted* by the ALEXANDRIANS and their buddies. They DISPUTE with Stephen over THE LAW! The law is the Word of God! Leave it to the ALEXANDRIANS and their pals to STIR UP THE PEOPLE against the man who preaches the Word of God and to set up false witnesses against him, accusing him of blaspheming the Word of God.

Today's Alexandrians work in exactly the same way. They accuse us "King James guys" of stirring up trouble, when all the time we just keep on preaching the AV1611 and believing it. And when we ignore their "scholarly" proclamation that only the "originals" were inspired and inerrant, they accuse us of blaspheming the Word of God! WHO is stirring up the trouble?

Whenever I have heard a man preach from one of the perversions or preach from the King James and correct it . . . I HAVE NEVER YET MADE A PUBLIC FUSS AND ATTACKED HIM, BARKING AT HIM LIKE A WILD COYOTE! But I have had so many Alexandrians do it to me, I've lost count of the number. Oh, well. The coyotes howl at the moon, but it just keeps on shinin'!

I think my reader can see that the contrast between Antioch and Alexandria in the Bible sheds quite a bit of light on both places. One for good . . . the other for evil. Let's move on.

> *Now they which were scattered abroad upon the persecution that arose about Stephen travelled as far as Phenice, and Cyprus, and ANTIOCH, PREACHING THE WORD to none but unto the Jews only. And some of them were men of Cyprus and Cyrene, which, when they were come to ANTIOCH, spake unto the Grecians, PREACHING THE LORD JESUS. And the hand of the Lord was with them: AND A GREAT NUMBER BELIEVED, AND TURNED UNTO THE LORD* (Acts 11:19-21).

CAN I TRUST MY BIBLE?

My, my! Wouldn't you say that some great things were going on at Antioch? At Antioch, they are preaching the WORD. At ANTIOCH, they are preaching THE LORD JESUS (which is EXACTLY the same thing as preaching the Word!). At Antioch, the hand of the Lord is on His people, and a great number of souls are being saved. Looks to me like God just might have a special place in His heart for ANTIOCH, eh, what?

I wonder how things are going for those disputers, resisters of the Word, and false witnesses over at Alexandria. Do you suppose those dudes are having a big revival over there? Well, we'll check on them later. Right now, we see that the news of God's blessings at ANTIOCH is spreading fast.

> *Then tidings of these things came unto the ears of the church which was in Jerusalem: and they sent forth Barnabas, that he should go as far as ANTIOCH* (Acts 11:22).

The members of the church in Jerusalem got all excited. They wanted to hear first-hand about what was going on at ANTIOCH, so they sent Barnabas to see it for himself and make a report. Barnabas called his travel agent, booked the earliest flight to ANTlOCH, then called the church up there and told them when to meet him at the airport.

When he landed, there was a whole crowd standing by the fence, waving their King James Bibles and singing, *"Get the new look from the Old Book!"*

DON'T LOOK AT ME LIKE THAT, YOU ALEXANDRIANS! I can see the sneer on your faces and hear your squeaky voices right now. "Hey, Lacy, don't you know there weren't any King James Bibles till 1611?"

Yeah. I know it. I . . . uh . . . just love my Book so much that I get a little carried away now and then. Of course, when I get

CAN I TRUST THE MODERN JEHOIAKIMS?

calmed down and we get a little further along, I'm going to show you that THEY HAD THE MANUSCRIPTS COLLECTING AT ANTIOCH FROM WHICH MY KING JAMES BIBLE WAS TRANSLATED!!! So if they had grabbed what manuscripts they had and brought them to the airport, and waved them at Barnabas, IT WOULD HAVE BEEN THE SAME THING AS WAVING THE KING JAMES BIBLE!

Go ahead, Alexandrian Jehoiakims. Choke on it. You boys don't believe there's a real Bible anywhere in this world, so you stay so sober all the time. We "King James nuts" HAVE the real Bible so we can have a little fun once in awhile, knowing that man shall not live by bread alone, but by EVERY WORD that proceedeth out of the mouth of God. Let me tell you, kiddies . . . life is a whole lot sweeter when you KNOW you HAVE every word of God IN YOUR HAND!

What's that you say, Alexandrians? You say, "There weren't no airport at Antioch!" Really, guys, I'd think that being such scholars as you are, you'd use better English than that!

What's that you say? You say I just quoted from the King James Bible, and it doesn't say anything about Antioch having an airport where Barnabas landed? Well, bless your pea-pickin' hearts. You're always telling me that my King James Bible is missing a whole lot of truth. So I'll tell you what. You know where I learned that Antioch had an airport in Barnabas's day? . . . FROM THE "ORIGINALS"!!!!!!!

What's that? You say the "originals" didn't mention an airport in Antioch? Well, I'll tell you what . . . YOU PRODUCE 'EM AND PROVE IT!

Now, for my Bible-believing friends . . . while we're waiting for the Alexandrians to produce their "originals" they're always bragging about, let's move on. Barnabas arrives in ANTIOCH.

CAN I TRUST MY BIBLE?

> *Who, When he came, and had seen THE GRACE OF GOD, was glad, and exhorted them all, that with purpose of heart they would cleave unto the Lord. For he was a good man, and full of the Holy Ghost and of faith: AND MUCH PEOPLE WAS ADDED UNTO THE LORD* (Acts 11:23- 24).

No one can deny that the grace of God was on the church at ANTIOCH. Barnabas was glad to see it, and he got so wrapped up in the blessings of God in ANTIOCH that he got a whole bunch of people saved himself. He got so excited about what God was doing in ANTIOCH, that he couldn't contain himself. He just HAD to share it with someone else. His mind went to young Saul of Tarsus, who had just been saved a few weeks. You will recall that Saul of Tarsus and Barnabas had become friends right after Saul's conversion (Acts 9:26-27). With God working so mightily in ANTIOCH, Barnabas was eager to get Saul there. He knew God had called Saul to preach, and he felt it would be good for the young convert to get in on what God was doing in ANTIOCH.

Barnabas knew Saul had gone back to his home in Tarsus (Acts 9:30), so he hopped on a Greyhound bus (That's in the "originals" . . . and I dare an Alexandrian to PROVE it's not!) and headed for Tarsus.

> *Then departed Barnabas to Tarsus, for to seek Saul: And when he had found him, HE BROUGHT HIM UNTO ANTIOCH. And it came to pass, that a whole year they assembled themselves with the church, and taught much people. And the disciples were called Christians first at ANTIOCH* (Acts 11 :25-26).

No one in his right mind could miss seeing the hand of the Lord in this situation. God wanted Saul at ANTIOCH FOR THAT YEAR. He wanted Saul to teach the church things He had already taught the young preacher . . . but He also wanted Saul to be

CAN I TRUST THE MODERN JEHOIAKIMS?

attached to the New Testament church in ANTIOCH, from whence would come HIS WORD, which would result in the King James Translation.

God had plans, and He was working them out. He also sent some prophets from Jerusalem so they would be in ANTIOCH at the same time Saul was.

And in these days came prophets from Jerusalem to ANTIOCH (Acts 11:27).

Barnabas had been saved and baptized in Jerusalem, so his church membership was in the First Baptist Church of Jerusalem. Saul had been baptized at Damascus, so his membership was in the First Baptist Church of Damascus. However, when Saul and Barnabas got to ANTIOCH and decided to stay for a year, they joined the First Baptist Church of ANTIOCH. If my reader should think I am kidding about them being BAPTIST churches . . . I assure you, I am NOT kidding! BAPTISTS ARE NOT PROTESTANTS!!! There were BAPTISTS before there was ever a Catholic church. . .hence, there were BAPTISTS before there were Protestant churches. Real BAPTISTS are the only people who can trace their heritage back through history through a trail of martyr blood RIGHT TO JESUS CHRIST and the CHURCH HE STARTED!!!

Objectors scream, "Well, if those New Testament churches were Baptist churches, WHY DIDN'T GOD SEE TO IT THAT THEY WERE CALLED BAPTIST CHURCHES IN THE BIBLE?"

Let me help you with that. Jesus Himself had BAPTIST baptism (Matthew 3:1, 13-17). The men with whom He started His church (Luke 6:13 Cf. I Cor. 12:28) had BAPTIST baptism (Acts 1:21-22). The name BAPTIST came from God. Check Matthew 3:1, and you'll see that John was called the BAPTIST *before* he ever baptized anyone, so he was not called the BAPTIST because he baptized people. GOD gave him the name BAPTIST. So if you were

CAN I TRUST MY BIBLE?

going to look for an identification for the church Jesus started, what would YOU call it?

Some will answer, "I would call it CHRISTIAN because the disciples were called CHRISTIANS first at Antioch!" Now, there's nothing wrong with the name "Christian." It means "like Christ." Certainly those of us who know Him should strive to be LIKE HIM, but the name "Christian" DID NOT COME FROM GOD! Our *enemies* named us Christians.

So if you are going to look for a name to go by that came from GOD . . . it is BAPTIST. However . . . if God had seen to it that they were called BAPTIST churches in the Bible . . . every kooky cult, every heretical church, and every denomination in the world would call themselves BAPTIST. It's bad enough right now with some modernist churches calling themselves "Baptist" . . . but think what a mess it would be if EVERYBODY called themselves by that name! So . . . God did not allow His New Testament churches to be called "Baptist Churches" in the Bible. He fixed it so you would have to do some real studying in the Book to find HIS identification for His church.

These selfsame people who are our Baptist forefathers were persecuted and slaughtered in the days of the Book of Acts but it didn't stop there. When the Catholic church came along (out of pagan Babylon), it took up persecution against the New Testament churches, calling them "Anabaptists." When the Protestant movement began under Martin Luther, the Protestants persecuted and slaughtered Baptists. Luther led a vicious attack against them, as did the bloody John Calvin, who started the Presbyterian church. Get ahold of some good history books that haven't been tampered with by Catholic and Protestant hands, and READ IT FOR YOURSELF!

Now, where was I? Oh, yes. ANTIOCH.

Saul of Tarsus and Barnabas joined the First Baptist Church of ANTIOCH . . . exactly where GOD wanted them. When God was

CAN I TRUST THE MODERN JEHOIAKIMS?

ready to send out preachers to spread His Word, guess where He got them. The First Baptist Church of ANTIOCH!!!

> *Now there were IN THE CHURCH [If they were IN the church, they were members.] at Antioch certain prophets and teachers; as BARNABAS . . . and SAUL* (Acts 13:1).

When the Lord needed men who were grounded in the WORD, He knew right where to get them. He didn't look in ALEXANDRIA, I can assure you of that! And He didn't look in some mugwump organization like Campus Crusade, Youth for Christ, or the Starvation Army! He went directly to a New Testament Baptist church! He went to the very church where He would one day gather the finished manuscripts of the entire New Testament, which would be called the RECEIVED TEXT.

As the church in ANTIOCH ministered unto the Lord:

> *. . . The Holy Ghost said, Separate me BARNABAS AND SAUL for the work whereunto I have called them. And when they had fasted and prayed, and laid their hands on them, they [the church] sent them away* (Acts 13:2-3).

Now let's watch what happens as Saul and Barnabas are sent forth from ANTIOCH by the Holy Spirit. They preach the WORD OF GOD in Salamis (Acts 13:5). At Paphos, Sergius Paulus called for Saul and Barnabas, desiring to hear THE WORD OF GOD. In Acts 13:9, Saul is called "Paul" for the first time. We read in Acts 13:12 that Sergius Paulus GOT SAVED, being astonished at the DOCTRINE OF THE LORD!

The DOCTRINE OF THE LORD is pure truth. Where did the doctrine come from? . . . THE WORD OF GOD that Paul and Barnabas preached! And where were they sent out from by the Holy Spirit? GLORY! They were sent out from the church where one day

CAN I TRUST MY BIBLE?

the manuscripts would be collected that would be the basis for our KING JAMES BIBLE!

That first missionary journey of Paul and Barnabas was signally blessed of God. Great numbers of people were saved in city after city, and more New Testament churches were founded. After many long months, the two preachers aimed for ANTIOCH.

And when they had preached THE WORD in Perga, they went down into Attalia: And thence sailed to ANTIOCH, from whence they had been recommended to the grace of God for the work which they fulfilled. And when they were come, and had gathered the church together, they rehearsed all that God had done with them, and how he had opened the door of faith unto the Gentiles. And there they abode LONG TIME with the disciples (Acts 14:25-28).

Paul and Barnabas liked it so well at that church where the Word of God was taught, preached, believed and revered, they stayed for a LONG TIME. The day came, however, when God was ready to send Paul out again. This time, He sent him FROM ANTIOCH, along with a new partner . . . Silas. And if you know the Book of Acts, you will recall what kind of work the Lord did through Paul and Silas as they went forth from the church in ANTIOCH, preaching THE WORD OF GOD.

I think this reveals to us the kind of place ANTIOCH holds in the heart of God. But what about ALEXANDRIA? Well, I would first remind you that Alexandria is in Egypt of Africa. Have you ever noticed God's attitude toward Egypt?

EGYPT was a place of licentiousness, rape, and murder (see Genesis 12:10-13). EGYPT was the vile land where God's chosen nation was held in hard bondage and made to be slaves. It was there that the king of Egypt ordered all the helpless little Hebrew baby

CAN I TRUST THE MODERN JEHOIAKIMS?

boys to be slaughtered (see Exodus chapter 1).

In Exodus 20:2, God called EGYPT a "house of bondage." In Deuteronomy 17:16, God tells His people to stay away from EGYPT, saying, ". . . Ye shall henceforth return NO MORE THAT WAY." God does not like EGYPT.

When Israel was a child [says God], then I loved him, and called my son OUT OF EGYPT (Hosea 11:1).

Many of the prophecies in the Bible have a NEAR fulfillment and a FAR fulfillment. In Hosea 11:1, God refers to Israel as His son, and says He called him OUT OF Egypt. When God's only-begotten Son, the two-year-old Jesus, was threatened by King Herod, Joseph took Mary and the young Child into Egypt; but just as soon as Herod was dead, God called His Son OUT OF EGYPT . . . thus fulfilling Hosea 11:1 as a FAR prophecy.

When Jacob was dying down in EGYPT, he called his son Joseph to his bedside and pled, ". . . bury me NOT, I pray thee, in EGYPT . . . carry me OUT OF EGYPT" (Gen.47:29-30). Jacob had the same feelings about EGYPT that God has.

We all know how God feels about SODOM. He destroyed it with FIRE. Sodom was a stench in the nostrils of God. He feels the same way about EGYPT. In Revelation 11:8, when God wants to censure Jerusalem for all of her wickedness and abominations, He calls the city Sodom and EGYPT. Now I ask you . . . if you were God, and you were going to preserve your Word . . . would you entrust it to EGYPT? . . . Hardly.

Now what about the Egyptian city, ALEXANDRIA? We have already seen in Scripture that men from that city RESISTED God's man Stephen and DISPUTED with him over the WORD OF GOD. Our history books tell us that ALEXANDRIA was a seed-bed of agnostic education and humanistic philosophy . . . both which are anti-God and anti-Bible. For dead sure, it was NOT a center

CAN I TRUST MY BIBLE?

for Bible preaching and soulwinning, as was ANTIOCH. However, ALEXANDRIA *is* known for Biblical error. Take Apollos, for instance.

> *And a certain Jew named Apollos, born at Alexandria, an eloquent man, and mighty in the scriptures, came to Ephesus. This man was instructed in the way of the Lord; and being fervent in spirit, he spake and taught diligently the things of the Lord, knowing only the baptism of John. And he began to speak boldly in the synagogue: whom when Aquila and Priscilla had heard, they took him unto them, and expounded unto him the way of God MORE PERFECTLY* (Acts 18:24-26).

Apollos was eloquent, and it is even said he was mighty in the Scriptures. He had been instructed in the way of the Lord, evidently at ALEXANDRIA, where he was born. But even though by ALEXANDRIAN standards he was mighty in the Scriptures, God used Aquila and Priscilla to STRAIGHTEN HIM OUT ON THE SCRIPTURES. You can bank on it. When Priscilla and Aquila "expounded" unto Apollos the "way of God MORE PERFECTLY," they expounded FROM THE SCRIPTURES.

Priscilla and Aquila were MIGHTIER in the Scriptures than was Apollos. It took THEM to square his thinking around.

WHO were Priscilla and Aquila? According to Romans 16:3-5, they were very close friends of Paul. They had risked their own lives to save Paul's, and they had a New Testament church meeting in their house. There is no question that they spent a great deal of time with Paul, who had spent a year in ANTIOCH as a young preacher, getting grounded solidly in the WORD OF GOD.

Do you see it? ANTIOCH was known as the city where the Word of God was preached and taught straight-as-an-arrow. ALEXANDRIA was known as a city where there was POOR BIBLE

CAN I TRUST THE MODERN JEHOIAKIMS?

TEACHING. If I were God, I certainly wouldn't trust that bunch with my Holy Word.

Let me mention one more thing about ALEXANDRIA as we find it in the Bible. In Acts chapter 27, Paul has been arrested and is being taken to Rome. The devil, who was "a MURDERER from the beginning" (John 8:44), wanted Paul dead. All he had to do was get him to Rome, Italy and put him in the hands of Nero Caesar. Nero would do his spiritual father's bidding and MURDER Paul. So when the devil contrived to get Paul to Nero at Rome, guess where the ship was from that would carry Paul to his execution? As Luke tells the story under the inspiration of the Holy Spirit, speaking of Paul and himself, he says,

> And when we had sailed over the sea of Cilicia and Pamphylia, we came to Myra, a city of Lycia. And there the centurion (who held Paul captive) found a ship of ALEXANDRIA sailing into ITALY; and he put us therein (Acts 27:5-6).

As the story proceeds, Luke tells about the ALEXANDRIAN ship being wrecked. He and Paul spent three months on the little island of Melita. When winter was over and the ships were sailing the high seas once more, the centurion, eager to get Paul to Rome, took him and Luke on board another ship. Guess where the ship was from!

> And after three months we departed in a ship of ALEXANDRIA ... (Acts 28:11).

And it was this ship that carried Paul to Rome where, according to history, he had his head chopped off. The city of ALEXANDRIA, and its country, EGYPT just doesn't have a favorable place in the mind of God. There is just no way He would entrust ALEXANDRIA, EGYPT with His precious, Holy Word!

I pointed out that the ALEXANDRIAN Apollos was a man

CAN I TRUST MY BIBLE?

of the Scriptures, but that he had experienced poor Bible teaching and had to be straightened out by Paul's close friends, Aquila and Priscilla. History tells us of a philosopher named Pantaenus, who founded the "Catechetical School" in ALEXANDRIA, EGYPT about A.D. 180. The school was established for the purpose of teaching the tenets of a religion based on humanistic philosophy. Pantaenus incorporated some "Christianity" into his doctrines, and began to gather some corrupted manuscripts of "scriptures." He knew they were corrupt, but used them to teach his students that there was no such thing as INFALLIBLE Scripture. His vile doctrine STUCK. Such untruth has been the philosophy of ALEXANDRIANS ever since!

After about twenty years as head of the "Catechetical School," Pantaenus stepped aside, allowing a humanist philosopher named Clement to take over as head of the school. Clement tied his philosophical views to "Christianity," and worked even harder at collecting corrupt manuscripts of the "scriptures."

My reader might ask, "Are you telling me that there were people producing corrupt manuscripts way back in A.D. 180?" They were doing it long before THAT, my friend. The devil had his Bible corrupters in full swing during PAUL'S ministry. Look what Paul wrote to the Corinthian church.

For we are not as many, which CORRUPT THE WORD OF GOD . . . (II Cor. 2:17)

Peter wrote that there were unlearned and unstable men who "wrested" the Scriptures Paul wrote, and said they were doing the same thing with other Scriptures (II Peter 3:15-16). You can't WREST the Scriptures without CORRUPTING THEM! Now watch what Peter said in the very next verse.

Ye therefore, beloved, seeing ye know these things before, beware lest ye also, being LED AWAY WITH THE ERROR OF THE WICKED, fall from your own

CAN I TRUST THE MODERN JEHOIAKIMS?

steadfastness (II Pet. 3:17).

The Holy Spirit through Peter's pen flat calls Scripture wresting "THE ERROR OF THE WICKED"! What the ALEXANDRIANS do to God's Word is the ERROR OF THE WICKED! And the warning is sounded here that steadfast Christians will fall from their steadfastness if they are led away by the ALEXANDRIANS who wrest and corrupt the Scriptures! Led away from WHAT? . . . FROM BELIEVING THAT GOD ALMIGHTY HAS GIVEN HIS WORDS TO US AND HAS PRESERVED THEM PERFECT AND WITHOUT ERROR!!!

Clement of ALEXANDRIA taught his students that the Bible was full of errors. He flat denied the deity of Jesus Christ and mocked the miracles that Jesus performed as recorded in the Gospels.

In about A.D. 230, Clement turned his school over to a man named Adamantius Origen, who held the same philosophies. Though Origen had a keen and brilliant mind, it was bent in the wrong direction by his spiritual father, the devil. It turned out, however, that Origen was a more wicked skeptic than Clement.

Origen became the most influential religious leader in his generation. Not only did he poison the minds of his students at the Catechetical School, but he also poisoned the minds of all who read his works. He produced a six-column "bible" called the Hexapla. Each of the columns had a different version of "scripture." He continually changed the words that did not agree with his liberal philosophical ideas. His approach to Scripture was that it was all to be spiritualized and never to be taken literal. The creation story was only a myth, and Adam and Eve were not actual people. The miracles recorded in Scripture were not miracles at all. They were just subjects of "poetry," and once in a while the poets got carried away.

Origen launched a vicious attack on the deity of the Lord

CAN I TRUST MY BIBLE?

Jesus Christ. His most famous work was his "Logos Doctrine." He pointed out in his writings that in Greek philosophy Logos was the name of the divine principle of creation and rational world order. He applied this principle to Jesus Christ, saying that Jesus was the Logos, a created god who shed some good philosophical light in the world.

The translators of the New World bible of the Jehovah's Witnesses wrested and corrupted John 1:18, making Jesus a created god, and the translators of the New American Standard version did EXACTLY THE SAME THING! Both sets of translators were ALEXANDRIANS who got their wicked ideas from Origen. Before Origen died at the age of sixty-nine, he had produced a complete set of corrupted manuscripts of "scripture," which he passed on to his followers in ALEXANDRIA. When people asked Origen's followers if the manuscripts were reliable as truth from God, they were told that they were the "best manuscripts" available, but that they were not perfect. Only the ORIGINAL manuscripts had been perfect. SOUND LIKE ANYTHING YOU'RE HEARING TODAY?

Thus, Origen was not only responsible for giving the world a set of manuscripts that were corrupt . . . he also left us with the philosophy that there is no such thing as an inerrant Bible on the face of the earth today. This is the ALEXANDRIAN philosophy that is still believed and taught from thousands of "Fundamentalist" pulpits around the world today . . . and that is forced into the minds of Bible College students in 99.44% of the Bible Colleges in America. Most "Fundamentalist" pastors, college professors, radio and television "preachers" in this country of ours are ALEXANDRIANS. The majority of them use bibles that have their roots in Origen of ALEXANDRIA. The sad thing is that a good many of them "use" the Antiochian King James Bible, but follow through the ALEXANDRIAN philosophy that there is no such thing as a perfect, inerrant Bible on the face of the earth, so they have the

CAN I TRUST THE MODERN JEHOIAKIMS?

right to correct the King James Bible where they disagree with it. Either way, it is corrupt ALEXANDRIAN philosophy.

I believe my reader can now understand the term "ALEXANDRIAN." The modern-day Jehoiakims who cut and tear at my King James Bible and toss it aside for other versions are ALEXANDRIANS.

Satan's polluted ALEXANDRIAN manuscripts were carefully kept by a follower of Origen, a man named Eusebius. Under Constantine, Eusebius was ordered to produce a bible that would appeal to the masses. Constantine had embraced "Christianity" for political purposes. I put it in quotes because it was not TRUE Christianity. Constantine was NOT a saved man. Eusebius the ALEXANDRIAN was happy to write manuscripts of his own, based on those of Origen. Eusebius's bible was used for centuries until it was taken over by Jerome who was called upon by the pope to prepare a bible that would favor the Roman Catholic teaching. Jerome's bible was produced from the ALEXANDRIAN manuscripts of Eusebius (copies, of course) and was officially accepted by the Roman Catholic church at the Council of Trent in 1546. It was Jerome who placed the Apocryphal books into the Catholic bible, announcing that God had revealed to him that they were part of the Scriptural canon. The pope and the other "holy daddies" of the Roman Catholic church believed Jerome, and the Apocryphal books were accepted as from God.

Time moved on and then came the nineteenth century. In England (where the King James Bible had been published), there were two ALEXANDRIAN snakes-in-the-grass that stuck their heads up. They were Brooke Foss Westcott and Fenton John Anthony Hort. In 1881 they published a two-volume edition of the New Testament in "original Greek." They had been working on the polluted text for some thirty years. They used the ALEXANDRIAN-based Origen-Eusebius-Jerome corrupted manuscripts as the basis

CAN I TRUST MY BIBLE?

for their "original Greek" new testament.

The Roman Catholic church has stuck to using the ALEXANDRIAN Vaticanus for translating their "scriptures," but it is from Westcott and Hort's corrupted ALEXANDRIAN text that ALL OTHER present-day bibles have been produced . . . *except the AV1611 King James Bible.* I know the "translators" of the so-called New King James version SAY they did their "translating" from the Masoretic Hebrew text for the Old Testament, and the Textus Receptus of the Greek for the New Testament, but if that is so, WHY DO SO MANY PASSAGES IN THE "NEW KING JAMES" HAVE ALEXANDRIAN RENDERINGS OF SO MANY WORDS AND PHRASES???? We will deal with the so-called New King James version later.

ALEXANDRIANS Westcott and Hort were blatant Christ rejecters. Neither even claimed to be a born-again, blood-washed son of God. They were liberal theologians to the "Nth" degree, and they were class "A" heretics. Origen, Eusebius, and Jerome were their heroes. Neither Westcott nor Hort ever stated that they believed the Bible was the inspired, inerrant Word of God. They have gone on record as saying it was to be handled and treated like any other book.

While doing their devilish work on their corrupt Greek text, both Westcott and Hort were professors at Cambridge University. They taught humanist theories to their students, along with evolution and the idea that none of the Bible could be taken literally. Let me give you a quote or two from them.

Professor Westcott had visited a Catholic church to observe a mass. He then toured the place. Afterward, he wrote about coming upon a kneeling booth that held the *pieta,* a statute of Mary holding a dead Christ (which scene never happened!). Describing it, Westcott said, "It is very small, with one kneeling-place; and behind the screen was a 'pieta.' Had I been alone, I could have knelt there for hours."

CAN I TRUST THE MODERN JEHOIAKIMS?

Another quote from Professor Westcott: "No one, now, I suppose, holds that the first three chapters of Genesis gives a literal history."

How do you like "them apples"? You Christians who have turned to the NIV, or the NASV, or the NEB, or the "Living Bible," or the "New King James," etc. are following BROOK FOSS WESTCOTT!

Let's hear from Professor Hort. In his day, "Evangelicals" were Bible believers. That is NOT someday! Listen to him: "Evangelicals seem to be perverted." "The book that has most engaged me is Darwin. My feeling is that the evolution theory is unanswerable." "I have been persuaded for many years that Mary-worship and Jesus-worship have very much in common." "I am inclined to think that such a state of Eden never existed." "The Romish view seems to be nearer, and more likely to lead to the truth than the Evangelical. We dare not forsake the sacraments or God will forsake us."

More rotten "apples." You Christians who give allegiance to teachers and preachers who use the ALEXANDRIAN bible versions are garnishing the tombs of Westcott and Hort as being reliable and "godly" men. THEY WERE NOT!!! They were LOST, Bible-perverting, Scripture-corrupting HERETICS!!!

Now, I've shown you the ALEXANDRIAN roots for all the "bibles" except the REAL English Bible, the AV1611 King James. Do you remember Job's powerful question . . . ?

Who can bring a clean thing out of an unclean? NOT ONE (Job 14:4).

I ask you . . . how can you get a pure Bible from impure men like Pantaenus, Clement, Origen, Eusebius, Jerome, Westcott, or Hort? Answer: YOU CAN'T!!! Who can bring a clean thing out of an unclean? NOBODY!!!

Jesus taught us the same thing.

CAN I TRUST MY BIBLE?

BEWARE OF FALSE PROPHETS, which come to you in sheep's clothing, but inwardly are RAVENING WOLVES. Ye shall know them BY THEIR FRUITS. Do men gather grapes of thorns, or figs of thistles? Even so every good tree bringeth forth good fruit; but a CORRUPT tree bringeth forth EVIL fruit. A good tree CANNOT bring forth evil fruit, neither can a CORRUPT tree bring forth GOOD fruit (Matt. 7:15-18).

I would have you to note the Lord's use of the word "CORRUPT" for a bad tree sort of ties with the use of the word "CORRUPT" in II Corinthians 2:17 when Paul said, *"We are not as many, which CORRUPT the word of God!"*

As we have seen in Scripture, ALEXANDRIA, EGYPT is shown to be a place of poor Bible teaching, and in general, is not looked upon by God as a good place. History has shown us that ALEXANDRIA is the seed-bed of Bible corruption.

We have already seen in Scripture how important ANTIOCH was to the pure Word of God. Now, let me give you a little history on ANTIOCH.

In about A.D. 150, there was a scholar in the church at ANTIOCH who founded a school he called "The School of the Scriptures." His name was Lucian. By this time there were many copies of the entire Bible available in ANTIOCH. When Lucian taught the Scriptures to his students, he told them they were holding the VERY WORD OF GOD in their hands, and that they should take it literally, not figuratively as was being taught by the philosophers in ALEXANDRIA.

Lucian stood against all the pagan philosophies of his day and exalted the Bible as God's inspired, inerrant Word. Since he was part of the church in ANTIOCH, he was a BAPTIST. So the church

CAN I TRUST THE MODERN JEHOIAKIMS?

in ANTIOCH was not only responsible for sending out Paul and Barnabas, then later Paul and Silas to preach the pure WORD OF GOD all over the Mediterranean world, but it was also responsible for exalting the pure Word of God and being used of God to PRESERVE it. ALEXANDRIA is the source of the philosophy that there is no perfect, inerrant Word of God on earth. ANTIOCH is the source of the ideology that there DOES exist the perfect, inerrant Word of God on earth . . . even as Almighty God said in His Word that there always WOULD be (Psalm 12:6-7, Isa. 40:8, Matt. 24:35, etc.).

Time moved on. Copies of the Greek and Hebrew manuscripts were made in ANTIOCH and taken all over the then-known world. When the printing press was invented, it was the desire of Bible believers to get the Scriptures put into print in Hebrew and Greek. There was a Greek scholar in Rotterdam named Erasmus. He desperately wanted to publish a New Testament in the Greek language. He had at his disposal manuscripts from ALEXANDRIA, which he poured over, but found them to be corrupt.

At the same time, Erasmus was given a set of manuscripts by a group of Waldensian churches. Is my reader acquainted with Baptist history? The Waldensians were BAPTISTS! The Catholics called them "Anabaptists," but they called *themselves* BAPTISTS! Erasmus wrote of them in a book he published in 1523, showing that he had great respect for them. Erasmus wrote that he believed in salvation by grace through faith in the Lord Jesus Christ and that we are redeemed by the blood . . . but there is nothing in history that gives record that he was ever baptized into a Waldensian church. However, his enemies dubbed him an "ANABAPTIST" . . . so it just might well be that this great man who had been forced into the Catholic church as an orphaned child ended up actually being a Baptist. A few years after his death in 1536, Pope Paul IV put Erasmus's writings on a black list of books that were forbidden to

CAN I TRUST MY BIBLE?

be read by Roman Catholics.

Rejecting the ALEXANDRIAN manuscripts, Erasmus turned to the ANTIOCHAN manuscripts and put out five printings of the New Testament in Greek. The forty-seven men who translated the King James Bible used the Masoretic Hebrew Text for the Old Testament and the Traditional Greek Text for the New Testament. The Traditional Text was the one given by the Waldensians to Erasmus, which he collated and printed in five editions. Twenty-two years after the King James Bible was published, the Traditional Text received a new name . . . the Received Text, or in Latin, Textus Receptus.

Thus we see that God has used men He chose to PRESERVE His Word from the time of the First Baptist Church of ANTIOCH to the present day. That's why I'm sticking with the AV1611 King James Bible! It, and it ALONE, is the preserved, perfect, inspired, inerrant Word of God in the English language!

I'm sorry to say that the ALEXANDRIAN cult is still going strong today. CAN I TRUST THE MODERN JEHOIAKIMS? Now that I have given you some Bible secular history about the ALEXANDRIANS, let's allow them to speak for themselves. I think you will soon figure out that they cannot be trusted.

Let me begin by quoting from a book which is the result of a "Summit Conference" held at Chicago's Hyatt Regency Hotel in October of 1978. The conference was conducted by a group of evangelicals known as The International Council on Biblical Inerrancy, which had been formed the previous year. The title of the book is *Can We Trust the Bible?* The book is made up of six sermons that were given at the conference. When I hear the word "council," an icy trickle slithers down my spine. It happened when I read the book . . . and my reader will soon see why.

The book was edited by Earl D. Radmacher, president of the Western Conservative Baptist Seminary in Portland, Oregon. Mr.

CAN I TRUST THE MODERN JEHOIAKIMS?

Radmacher says in his preface, "It is the prayer of the ICBI that as those messages of October 1978 are now presented in printed form, the Spirit of God shall so move upon you, the reader, that you will exclaim with us, 'What the Bible says, God says—through human agents and without error.'"

Hey! That sounds pretty good! "What the Bible says, GOD says—through human agents and WITHOUT ERROR!" I only wish I could tell you that the Bible Mr. Radmacher is talking about was one that he could *hold in his hand,* lift it high, and make that prolific proclamation. But, alas, it is not so.

In his preface, Mr. Radmacher quotes a Dr. James A. Borror, who says, "To the extent that you weaken inerrancy, to that extent, you weaken inspiration. To the extent that you weaken inspiration, to that extent you have a garbled revelation. To the extent that you have a garbled revelation, to that extent you have a weakened authority. And when you weaken the authority of the Bible, you launch upon a shifting sea of subjective uncertainty."

Sounds pretty good, too, eh? But, now let these two men tell you what they mean by "inerrancy." Mr. Radmacher says in the same preface, "There are those who believe that you can have an authoritative Scripture without insisting that it be without error in factual data such as history or science. On the other hand, there are those who insist that a doctrine of inspiration without inerrancy of the autographs [ORIGINAL WRITINGS] ultimately and logically results in Scriptures without final and absolute authority."

The capitals are mine, but the words in parenthesis are Mr. Radmacher's. The two sides of thought presented by him show us the thinking of many evangelicals and "fundamentalists" today. Some say it is possible to have an authoritative Bible even though it is in error on factual data such as history and science. Of course, this would be total nonsense, and it is evident that Mr. Radmacher does not hold this view. He holds the view that if you say the "original

CAN I TRUST MY BIBLE?

writings" (autographs) had errors, ultimately and logically you would have Scriptures without final and absolute authority. I totally agree. If the Scriptures God gave to the holy men who wrote them down had errors, you sure could not have inerrant Scriptures today.

BUT! . . . Mr. Radmacher shoots himself out of the saddle when he says in the preface, "A deep and growing concern over the strategic importance of the inerrancy of the AUTOGRAPHS brought into existence, in 1977, The International Council of Biblical inerrancy." Big deal. What in the name of Adamantius P. Origen is so important about inerrant "autographs" if we do not have an inerrant Bible to hold in our hands and read TODAY???

So the ICBI was formed, and the conference was held in order to uplift "THE BIBLE," which not one man or woman who had a part in it has ever SEEN WITH THEIR EYES or HELD IN THEIR HAND! Mr. Radmacher closes off his preface by quoting Philippians 2:15-16 from the perverted New American Standard Version, which has its slimy roots in ALEXANDRIA. The six men whose sermons are printed in *Can We Trust the Bible?* are every one an ALEXANDRIAN.

They are James I. Packer, who quotes the ALEXANDRIAN New International Version throughout his sermon . . . Edmund P. Clowney, whose "bible" is the ALEXANDRIAN American Standard Version . . . Robert C. Preus, who quotes from the King James Version "unless otherwise noted," and also quotes from the nefarious ALEXANDRIAN Revised Standard Version, which is a product of the Communist infiltrated National Council of Churches. Next is James M. Boice, who stays strictly with the ALEXANDRIAN New International Perversion. Another is R.C. Sproul, who quotes his entire message from the ALEXANDRIAN Revised Standard Perversion . . . and last is W.A. Criswell, whose sermon is entitled, "What Happens When I Preach the Bible as Literally True?" His message was good. He quoted from the King

CAN I TRUST THE MODERN JEHOIAKIMS?

James Bible throughout.

However . . . though he went so far as to say that the Book in his hand was the Word of God, he NEVER identified WHAT BOOK he had in his hand . . . and left the impression that the books the other preachers in attendance had in their hands were ALSO the Word of God. Once he lamented that the chapter divisions in the King James Bible were bad; and in another place, he quoted John 5:24 but threw in two words that are used in ALEXANDRIAN versions. Dr. Criswell left me wondering just WHICH Bible is "THE Bible" . . . and WHICH ONE is literally true. By his presence at the ICBI conference, and being on the platform with a wolf pack of ALEXANDRIANS, I assume he is one of them.

It would have been different if he had stood up and told the crowd that it was foolish to meet together and declare that the forever-lost "original autographs" were inspired and inerrant when they have no such Bible TODAY. But, alas, he never said any such thing. Not one time did he assert that the Almighty God who breathed out the words that make up the originals had PRESERVED them inspired and inerrant TODAY in the very Book he held in his hand.

So what am I to believe? Dr. Criswell is an ALEXANDRIAN. What's the old saying? . . . "Birds of a feather flock together" (Amos 3:3).

So the book *Can We Trust the Bible?* leaves me WITH NO BIBLE TO TRUST. The ICBI conference emphasized the inerrancy of the "original autographs," WHICH NOBODY HAS IN THEIR POSSESSION TODAY. How can I trust the "original autographs" if I have no idea what the "original autographs" said? If I am to believe these ICBI men, there is no Bible I can hold in my hand today and say, "This is the inerrant Word of God."

Then to borrow Dr. James A. Borror's philosophy . . . we have a "weakened inerrancy." He said, "To the extent that you weaken

CAN I TRUST MY BIBLE?

inerrancy, to that extent you weaken inspiration." I conclude, then, that since only the "original autographs" were inerrant, only the "original autographs" were inspired. We have no inerrant, inspired Book TODAY.

Borror went on to say, "To the extent that you weaken inspiration, to that extent you have a garbled revelation." And that is EXACTLY what they had at the ICBI conference . . . A GARBLED REVELATION. There were six men who spoke from FOUR different books they called the "Bible." The WORDS in these four different books are vastly different. They say DIFFERENT things which teach DIFFERENT doctrines (on such subjects as the Virgin Birth, the Deity of Christ, the Blood Atonement, Salvation by Grace, to name a few). Talk about a garbled revelation! It's total CONFUSION! God is not the author of confusion (I Cor. 14:33). Neither is He the author of a garbled revelation. That's why He wrote only ONE Book. Anything else is CONFUSION.

Borror says, "To the extent that you have a garbled revelation, to that extent you have a weakened authority." I agree. WHERE is the authority for the folks in the ICBI? By their own words, their authority lies in the "original autographs," which none of them have ever seen, or ever will see. Talk about a weakened authority! Since they do not HAVE the "original autographs" . . . THEY HAVE NO AUTHORITY!

Borror finishes with, "When you weaken the authority of the Bible, you launch upon a shifting sea of subjective uncertainty." And that is EXACTLY where the ICBI people are! They HAVE no Bible as their authority! THEIR "Bible" went back to the dust ages ago! They cannot SEE their Bible . . . they cannot HOLD IT IN THEIR HAND . . . they cannot READ their Bible . . . and neither can they STUDY their Bible. They are riding the choppy waves of a shifting sea of subjective uncertainty!

In their sermons, all six of the men referred to "THE BIBLE"

CAN I TRUST THE MODERN JEHOIAKIMS?

time and time again. A listener would actually believe the preachers had "THE BIBLE" in their hands . . . but NOT ONE TIME did any of them SAY the book they were preaching from was the inspired, inerrant Word of God. I have already shown you that they believe the only inerrant, inspired "BIBLE" was the "original autographs." As so often with ALEXANDRIANS, they talked out of both sides of their mouth. They spoke of "THE BIBLE" in the present tense, as if they had it . . . then turned around and declared that only the "original autographs" were actually "THE BIBLE."

The cold, hard fact of the matter, is that there never was a time when all sixty-six books of original manuscripts were together as a collected BIBLE. By the time David wrote the Psalms, the books of Moses (Genesis, Exodus, Leviticus, Numbers, and Deuteronomy) had been copied many times, because the original parchments had crumbled and gone back to the dust. By the time Malachi wrote the last book of the Old Testament, David's original autographs had been destroyed by centuries of time . . . along with Solomon's, Isaiah's, Jeremiah's, etc.

By the time the New Testament was being written, ALL of the original autographs of the Old Testament were out of existence, and only COPIES of COPIES of COPIES of COPIES remained. So when the ALEXANDRIANS talk about "THE BIBLE," meaning the collection of sixty-six books of "original manuscripts," they are talking about a PHANTOM BIBLE that never DID exist!!!

As a perfect example of ALEXANDRIAN double-talk, let me give you a portion of a doctrinal statement from an independent Baptist church in a southern state. Asking me for a meeting, the pastor wrote, and enclosed the statement so I would know where he stood doctrinally. Within the brochure that bore the doctrinal statement was the plan of salvation with many Scripture verses quoted. All of them were from the King James Bible, which pleased me. However, when I read the doctrinal statement, I found the tenets

CAN I TRUST MY BIBLE?

of ALEXANDRIANISM. The very first subject in the doctrinal statement was the Word of God, and I quote, "We believe in the Scriptures of the Old and New Testaments as verbally inspired of God IN THE ORIGINAL WRITINGS, and that they ARE of supreme and final authority in faith and life."

This is the typical doctrinal statement concerning the Word of God in the average independent Baptist church in America. Please note the words I capitalized in the statement. Do you see the ALEXANDRIAN double-talk? This southern church says they believe in the verbally inspired Scriptures IN THE ORIGINAL WRITINGS. Fine. So do I. Lacking in the statement, however, is anything about believing in inspired Scriptures TODAY. Yet . . . with only a PHANTOM BIBLE which they have never seen, and never WILL see, they say the Scriptures ARE of supreme authority in faith and life. How can they say "ARE" (present tense) when the only inspired Scriptures were the "original writings"??? This is nothing but *Class A* ALEXANDRIAN double-talk!

By the way . . . I went ahead and accepted the invitation since the pastor at least USED the King James Bible. While there, I did not come on like gangbusters about the double-talk in his doctrinal statement, but I DID preach a sermon on the King James Bible. Afterward, the pastor and I got into a discussion about the Book, and before the meeting was over, he renounced his ALEXANDRIAN ways! HALLELUJAH!

I can trust the pastor, now . . . but I couldn't have trusted him to teach me anything when he thought the only real Bible was a collection of "original parchments" that long ago cracked, crumpled and disintegrated with the passing of time. That would leave HIM as the authority . . .and not the PRESERVED WORD OF GOD!

Can we trust the modern-day Jehoiakims who take their penknives and slice up the Word of God by denying its PRESERVATION at the hand of its Author, and tell us that the only

CAN I TRUST THE MODERN JEHOIAKIMS?

inspired, inerrant Scriptures were the "original autographs"?

I have before me a book entitled *God's Inerrant Word*, which is the result of "An International Symposium on the Trustworthiness of Scripture" that was held at Ligonier, Pennsylvania, in the fall of 1973. The book contains eleven sermons that were preached at the symposium, all of which are supposed to strengthen the believer's faith in the trustworthiness of Scripture. The only problem is . . . no one who preached at the symposium could hold up a Book and say, "Here is the trustworthy Scripture."

On page 7 of the book is the "Ligonier statement." It reads as follows: "We believe the Holy Scriptures of the Old and New Testaments to be the inspired and inerrant Word of God: We hold the Bible AS ORIGINALLY GIVEN through human agents of revelation, to be infallible and see this as a crucial article of faith with implications for the entire life and practice of all Christian people. With the great fathers of Christian history, we declare our confidence in the total trustworthiness of the Scriptures, urging that any view which imputes to them a lesser degree of inerrancy than total, is in conflict with the Bible's self-testimony in general and with the teaching of Jesus Christ in particular. Out of obedience to the Lord of the Church, we submit ourselves unreservedly to his authoritative view of Holy Writ."

My reader can readily see here that the "Scriptures" they speak of are those "ORIGINALLY GIVEN." We're back to the same old ALEXANDRIAN hodge-podge. All this wordy stuff sounds like these gentlemen are real soldiers of theTruth, doesn't it? Yet if they were asked to produce a copy of this "Holy Writ" they so bravely defend, THEY COULDN'T DO IT! They defend a PHANTOM BIBLE that never existed . . . because I have already pointed out that there never has been a time when all the "original autographs" were together in a collection of sixty-six books.

Since what we are reading here is typical of ALEXANDRIAN

CAN I TRUST MY BIBLE?

PHILOSOPHY everywhere, let us examine it closely. I want my reader to realize that you cannot trust the modern Jehoiakims, who are ALEXANDRIAN to the core. How could they possibly teach you the truth when they do not have the TRUTH in their hands to teach?

There are four typical ALEXANDRIAN declarations made in the Ligonier Statement that I want to point out. I call to your attention these words in the Statement: "We believe the Holy Scriptures of the Old and New Testaments to be the inspired and inerrant Word of God: We hold the Bible, AS ORIGINALLY GIVEN through human agents of revelation to be infallible."

DECLARATION NUMBER ONE: "We . . . see this as a crucial article of faith with implications for the entire life and practice of all Christian people."

I will not deny that it is crucial that there had been infallible, inerrant writings of Scripture to begin with. Since the original writings WERE Scripture, they were, of course, infallible and inerrant. But what good is faith in "original autographs" that went back to the dust centuries ago? If we do not have "Holy Writ" NOW . . . if we do not have an infallible, inerrant Bible NOW . . . then where is the guidelines for the "entire life and practice of all Christian people" NOW???

I will deal with this in more detail in the chapter on PRESERVATION, but suffice it to say here that if God were not able to PRESERVE His Holy Writ down to this day, He isn't worth our trust or our service.

DECLARATION NUMBER TWO: "We declare our confidence in the total trustworthiness of the Scriptures."

Sounds good, doesn't it? But we have a slight problem here. Ask one of these boys to place a copy of the inerrant, inspired "Scriptures" in your hand. They would look at you as if you had

CAN I TRUST THE MODERN JEHOIAKIMS?

just lost all your marbles. I know this by experience. I've done it to many of them, and they give me that "What asylum did you just escape from?" look. The "Scriptures" in which they declare their total confidence DO NOT EXIST. We've already heard it from their own mouths: *"We hold the Bible AS ORIGINALLY GIVEN . . . to be infallible."*

Too bad there are no Scriptures TODAY in which they place their confidence.

DECLARATION NUMBER THREE: "Any view which imputes to them [the "originally-given" Scriptures] a lesser degree of inerrancy than total, is in conflict with the Bible's self-testimony in general and with the teaching of Jesus Christ in particular."

Again, I agree that the Scriptures as "originally given" were absolutely inerrant and infallible, but I will challenge them on the "Bible's self-testimony" bit. WHERE DOES IT SAY IN *ANY* BIBLE THAT *ONLY* THE "ORIGINALLY-GIVEN" SCRIPTURES WERE INERRANT OR INFALLIBLE?

Time and time again in His Book, the Lord has declared that He would PRESERVE the *WORDS* forever. But never once are the "original writings" ever mentioned.

And as for *"with the teaching of Jesus Christ in particular"* . . . I double-ding-dong-dead-dog DARE an Alexandrian to show me ANY Bible ANYWHERE where Jesus Christ ever mentioned the "original writings"!!!' As I will demonstrate later in the book, Jesus called COPIES *"scripture,"* and preached from them! Not only that, but He told people to search the Scriptures, and the Scriptures He referred to were a TRANSLATION from Hebrew into Aramaic!!!

DECLARATION NUMBER FOUR: "Out of obedience to the Lord of the Church we submit ourselves unreservedly to his authoritative view of Holy Writ."

Hogwash.

CAN I TRUST MY BIBLE?

What edict or command of the Lord's are they obeying as they "unreservedly" submit themselves to His authoritative view of Holy Writ? WHERE in the "original writings" did God ever authorize ANYBODY to place their faith in the "original writings"? As we have already seen, once Jeremiah's Scripture was COPIED, the "original writings" were thrown in the river! I repeat what I have already said before . . . God did not inspire the papyrus on which the words were written! He inspired the WORDS! The Alexandrians may have their faith in the "original papyri" . . . but this author has his faith in the ALMIGHTY GOD who said He inspired the WORDS and will preserve the WORDS.

The first sermon in this book before me entitled "God's Inerrant Word" is by a John Warwick Montgomery, who also edited the book. In his sermon, "Biblical Inerrancy: What is at Stake?" Mr. Montgomery readily admits that the "original autographs" are long gone. Commenting on this he says, "If the Bible is inerrant, where is that inerrancy to be located? Not in translations of the text, since these are but approximations of the original; not in printed texts, for these are but representations of manuscript copies, subject to correction by comparison with them; not in the manuscript copies themselves, since they likewise endeavor, with greater or less fidelity, to reproduce the manuscripts on which they are dependent. Unless, therefore, one wishes to maintain that a given stream of transmission or translation was kept inviolable by God (and Scripture itself nowhere gives ground for such affirmation), inerrancy must be said to reside in the original manuscripts written by the biblical authors, i.e., in the autographs of Scriptures."

Here we go again. More ALEXANDRIAN double-talk. Mr. Montgomery, like all ALEXANDRIANS, makes no sense at all. He says inerrancy is not found in TRANSLATIONS since they are only APPROXIMATIONS of the "original." In other words, he is saying that no translation can be inerrant. Ho-hum, where have I

CAN I TRUST THE MODERN JEHOIAKIMS?

heard THAT before? He says inerrancy is not found in PRINTED texts, because printed texts are but representations of manuscript COPIES. So, of course, no PRINTED "Bible" of any kind could possibly be inerrant.

Then this ALEXANDRIAN "scholar" says with an obvious sneer, "Unless, therefore, one wishes to maintain that a given stream of transmission or translation WAS KEPT INVIOLABLE BY GOD (AND SCRIPTURE NOWHERE GIVES GROUND FOR SUCH AN AFFIRMATION), inerrancy must be said to reside in the ORIGINAL MANUSCRIPTS written by the biblical authors, i.e., in the AUTOGRAPHS of Scripture."

Didn't I tell you, dear reader, that the Alexandrians ride this "original autographs," "original writings," "original manuscripts" thing to the point of nausea? Well, make a short dash to the medicine cabinet, take a dose of Pepto Bismol, and let's proceed.

This guy is such a typical ALEXANDRIAN that I want to stay with him just a little longer. Let me point out his absolute nonsense.

Take his statement, "Scripture nowhere gives ground for such an affirmation." The statement is absolute NONSENSE. Since nothing can be "SCRIPTURE" except the "original manuscripts," WHAT Scripture is he talking about? Has HE seen the "originals"? Nope. Then, WHAT Scripture is he reading to know that "Scripture nowhere gives ground for such an affirmation"?

You will note some more nonsense. Notice he says, "Scripture GIVES . . ." That's *present tense,* isn't it? But he has just told us that there is NO Scripture today, because the ONLY Scripture WAS the "original autographs" which are long gone.

Mr. Montgomery apparently is reading SOMETHING *today* that he calls "Scripture," wouldn't you say? But whatever he is reading is either a TRANSMISSION of the original language of

CAN I TRUST MY BIBLE?

Hebrew and Greek which he is able to readily read and understand, OR . . . it is a TRANSLATION into English. But he is a naughty man to refer to either a TRANSMISSION or a TRANSLATION as "Scripture" since he insists that "inerrancy MUST be said to reside in the 'original manuscripts.'"

This "Scripture" he refers to . . . is it PRINTED? Tch. Tch. Mr. Montgomery. Really. How two-faced of you. You just told us that inerrancy does not lie in PRINTED texts. Yet you allude to "Scripture," which has GOT to be something that you have read with your own eyes. Since you do not have the "original manuscripts," and I doubt that you even have COPIES of the original handwritten manuscripts . . . I assume that whatever you are referring to as "Scripture" is something that CAME OFF A PRINTING PRESS. Oh, for shame! There is no way I could ever trust YOU, sir!

MORE nonsense . . . Mr. Montgomery says that Scripture nowhere gives affirmation for one to maintain that a given stream of TRANSMISSION or TRANSLATION was kept inviolable by God. Now he can make this statement without any Scripture to HOLD IN HIS HAND AND READ, I cannot figure out, but what he says is NOT SO! I will devote the next three chapters to proving my point. The god of the ALEXANDRIANS, of course, is too anemic, weak, and puny to maintain a steady, inerrant stream of transmission and/or translation . . . but the ALMIGHTY GOD OF THE BIBLE can handle it! He SAID He would . . . and He is DOING IT!

God's ANTIOCHAN Bible still lives in many languages on earth today. I have one in English laying on the desk in front of me at this moment. Of course, the "original manuscripts" of the ALEXANDRIANS is non-existent at this point in history, but those boys still continue to quote from manuscripts they have never seen, nor will EVER see.

This, however, is typical ALEXANDRIANISM. For several years, I have been purchasing historical books from Time-Life

CAN I TRUST THE MODERN JEHOIAKIMS?

Books, headquartered in Richmond, Virginia. In a book entitled, *Feats and Wisdom of the Ancients*, the authors have written a chapter on the great library of Alexandria, Egypt, which was founded near the end of the 4th century B.C. by Ptolemy I, a Greek general under Alexander the Great.

Following Alexander's death in 323 B.C., it fell to Ptolemy to rule Egypt, including the port city of Alexandria to which Alexander had given his name. In a grand scheme to make Alexandria the learning center of the world, Ptolemy established a university and attached it to the library. Within a short period of time, there were some fourteen thousand students at the university studying physics, engineering, astronomy, medicine, mathematics, geography, biology, philosophy, and literature.

The library was divided into two parts. The main facility, known as the Royal Library, was housed in a building next to the university. Some distance away in the city's old Egyptian quarter was the second library, housed in the Serapeum, the pagan temple of Serapis.

Now let me give it to you exactly as it is written in the book:

"Both buildings were repositories for books HANDWRITTEN ON PAPYRUS SCROLLS. To assemble a book collection superior to all others, the Ptolemys and their librarians spared no effort. While many rolls were purchased fairly by the Ptolemy's minions, ships docking at Alexandria HAD TO SURRENDER ANY WORKS ON BOARD to the library, after which cheap copies would be returned to their hapless owners. Obviously, since copyists sometimes made mistakes, ORIGINALS . . . of valued works were considered far more desirable."

Did you get that? Deep in the fibre of ALEXANDRIANS is an attachment to ORIGINALS . . . so much so that they actually STOLE original writings from ships that docked in Alexandria

CAN I TRUST MY BIBLE?

so that they could replace them with cheap copies and keep the ORIGINALS!!!

My reader can readily see that ALEXANDRIANS have never changed their stripes. Even to this day, they make a BIG THING of the "originals."

Recently I received copies of a "public forum" put in print by Evangelist J. H. Melton of Milton, Florida, which he addresses to "The Baptist Brethren." The "forum" is in the form of several letters written by Melton in response to letters he had received from some Baptist pastors. In the "forum," Mr. Melton says, "The rabid insistence that the King James Version is inerrant is RANK HERESY. The ORIGINAL MANUSCRIPTS-the AUTOGRAPHS- of the sixty-six books of the Word of God WERE infallible, inerrant, verbally inspired. The Word of God TEACHES that the Holy Spirit chose holy men of old to receive the Divine Revelation, which TODAY we call the Word of God. The Holy Spirit so controlled the holy men who recorded the Divine Revelation that they could not err, even in a word they chose to use. This pertains to the whole of the Bible, Old Testament as well as New Testament. We believe in verbal plenary inspiration. We believe that the very words were inspired; and this pertains to every book, every CHAPTER, and every VERSE of the ORIGINAL MANUSCRIPTS."

Again . . . we have typical ALEXANDRIAN thinking, but watch how Mr. Melton contradicts himself. I have capitalized some words in his statement to help my reader pick out the self-contradictions. You picked up, of course, the reference to the "original manuscripts." Please note that he said the "original manuscripts" (the "autographs") WERE infallible, inerrant, verbally inspired. I assume he uses the past tense (WERE) because the "original manuscripts" are long gone.

He turns right around and contradicts himself by saying, "The Word of God TEACHES . . . TODAY . . . etc." Pardon me,

CAN I TRUST THE MODERN JEHOIAKIMS?

but "teaches" is *present* tense. Something that "we" call the Word of God TODAY "teaches." But Mr. Melton, we do not HAVE the "original manuscripts" TODAY!!! What is this "Word of God" that TEACHES TODAY???

In another part of the "forum," Mr. Melton says, "Anyone and everyone in THIS DAY and EVERY DAY since the writing of the New Testament HAS the Word of God preserved in THE GREEK MANUSCRIPTS." Yet Mr. Melton has just gone on record as saying that only the original manuscripts (the autographs) were inspired and inerrant. Does he HAVE the "original Greek manuscripts"? I trow not. Then we have more ALEXANDRIAN double-talk.

In another part of the "forum," Mr. Melton says (and these are HIS capitals), "THERE NEVER HAS BEEN, THERE IS NOT NOW, THERE NEVER WILL BE BUT ONE INERRANT, INFALLIBLE, VERBALLY INSPIRED WRITING-THE ORIGINAL MANUSCRIPTS OF THE SIXTY-SIX BOOKS COMPRISING THE ONE BOOK, THE BIBLE, THE WORD OF GOD!"

Yet he says, "Anyone and everyone in THIS DAY and EVERY DAY since the writing of the New Testament HAS the Word of God preserved in the Greek Manuscripts."

I must hasten to point out that the Old Testament was NOT written in Greek. Mr. Melton has not mentioned the Hebrew manuscripts here. Furthermore . . . he is telling us that nobody today has the Word of God. He says, "There never has been, THERE IS *NOT NOW*, there never will be but ONE infallible, verbally inspired writing-THE ORIGINAL MANUSCRIPTS of the sixty-six books comprising the one Book, the Bible, the Word of God."

Mr. Melton will have to admit that the "original manuscripts" are out of existence. So what he is saying is that THERE IS NO WORD OF GOD TODAY. Yet I have seen Mr. Melton stand in pulpits and hold the King James Bible in his hand and CALL it the

CAN I TRUST MY BIBLE?

Word of God!!!

Another thing . . . I repeat what I said earlier: There was NEVER a time when the original manuscripts of all sixty-six books were TOGETHER in one Book! By the time the New Testament was written, ALL of the Old Testament original autographs had passed from existence. And what's more, Mr.Melton says he believes that the very words were inspired, and "this pertains to every book, every CHAPTER, and every VERSE of the ORIGINAL MANUSCRIPTS."

Elsewhere in the "forum," Mr. Melton states: "I received my Bachelor of Arts degree from Baylor in 1942 and my Master of Theology degree from Southwestern Baptist Theological Seminary in 1945. I have had seventeen courses in Greek and Hebrew in college." Tch. Tch. Then Mr. Melton, surely you ought to know that THERE WERE NO CHAPTERS AND VERSES IN THE "ORIGINAL MANUSCRIPTS" (unless you would want to call the 150 Psalms "chapters")!!!

I'm telling you, dear reader, YOU CAN'T TRUST THESE ALEXANDRIANS! There is too much double-talk and there are too many inconsistencies in what they believe and teach.

In the "forum," Mr. Melton says, "I teach and preach from the King James Version, BUT I CERTAINLY RESERVE THE RIGHT TO IMPROVE AND/OR CORRECT THE KING JAMES TRANSLATION. I AM NOT A BIBLE CORRECTOR, BUT A TRANSLATION CORRECTOR. Scriptural Baptists contend that we are not Protestants. That is right. How contradictory for us to insist on the inerrancy of a Protestant translation."

Talk about "contradictory." I have seen Mr. Melton stand in pulpits and CALL the King James translation (which he held in his hand) the BIBLE. Now he says it is NOT the Bible. Mr. Melton, sir, if the King James translation is NOT the Word of God, and if it is

CAN I TRUST THE MODERN JEHOIAKIMS?

NOT the Bible, why don't you get honest and QUIT CALLING IT THAT???

And if you don't like the Protestant translation, WHY DO YOU *USE* IT? WHY DON'T YOU USE THE *BAPTIST* TRANSLATION?

What's that you say? There ISN'T a Baptist translation? You are so correct, sir. And why is there NOT a Baptist translation? Let me answer that question for you.

First, let me state that anyone who knows Al Lacy knows there is not anyone MORE *Baptist* than I am. For years I have been labeled a BIG "B" Baptist for the strong stand that I take. That's fine with me. The forerunner of the Lord Jesus Christ was a BIG "B" Baptist. Check it out in the Bible. John the Baptist ALWAYS has a BIG "B" on his name. Jesus was baptized by a BIG "B" Baptist, and so were the men with whom He began His New Testament Church. That puts me in pretty good company.

At the time that the English language was at its peak, God desired to give the English-speaking people HIS WORD in their language so they could evangelize the world for the last four hundred years (or so) of this age. He chose to use scholarly men to do the translating. In the early seventeenth century, *Baptists were not living long enough to become scholars!!* They were being persecuted and slaughtered by Catholics and Protestants alike. The forty-seven men who undertook the production of the Authorized version of 1611 were language scholars of unparalleled ability. They were Anglicans and Puritans who held the highest reverence for the Word of God and humbly and honestly labored to translate it correctly. Even though they were not aware of it, it is my belief that the Holy Spirit hovered over them as they labored and saw to it that His Word was preserved perfect, infallible, inspired, and inerrant for the English-speaking people.

If that is not the case . . . where do we look for the perfect,

CAN I TRUST MY BIBLE?

infallible, inspired, and inerrant Word of God? The ALEXANDRIANS tell us we must look to the "original autographs," which are out of existence, and have been for centuries. Then they turn around and speak of the Word of God in the PRESENT tense, but couldn't place a copy of it in your hand if their lives depended on it.

Mr. Melton says anyone and everyone in this day HAS the Word of God preserved in the Greek manuscripts. He ignores the fact that the Old Testament was not written in Greek; but by passing that, I ask, WHICH GREEK manuscripts, Mr. Melton? In your "public forum," you state that there is not one one-thousandth of a difference between the Westcott and Hort Text and the Textus Receptus, and that "no major doctrine is affected by that difference." Such a statement is a sign of gross ignorance and is not even worthy of comment. But I would like to ask this: Why do you defend the Westcott and Hort Text when you don't even believe that IT is the Word of God? You repeatedly state that the ONLY Word of God there has ever been are the "original manuscripts." Certainly Westcott and Hort's text is not the "original manuscripts."

Seems to me that Mr. Melton would come under the category often spoken of by Chief Sitting Bull of the Lakota Sioux Nation. "White man speak with FORKED TONGUE." But he is not alone. The rest of his ALEXANDRIAN friends talk the same way. It comes from literally thousands of "fundamental" pulpits across this land of ours and from the faculties of most "fundamental" Christian colleges and universities in America. First they tell you that the ONLY inspired, infallible, inerrant Word of God WAS the "original autographs" . . . then they call the King James Bible the Word of God in their pulpits and classrooms, and in the same breath "correct" it with the "original" Hebrew and Greek.

Now I ask my reader . . . can you trust men like this? I have more respect for the ALEXANDRIANS who use the NIV or the NASV or the LB or the NKJV than I do those who "use" the King

CAN I TRUST THE MODERN JEHOIAKIMS?

James then employ their Jehoiakim penknives to cut it to shreds. As with Mr. Melton, they reserve the right to "improve and/or correct the King James Translation." They call the King James the Word of God, then "improve" and "correct" the Word of God with their great knowledge of the "original manuscripts" which they have NEVER seen. This constitutes criminal deception, known also as FRAUD.

The REAL Bible says, "... *Provide things HONEST in the sight of ALL men"* (Rom. 12:17). If you ALEXANDRIANS who "use" the King James Bible and correct it were HONEST, you would quit telling your hearers that it is the Word of God, and you would quit calling it the "Bible." If you were honest, you would readily admit that you do not believe the old Book is the Word of God. If you were anything other than cold-eyed FRAUD, you would admit that the "Hebrew" and "Greek" you quote is not from the "original manuscripts" (since they are out of existence), but from COPIES, which no doubt are full of errors. If you were HONEST, you would tell your hearers that the only thing you believe to be the Word of God crumbled back to the dust thousands of years ago, and that NOBODY ON EARTH TODAY HAS THE WORD OF GOD!!!

This, of course, would cost you your paycheck and the respect you so dearly desire as a great scholar. And if you were REALLY honest, you would admit that in all of your preaching and teaching as you "correct" and "improve" the King James Bible, it really boils down to the fact that YOU want to be the final authority! Of course, you ALEXANDRIAN "scholars" won't admit that YOU want to be the final authority because you ARE cold-eyed, forked-tongue FRAUDS!

The REAL Word of God says,

Whatsoever things are TRUE, whatsoever things are HONEST ... think on THESE things (Phil. 4:8).
Let us walk HONESTLY ... (Rom. 13:13).

CAN I TRUST MY BIBLE?

> *Now I pray to God... that ye should do that which is HONEST...* (II Cor. 13:7).
>
> *LIE NOT to one another...* (Col. 3:9).
>
> *... LIE NOT AGAINST THE TRUTH* (James 3:14).

When Paul defended his ministry and that of the men who were traveling with him, he said they were *"Providing for HONEST things,* not only IN THE SIGHT OF THE LORD, but also IN THE SIGHT OF MEN" (II Cor. 8:21). I would remind you ALEXANDRIANS who CALL the King James Bible the Word of God and CALL it the "Bible"... then "correct" and "improve it" with the "original" Hebrew and Greek which you have never laid eyes on... GOD IS WATCHING! HE sees and hears you talking with fraudulent words. You WILL stand before Him one day (Rom. 14:12). What do you plan to say to Him when He tells you to hand over your Jehoiakim penknife? I wouldn't want to be in YOUR sneakers, pal!

Let me show my reader some MORE ALEXANDRIAN double-talk. I'm riding this thing hard because I want you to see that you cannot trust the modern Jehoiakims to lead you in spiritual matters. They HAVE no Bible to preach, teach, study, read, or point you to.

I have before me a large book entitled *Encyclopedia of Bible Difficulties,* by ALEXANDRIAN Gleason L. Archer, Jr., who holds a B.D. from Princeton Theological Seminary, an LL.B from Suffolk University Law School, and a Ph.D. from Harvard Graduate School. Many of these ALEXANDRIANS are highly educated but don't show the common sense that God gave a soda cracker.

Archer opens his introduction by saying, "Throughout the history of the Christian church, it has been clearly understood that the Bible as ORIGINALLY GIVEN by God was free from error." A few lines later, he says, "Whether or not they avowed themselves to

CAN I TRUST THE MODERN JEHOIAKIMS?

be 'Fundamentalists,' all those who laid claim to being Evangelicals stood shoulder to shoulder in their insistence that the Old and New Testaments, as ORIGINALLY GIVEN, were free from error of any kind." As always with ALEXANDRIANS, there is a total lack of anything in Mr. Archer's book about any Bible TODAY that is free from error.

Page after page after page, the educated doctor labors to prove that the ORIGINAL MANUSCRIPTS were without error. Fine. I agree. Of course the original manuscripts were without error. But then he stumbles his ALEXANDRIAN toes and says on page 27, "Now that the inerrancy of the original manuscripts of Scripture has been established as essential to its inerrant authority, we must deal with the very real problem of the COMPLETE DISAPPEARANCE OF THE AUTOGRAPHS THEMSELVES. *Even the earliest and best manuscripts that we possess are NOT totally free of transmissional error.*"

That is a blasphemous insult to the God who said He would PRESERVE His WORDS forever (Psalm 12:6-7)!!! It is a slap in the face of the Lord Jesus Christ, who said, "Heaven and earth shall pass away, but my WORDS shall Not pass away" (Matt. 24:35). And it is an insolent outrage against the Holy Spirit who told Isaiah to write, *"My WORDS which I have put in thy mouth, shall not depart out of thy mouth, nor out of the mouth of thy seed, nor out of the mouth of thy seed's seed, saith the Lord, FROM HENCEFORTH AND FOR EVER" (Isa. 59:21).*

Who are we going to believe, dear reader . . . the ALMIGHTY GOD who cannot lie . . . or the ALEXANDRIANS who are stuffed plumb full of wild gooseberries?

Even in the face of what God's pure, perfect Word in the English language says, Archer blasphemes again on the same page by saying, "Even the finest extant manuscripts of the Hebrew--Aramaic Old Testament and the Greek New Testament ARE NOT

CAN I TRUST MY BIBLE?

WHOLLY WITHOUT ERROR."

Poor God. He just couldn't manage to PRESERVE his WORDS. Tch. Tch.

You know what the problem is? Simple. The god of the ALEXANDRIANS is NOT the God of the BIBLE!!!

This educated ALEXANDRIAN adds to his blasphemy by saying on page 28 (in defense of the ORIGINAL MANUSCRIPTS), "The sovereign Lord who could use the wooden staff of Moses to bring down the ten plagues upon Egypt and part the waters of the Red Sea can surely use a fallible human prophet to communicate His will and His truth without blundering or confusion of any kind. The inerrancy of God's written Word as it was ORIGINALLY INSPIRED is a necessary corollary to the inerrancy of God Himself. We must therefore condemn an attitude of indifference concerning the inerrancy of the ORIGINAL MANUSCRIPTS of the Bible as a serious theological error."

Well, Buster, what about YOUR theological error when you say, "Even the finest extant manuscripts of the Hebrew-Aramaic Old Testament and the Greek New Testament ARE NOT WHOLLY WITHOUT ERROR"? The Author of the Word of God said He would PRESERVE His WORDS FOREVER! If He did that (AND HE DID!), then there is a set of manuscripts that are free of error! You will find them in the Masoretic Hebrew and the Greek Received Text! They are copies of copies of copies of copies of copies of copies . . . yes, but if God can use fallible human men to write His ORIGINALS . . . why can't He use fallible human men to make COPIES of the originals?? I assure you . . . He CAN!!! He DID!!! And the same God can use infallible human men to TRANSLATE His Word from one language to another and still keep it inerrant, infallible, and INSPIRED!!!

Good doctor . . . YOU condemn the theological error of those who say the "original manuscripts" had errors. Fine. So do

CAN I TRUST THE MODERN JEHOIAKIMS?

I. But I also condemn YOUR theological error that God has not preserved errorless Greek and Hebrew manuscripts TODAY. I smell some rotten baloney around here somewhere. GOD said He would PRESERVE His WORDS *forever.* YOU say He has not done it. It isn't hard for me to tell where the ROTTEN SMELL is coming from!

Speaking of nefarious odors, let's follow them and see where else they lead. (I guarantee you this . . . they will ALL lead eventually to ALEXANDRIA!).

Bob Jones University in Greenville, South Carolina has for years advertised itself as the great "Bastion of the Faith" . . . the "Fortress of Fundamentalism." Let's see what Stewart Custer has put in print on the Bible question. He is the chairman of the Bible department at Bob Jones. I quote Custer's word: "I defend every word in the ORIGINAL AUTOGRAPHS of the Greek and Hebrew texts of the Bible. The Greek and Hebrew manuscripts which agree most closely with the AUTOGRAPHS are to be followed. We have some that go back to within twenty-five years of the writing of the AUTOGRAPHS. They are known as the ALEXANDRIAN Text."

Is my reader getting a good whiff?

Mr. Custer proceeds, "The King James Version is a good English translation. I have used it all my life and highly recommend it. *There is no perfect English translation;* this is why we study the Greek and Hebrew. The Bible is indeed the Word of God insofar as it agrees with the wording of the ORIGINAL Greek and Hebrew AUTOGRAPHS. The ORIGINAL Greek and Hebrew manuscripts ARE the inerrant Word of God."

It seems that this ALEXANDRIAN (like ALL of them) has some problems with his position. He says he defends every word in the ORIGINAL AUTOGRAPHS. Is Mr. Custer going to tell us that he HAS the "original autographs"? I don't think he would go THAT far! No, he does not have in his possession the "original autographs."

CAN I TRUST MY BIBLE?

Even if he DID . . . how would he know they were the "original autograps"? They were rubber-stamped as such?

Since Mr. Custer does not HAVE the "original autographs" . . . and cannot get his hands on them . . . and has never SEEN them . . . how in the name of Bugs Q. Bunny can he DEFEND every word in the "original autographs"??? He speaks of the Greek and Hebrew manuscripts and says he has some that go back to within twenty-five years of their writing. Then he identifies them as the ALEXANDRIAN Text. Really now, Mr. Custer. You have manuscripts that go back to within 25 years of the autographs that MOSES wrote? Or that DAVID wrote? Or that even MALACHI wrote?

Maybe you didn't mean the HEBREW autographs. Okay . . . are you telling me you have manuscripts that go back to within twenty-five years of the time MATTHEW wrote his Gospel? How about MARK? Or LUKE? Or even JOHN? You have manuscripts that go back to within twenty-five years of the time PAUL wrote his epistles? Or PETER? JUDE? JAMES? Let's say that you really DO have manuscripts that date with in twenty-five years of the time that JOHN wrote the Revelation . . . What you have did not come from ANTIOCH. Admittedly, they came from the nefarious ALEXANDRIA, EGYPT.

We have already seen from Scripture what GOD thinks of Egypt . . . and of ALEXANDRIA. The stuff you have that came from ALEXANDRIA is what produced such rotten translations as the Revised Standard Version, the New English Version, the old American Standard Version, the New American Standard Version, the New World Translation of the "Jehovah's Witnesses," the New International Version, ALL the Roman Catholic Versions, and Jerry Falwell's so-called "New King James" Version.

Mr. Custer, you say that the Greek and Hebrew manuscripts which agree MOST CLOSELY with the original autographs are

CAN I TRUST THE MODERN JEHOIAKIMS?

known as the ALEXANDRIAN Text. By "MOST CLOSELY" I assume you mean that even the ALEXANDRIAN Text is shy of being perfect. What I want to know is . . . SINCE YOU HAVE NEVER SEEN THE ORIGINAL MANUSCRIPTS . . . HOW DO YOU KNOW THAT THE ALEXANDRIAN TEXT AGREES "MOST CLOSELY" WITH THE ORIGINAL MANUSCRIPTS??? Seems to me you are expressing an opinion for which you have NO BACKING.

Ho Hum. More typical ALEXANDRIAN HOGWASH.

Another thing . . . In his typical ALEXANDRIAN double-talk, Mr. Custer says, "The Bible is indeed the Word of God insofar as it agrees with the wording of the ORIGINAL Greek and Hebrew AUTOGRAPHS." Now, what "Bible" is THIS? You say there is no perfect English translation. Then please, please, sir . . . WHAT "Bible" is indeed the Word of God insofar as it agrees with the wording of the ORIGINAL Greek and Hebrew AUTOGRAPHS? Certainly it could not be the KING JAMES BIBLE! It was not translated from the ALEXANDRIAN Text, which YOU say agrees "most closely" with the "original" Greek and Hebrew manuscripts. And I also would like to ask . . . since the KING JAMES BIBLE came from the ANTIOCHAN Text, which according to you is inferior to the ALEXANDRIAN Text . . . WHY HAVE YOU "USED" IT ALL OF YOUR LIFE, AND WHY DO YOU HIGHLY RECOMMEND IT?

Such conduct seems highly hypocritical to me. I wouldn't trust Mr. Custer as far as I could throw the Eiffel Tower! After all this double-talk, he caps it off by saying, "The ORIGINAL Greek and Hebrew manuscripts ARE the inerrant Word of God." This is QUADRUPLE TALK! What does he mean "ARE"? They don't exist!

Dear reader . . . are you getting the message? YOU CANNOT TRUST THESE MODERN JEHOIAKIMS! They will only confuse

CAN I TRUST MY BIBLE?

you and lead you astray with their split-tongued doctrinal teaching. According to THEM, no one on earth has the Word of God TODAY. If you want to know what God has to say to the human race, you have to ask the ALEXANDRIANS. THEY are the final authority! THEY, like Roman Catholic priests, have an inroad with God. We must look to THEM for final truth.

You will find it this way all over America. "Fundamental" pulpits and "Fundamental" colleges and universities are poisoning the minds of Christians and unsaved people alike with their ALEXANDRIAN heresy. Their penknives are kept razor-sharp, and they are ready, willing, and able to rip up the REAL Bible while "using" it or supplanting it altogether with perverted ALEXANDRIAN "bibles."

Let's hear from one more ALEXANDRIAN before moving to the next chapter. I refer to John MacArthur, head "elder" of the Grace Community Church, Sun Valley, California. Mr. MacArthur, who is known for his vicious attack on the precious blood of my Savior, has prepared a booklet to answer questions concerning various Bible versions. He says in the booklet, "Let me share with you my own conclusions after studying these issues. Bible versions such as the New International Version and the New American Standard Bible have been translated by godly men of demonstrated academic repute from the very best manuscript evidence that is now available today. May I add, the manuscript evidence that is now available is FAR SUPERIOR to that which was available to the King James Version's translators in 1611."

How do you like "them apples," dear reader? Poor God slipped up, didn't He? Instead of seeing to it that the English-speaking people (whom He would use to evangelize the world from the seventeenth century to the end of this age) had the SUPERIOR manuscripts BEFORE the great missionary and evangelistic movements began... He waited until this age was ALMOST OVER

CAN I TRUST THE MODERN JEHOIAKIMS?

to let the FAR SUPERIOR manuscripts surface! And since Mr. MacArthur brings up the New International and the New American Standard versions, saying they were translated from the very best manuscripts we have today, he HAS to mean the ALEXANDRIAN manuscripts, since they are the manuscripts from which the New International perversion and the New American Standard perversion were translated.

So we see that it was not the God of the Bible who slipped up, after all. It was the god of the ALEXANDRIANS. Here we are about to wrap up this age . . . and the god of the ALEXANDRIANS finally comes up with the "SUPERIOR MANUSCRIPTS"!!! I guess the old boy just forgot. Maybe he's got Alzheimer's disease.

Mr. MacArthur states that the NIV and the NASV were translated by "godly men of demonstrated academic repute." How can he possibly make this statement? John MacArthur has ABSOLUTELY NO IDEA WHO THE MEN WERE THAT TRANSLATED THE NASV!!! The Lockman Foundation has never revealed their identities and still refuses to do so today! And as for the "godly" men who produced the NIV . . . I'm smelling some more rotten baloney! In the Preface of the NIV, they list thirteen different denominations that were represented on the Translation Committee. THREE of those denominations are part of the World and National Council of Churches. One of them is Charismatic, which means they are tongues-speaking, flesh-flourishing, vision-seeking, heretics who have such "godly" people as Oral Roberts, Tammy Faye Bakker, and Jimmy Swaggart as their leaders. Another one is the "Church of Christ," which is nothing short of a devil-inspired CULT. Come on, MacArthur, have you any idea what "godly" means?

Further in the booklet, Mr. MacArthur says, "We do not have the ORIGINALS of any of the books of the Bible. God never promised the perfect preservation of the originals, but He did promise to preserve the CONTENT. They are preserved within the body of

CAN I TRUST MY BIBLE?

the CURRENTLY EXISTING manuscripts."

Of course, Mr. MacArthur has already told us WHICH manuscripts these would be . . . the "FAR SUPERIOR" *Alexandrian* manuscripts. Here lies some more ALEXANDRIAN double-talk. I would like for Mr. MacArthur to show me in ANY "bible" ANYWHERE that it says God promised to preserve the CONTENT. Foulsmelling BALONEY!!! We have already seen many Scriptures that flat declare from the mouth of the Almighty God that He will preserve His WORDS!!!

If the WORDS are not kept perfect and inspired, the CONTENT won't be worth the paper it's printed on.

Referring to the NIV and the NASV, Mr. MacArthur says, "I would have no reservation in recommending these versions, yet I myself choose to continue USING the Scofield Reference Bible because it is the text with which I am most familiar."

More forked tongue. The Scofield Reference Bible is the OLD Scofield Bible. Unlike the New Scofield, it has the untouched KING JAMES TEXT. This shows you how much conviction Mr. MacArthur has about ANYTHING. He "uses" a bible that came from inferior manuscripts, but he stays with it because it is the one with which he is most familiar. This guy really has convictional BACKBONE, wouldn't you agree?

Or would you?

I could go on quoting ALEXANDRIANS until my reader would run out of Pepto Bismol . . . but I think we've seen enough to draw a conclusion. The question is: CAN I TRUST THE MODERN JEHOIAKIMS?

The answer is YES! You can trust them to use continual double-talk. You can trust them to attack the REAL Bible, even if they "use" it. You can trust them to talk out of two sides of their mouths . . . speaking as if they ACTUALLY HAD READ THE ORIGINAL MANUSCRIPTS . . . then saying such manuscripts

CAN I TRUST THE MODERN JEHOIAKIMS?

really do not exist. You can trust them to stand on the stepladder of "scholarship" above you and subtly attempt to get you to look to THEM as the final authority.

But one thing for sure . . . YOU CANNOT TRUST THEM TO BE HONEST!!!

CAN I TRUST MY BIBLE?

III

CAN I TRUST MY BIBLE'S TRANSLATION?

There was a time that every person on this planet spoke ONE language; but when a great multitude of them gathered on a plain in the land of Shinar, they decided to build a city, and in the midst of the city, a tower. Their plan was to build the tower so high that they could step right off its pinnacle into God's Heaven.

God decided it was time to put such nonsense to a halt, so He worked a special miracle and suddenly changed the one language into MANY languages, thus confounding the multitudes so that they could not understand one another's speech. After a while, they grouped off with those whose speech they *could* understand, and scattered from Shinar upon the face of all the earth. Thus the tower is called the "Tower of Babel" because as the people talked in their one language and God suddenly changed it into MANY languages, they seemed to "babble" to each other.

This fascinating story is found in Genesis 11:1-9. Ever since that time, the peoples of different locations on earth have spoken different languages.

After our Lord Jesus was crucified and rose from the grave, He spent forty days here on earth and then ascended back to Heaven. Just before His Ascension, He gathered His New Testament church together on top of the Mount of Olives and gave them what we often

CAN I TRUST MY BIBLE?

call the "Great Commission." In Mark's Gospel it reads thus:

> ... *Go ye into ALL THE WORLD, and preach the gospel to every creature* (Mark 16:15).

In Matthew's Gospel, it reads thus:

> *Go ye therefore, and teach ALL NATIONS, baptizing them in the name of the Father, and of the Son, and of the Holy Ghost: Teaching them to observe all things whatsoever I have commanded you: and, lo, I am with you alway, even unto the end of the world* (Matt. 28:19-20).

You will notice that the church is to go into ALL THE WORLD ... that is, go into ALL NATIONS and preach the Gospel to them. Once they have repented, believed, and obeyed the Gospel (Mark 1:15; II Thess. 1:8), they are to be baptized and then taught ALL THINGS whatsoever Jesus has commanded. This would be the ENTIRE sixty-six books of the Bible.

It is an historical FACT that the men to whom Jesus gave the "Great Commission" spoke Aramaic. Speaking to them in their Aramaic language, the Lord told them to go into ALL THE WORLD and teach ALL NATIONS how to be saved. After they got saved, they were to be baptized and then were taught THE WHOLE BIBLE.

QUESTION: WAS the Lord Jesus aware that all nations in all the world did NOT speak Aramaic?

OBVIOUS ANSWER: Of course.

ANOTHER QUESTION: Since saving faith only comes from the Word of God (Rom. 10:17), and the original languages of the Word of God were Hebrew and Greek ... would these men need the Word of God in THEIR language so they could preach and teach it?

OBVIOUS ANSWER: Of course ... especially since part

CAN I TRUST MY BIBLE'S TRANSLATION?

of ALL THE WORLD was their own people (who for the most part did not understand Hebrew and Greek). Therefore . . . ONE BIG THING would be necessary. These men would have to have a TRANSLATION of the Word of God from Hebrew and Greek into Aramaic so they could preach it to their own nation.

ANOTHER QUESTION: How would the missionaries of the New Testament church preach the Word of God to the people of ALL NATIONS without TRANSLATING it into the languages of the people to whom they went?

OBVIOUS ANSWER: They couldn't.

Thus we come to an OBVIOUS conclusion . . . in order for the Great Commission to be obeyed, THERE WOULD HAVE TO BE TRANSLATIONS OF THE WORD OF GOD INTO MANY LANGUAGES!!!

NEXT QUESTION: The people of WHAT language have been evangelizing the world since early in the seventeenth century?

OBVIOUS ANSWER: The ENGLISH-speaking people.

Has my reader ever heard of black people in Africa leaving their dark continent to be missionaries to China? Have you ever known of Germans to leave the Old Country to be missionaries to Australia? Have you ever seen Japanese people leave Japan to be missionaries to Norway? Have you ever known of Eskimos leaving the cold arctic northland to be missionaries to the islands of the South Pacific? Have you ever known of Spaniards in Spain leaving their land to preach the Gospel of Jesus Christ to the people of Korea?

The answer to all of these questions is NO! The ONLY people who have traveled this globe in the last four hundred years carrying out the Great Commission are the ENGLISH-speaking people!

NEXT QUESTION: Did GOD have anything to do with this great missionary movement?

CAN I TRUST MY BIBLE?

Only a retarded numbskull would give a negative answer.

NEXT QUESTION: What instrument does God use to bring people to SAVING faith . . . to CONVERT the soul . . . to give the NEW BIRTH?

SCRIPTURAL ANSWER: The Word of God!

Without SAVING FAITH . . . without being CONVERTED . . . without being BORN AGAIN . . . a person will die in his sins and spend eternity in the Lake of Fire (Revelation 20:15; 21:8).

For by grace are ye saved through FAITH . . . (Eph. 2:8).

. . . Except ye be CONVERTED . . . ye shall not enter into the kingdom of heaven (Matt. 18:3).

. . . Except a man be BORN AGAIN, he cannot see the kingdom of God (John 3:3).

WHERE do we obtain SAVING FAITH? By WHAT INSTRUMENT are we CONVERTED? What does God use to give us the NEW BIRTH?

Let GOD tell you.

So then FAITH cometh by hearing, and hearing by the WORD OF GOD (Rom. 10:17).

The LAW OF THE LORD is perfect, CONVERTING the soul: . . . (Psalm 19:7).

Being BORN AGAIN, not of corruptible seed, but of incorruptible, by the WORD OF GOD, which liveth and abideth forever (I Pet. 1:23).

Of his own will BEGAT he us with the WORD OF TRUTH . . . (James 1:18).

Now, let's closely examine what God tells us here. We are saved by FAITH, and that SAVING FAITH comes from the WORD

CAN I TRUST MY BIBLE'S TRANSLATION?

OF GOD. The perfect LAW OF THE LORD (which is His Word) is what CONVERTS the lost soul. We are BORN AGAIN by the WORD OF GOD, which IS the WORD OF TRUTH.

I have already shown my reader the humanistic philosophy of the ALEXANDRIANS from their own mouths. Remember? They say the ONLY inerrant Word of God that ever existed was the "original autographs." They have told us time and again that there is NO perfect translation. Then pray tell . . . how could ANYBODY get saved unless they heard and read the "originals"???

THINK ABOUT IT! IT takes the PERFECT Law of the Lord to convert a lost soul. It takes the INCORRUPTIBLE seed to give the New Birth. God can only BEGET us with the Word of TRUTH. If there is NO perfect translation . . . and if even the Masoretic Hebrew and the Antiochan manuscript copies we have today have errors . . . THERE IS NO WAY ANYBODY COULD EVER GET SAVED!!!

The Alexandrians that I quoted in the previous chapter all claim to be saved. But how is that possible? Not ONE of them has ever seen or handled the "ORIGINAL MANUSCRIPTS." And if the truth were known, NOT ONE of them knew Hebrew and Greek when they made their profession of faith in Christ. If they are saved, they got saved by hearing the perfect, inerrant, incorruptible, inspired Word of God in ENGLISH!!! But if they are correct in saying there is no perfect English translation . . . they are LOST! If there is no PERFECT, FLAWLESS, INERRANT, INSPIRED, INCORRUPTIBLE translation in English . . . then NOBODY who speaks only English can get saved!

James tells us that God BEGAT us with the Word of TRUTH. If ANY BOOK that is called a "Bible" has even ONE error in it . . . it is NOT the Word of TRUTH!!!! Therefore, it cannot bring about the New Birth.

In this chapter, I am asking, CAN I TRUST MY BIBLE'S TRANSLATION? The answer is plain and simple . . . NOT IF

CAN I TRUST MY BIBLE?

YOUR BIBLE HAS ERRORS! If it has even ONE error, it is NOT the Word of TRUTH! You cannot trust it! Because I'll guarantee you . . . if it has ONE error, it will have a whole lot more! How can you trust a "bible" that is not perfect? If there are imperfections . . .WHO is to identify the imperfections? The ALEXANDRIANS? NO! NO! NO! We have already seen that we most assuredly cannot trust THEM!

How can you be sure you are saved and going to Heaven if your translated Bible has errors? Maybe the passages you are trusting concerning your salvation are in ERROR.

Do you see what we are down to? We are in total dependence upon the ALMIGHTY GOD to KEEP HIS WORD INTACT as He SAID He would do! Unless it is possible for God to keep His perfect, inerrant, infallible, incorruptible, inspired Word ABSOLUTELY PURE though it is *copied* over and over again down through the centuries in the original Hebrew and Greek languages—and though it is *translated* into other languages—NOBODY ON EARTH CAN GET SAVED TODAY!!!

QUESTION: CAN God do that? HAS God done that?

To say He CANNOT or that He HAS NOT is to CALL GOD A LIAR! He SAID He WOULD! And He says He DID! Right smack-dab in the heart of the Old Testament, God says,

> *This shall be WRITTEN for the generation TO COME: and the people which SHALL BE created shall praise the LORD* (Psalm 102:18).

When it is WRITTEN, it is SCRIPTure. God is plainly saying that the Scriptures were being written for people who had not yet even been born on the earth. Now, that sounds to me like the Almighty God had definite plans to PRESERVE His holy, infallible, inerrant, inspired Word for the generation TO COME. Would all of these people know Hebrew and Greek? Of course not. Then . . .

CAN I TRUST MY BIBLE'S TRANSLATION?

He would have to see to it that His Word was translated into other languages! If, as the educated, scholarly ALEXANDRIANS tell us . . . that there were never any Scripture except the "originals" . . . and God knew the "originals" would crack, peel, fall apart and disintegrate . . . WHY DID HE SAY THE SCRIPTURES WERE WRITTEN FOR PEOPLE WHO HAD NOT YET BEEN CREATED ON EARTH???

QUESTION: Were ANY of the "original parchments" in existence when Paul was on earth?

ANSWER: NO! Even the best of papyrus scrolls treated in oil would not have lasted more than a hundred years. When Paul was on earth, the newest of Old Testament parchments had crumbled back to dust over three hundred years previously. Yet look what Paul writes under the inspiration of the Holy Spirit when the only Scriptures he could possibly refer to were COPIES of the originals.

For whatsoever things were written AFORETIME were written for OUR LEARNING, that we through patience and comfort of the SCRIPTURES might have hope (Rom. 15:4).

Sure sounds like a fulfillment of Psalm 102:18 to me!

Even though all he had were COPIES of the original autographs, Paul said under Holy Spirit inspiration that he HAD the Scriptures . . . and SO DID THE PEOPLE TO WHOM HE WAS WRITING! Whenever you see the words "scripture" or "scriptures" in the Bible, it is talking about God's PERFECT, INFALLIBLE, INERRANT, INSPIRED, INCORRUPTIBLE WORD! If there are errors in it . . . it is NOT Scripture! God is not the Author of something written imperfectly or in error! He is not the Author of corruptible "scriptures"! God is PERFECT . . . and His Word is PERFECT!

Away with this Satanic trash that only the "original

CAN I TRUST MY BIBLE?

autographs" were perfect and inspired . . . and away with the same devilish dribble that there is no such thing as a perfect translation! Satan is the father of a lie . . . and he sure fathered THAT ONE!

God the Holy Spirit caused Paul to write in SCRIPTURE that the Old Testament SCRIPTURES were written for OUR learning, that WE through patience and comfort of the SCRIPTURES might HAVE (present tense) hope! Sure sounds to me like they HAD the Scriptures in Paul's day, but it sure doesn't stop there. Any of God's children who can read the book of Romans TODAY can lay claim to the same truth. God gave us His infallible, inerrant, perfect Word for our learning so that we could HOLD THE SCRIPTURES IN OUR HANDS AND LEARN FROM THEM. We might have patience, comfort, and hope. What patience, comfort and hope is there to be gained "through the scriptures" if we do not HAVE the Scriptures???

If we do not have a perfect translation, we do not HAVE the Scriptures . . . and don't let some double-talking ALEXANDRIAN tell you any different! Just because the ALEXANDRIAN'S puny little sissy-britches effeminate god cannot get his word into more than the "original" languages . . . don't think the Almighty God of the Bible cannot do it! He gave the Great Commission, knowing full well that the "original autographs" would pass out of existence . . . and knowing full well that in order for His New Testament church to carry the Commission to its fulfillment, His Word would have to be translated into other languages. If such a thing were impossible, HE WOULD NEVER HAVE GIVEN THE COMMISSION!

It grinds my gizzard and burns my collar when I hear the Alexandrians say, "There is no such thing as a perfect translation." They are flat accusing God of being weak, frail, fraudulent, uncaring, and stupid. Like I say . . . I wouldn't want to be in their sneakers when they face Him!!!

Recently, I received a packet in the mail from an

CAN I TRUST MY BIBLE'S TRANSLATION?

ALEXANDRIAN named Milton Carr. I have never heard of him, but I get lots of mail from people whom I have never met and who attempt to straighten me out on my "King James only" error. Mr. Carr is apparently connected somehow with a Baptist church in Castle Dale, Utah. He may be the pastor. I don't know. He never says.

Anyway, he enclosed two articles in the packet. One was the photostatic copy of a book some unidentified ALEXANDRIAN wrote to destroy faith in the King James Bible. The writer says in essence, that the King James Bible cannot be trusted because it has gone through a great number of "revisions." That is a LIE! My dictionary says to revise is to "look over and correct." Other than printers' errors (which were taken care of quickly), there has been no revising. There was nothing to CORRECT. There were CHANGES, yes. The English language underwent a vast change in the first 158 years after the 1611 edition was published. Most of it was in spelling. Up until the early eighteenth century, there were no set rules as to the spelling of English words. This is why in the original 1611 version there are often several spellings for the same word. When this began to be changed, new EDITIONS of the King James Bible were printed.

There is a difference between a revision and an edition. The dictionary says to *edit* is to "prepare for publication." It says an *edition* is "the form in which something is published." The FORM of the King James Bible was changed six times after the original 1611 edition due to changes in spelling and punctuation in the English language . . . but there were NO *revisions!*

Tossing this pack of lies aside, I looked at the other article. It was a "paper" prepared by Mr. Carr, in which he extols the New International perversion. But, again (as always), it is filled with ALEXANDRIAN double-talk.

Carr's "paper" is more or less a plea to the "brethren" to

CAN I TRUST MY BIBLE?

stop fighting over Bible versions. Speaking of the controversy that is hot amongst "Fundamentalists," he says, "At present there is a controversy raging among fundamental preachers across this country which is causing good men to malign and devour one another as though they were fighting the devil himself—and all the while they are mutilating the body of Christ."

From the context of his statement, I assume he thinks there is some kind of mystical, universal, invisible "body" of Christ that is being mutilated by the controversy over Bible versions. It's beyond me how a mystical, universal, invisible "body" could be mutilated. But, putting that statement aside . . . maybe someone should inform Mr. Carr that those of us who stand for the King James Bible as the ONE AND ONLY Bible in the English language as the pure, perfect, inspired, inerrant Word of God ARE fighting the devil himself!!!

When God says He will preserve EVERY WORD forever . . . and the ALEXANDRIANS say He WILL NOT do any such thing . . . WHO is behind calling God a liar? The DEVIL!!! And the ALEXANDRIANS are giving place to the devil by saying there is NO perfect Word of God on the earth TODAY!

Mr. Carr quotes Scripture on pages 2, 6, and 7 of his "paper" in an attempt to get the "brethren" to love each other and not to scrap over Bible versions. Amazingly enough, all of his Scripture quotations are from the KING JAMES BIBLE. Yet in the "paper," he labors to show 344 times where the New International perversion is BETTER translated than the King James! WHY DIDN'T HE QUOTE FROM THE BLESSED NEW INTERNATIONAL PERVERSION???

James commented on this type of thing: *"A DOUBLEMINDED man is unstable in ALL his ways"* (James 1:8). Being double-minded, Mr. Carr then comes forth with his DOUBLE talk.

On page 2 of his "paper," Mr. Carr says, "There are those who believe and teach that the so-called Textus Receptus has been

CAN I TRUST MY BIBLE'S TRANSLATION?

divinely preserved by God as the 'one and only inspired Greek text' of the New Testament . . . and furthermore, that the 1611 King James Version of the Bible is the one and only divinely inspired translation of the Textus Receptus—therefore making the King James Version the only Bible which is the very Word of God. Their reasoning and logic is rather asinine."

Seems to me that MR. CARR'S reasoning is QUITE asinine. How could there POSSIBLY be more than ONE real Bible in ANY language? God said He would preserve EVERY WORD! If you have TWO Bibles . . . ONE of them CANNOT POSSIBLY BE THE WORD OF GOD. The WORDS are different. Jesus told the devil, *". . . man shall not live by bread alone, but by EVERY WORD that proceedeth out of the mouth of God"* (Matt. 4:4).

Since the WORDS are different in every version . . . only ONE can be the real Word of God. Common sense tells me immediately that the REAL one cannot be an ALEXANDRIAN bible. It MUST be the ONE AND ONLY *ANTIOCHAN* Bible. The ANTIOCHAN Bible in English is the precious old AV1611 KING JAMES BIBLE!

Now, here comes the double-talk. On page 3 of his "paper," Mr. Carr says, "I believe the King James Version is a reliable and good translation. (I have studied, memorized, and preached the King James Version for some thirty-odd years.) I repeat—I believe that the King James Version is a reliable and good translation."

My question is . . . How can the King James Bible be a "reliable and good" translation if it has 344 places where it is wrong?

Mr. Carr proceeds, "In three hundred and seventy years the English language has changed tremendously. And because of this and some other reasons, I believe that there are some other translations that are better for today than the King James Version."

CAN I TRUST MY BIBLE?

This is typical ALEXANDRIAN reasoning . . . full of HUMANISM. Where is GOD in all of this "other versions" stuff, Mr. Carr? HE said He would preserve EVERY WORD. Jesus said, *"Heaven and earth shall pass away, but my WORDS shall NOT pass away"* (Matt 24:35).

The humanistic ALEXANDRIANS throw God clear out of their thinking and look totally at MAN in this picture, thus reasoning that MAN cannot keep God's words perfect and pure, so since God turned it all over to MAN, there is no perfect Hebrew or Greek manuscript; and consequently, there is no perfect translation.

Since we ANTIOCHANS believe God . . . we KNOW that somewhere on earth is a BOOK that has EVERY ONE OF THE WORDS GOD WANTS US TO HAVE. In English . . . it is the precious old KING JAMES BIBLE!

In spite of all that the DEVIL and the ALEXANDRIANS can do, God still promised to preserve EVERY WORD of His Bible. In Jeremiah 1:12, the Lord refers to His veracity and says, *"I will hasten my word to perform it."* Again referring to His veracity, the Lord says,

My covenant will I not break, nor alter the thing that is gone out of my lips (Psalm 89:34).

You ALEXANDRIANS can go on insulting God by insisting that there is no perfect Hebrew or Greek text and that there is no perfect translation all you want . . . but there is a reckoning day coming! Like I keep saying . . . I sure am glad I won't be in YOUR sneakers!

And another thing, Mr. Carr . . . the New International Version, which you extol so highly has been off the press since 1973. If it is so much better than the King James Bible, WHY IN THE NAME OF DONALD DUCK HAVE YOU NOT BEEN TEACHING AND PREACHING FROM IT SINCE 1973??? Could it be that you have

CAN I TRUST MY BIBLE'S TRANSLATION?

noticed the LACK OF GOD'S BREATH on the NIV, which is so obvious on the GOOD OLD KING JAMES?

In John MacArthur's booklet in which he attacks the King James Bible, he says, "There is a growing literature crusade which claims that 'God wrote only one Bible.' By 'one Bible,' they mean the King James Version Bible written in 1611. They conclude that the King James Version is the only English version which faithfully preserves the original writings. They build their case upon such doctrines as the preservation of Scripture and the inerrancy of Scripture."

Again, we see ALEXANDRIAN philosophy coming from Mr. MacArthur, which is typical of his ilk. The ALEXANDRIANS just can't seem to get it in their heads that God DID produce only ONE Bible. Anything else would be total CONFUSION, and God is NOT the Author of confusion (I Cor. 14:33). God did not have several men write the first five books of the Bible. Why should He do that? There was only ONE Moses and only ONE Pentateuch. So why should God have several versions of the Pentateuch? That would necessitate DIFFERENT WORDS being used, which would only cause confusion. God is NOT the Author of confusion.

There is only ONE BOOK of Proverbs. There was only ONE King Solomon. Why should God have several men write different versions of Proverbs? It would only serve to cause CONFUSION, and God Is NOT the Author of confusion.

I can just hear some wiseacre ALEXANDRIAN cry out, "Well, how come there are FOUR Gospels in the New Testament? Aren't they FOUR versions of the SAME story?"

In one sense they are, but in the strictest sense, they are not. God chose to have Matthew present Jesus as King of the Jews. Mark presents Him as the Servant of the Father; Luke presents Him as the Son of Man, and John presents Him as the Son of God. In order for

CAN I TRUST MY BIBLE?

God to give us the FULL PICTURE of the earthly life of the Lord Jesus, it took a perfect BLENDING of seeing Him from four sides. The four Gospels NEVER contradict one another, but rather tell the story to its FULLEST beauty. Though God used FOUR different men to write the Gospels, the four books have the same AUTHOR. So in the strictest sense, the books of Matthew, Mark, Luke and John are NOT four "versions." God gave ONE BOOK of Matthew, ONE BOOK of Mark, ONE BOOK of Luke, and ONE BOOK of John. Anything else would have caused confusion, and God is NOT the Author of confusion.

When God was ready to close off the Bible with the Revelation of Jesus Christ, He did not put SEVERAL men on the isle of Patmos. He only put ONE. God wanted only ONE written manuscript to come from the Patmos experience . . . not several. Such a thing would have produced manuscripts with DIFFERENT WORDS. This would only bring CONFUSION, and God is NOT the Author of confusion.

Someone might say, "Yes, but even if God had placed several men on the isle of Patmos and had the Holy Spirit breathe out the words, each and every manuscript would have the EXACT same words."

Correct! So why have more than one writer for any given section of Scripture? If there was MORE than ONE version of any writing of Scriptural books in the beginning, there would be nothing but CONFUSION. That's why there cannot be more than ONE version of the Bible in any given language. TWO versions or more only cause CONFUSION. God is NOT the Author of confusion. Therefore, God DID only write ONE Bible. If He had written TWO or more, He would be the Author of confusion.

Altogether in the English language, there have been a total of over ONE HUNDRED versions of the "Bible." There are about thirty available today in the "Christian" bookstores. Is God behind

CAN I TRUST MY BIBLE'S TRANSLATION?

all these versions? NO! Every one of the versions has DIFFERENT WORDS. DIFFERENT WORDS CAUSE CONFUSION! Since God is NOT the Author of confusion, He is behind only ONE of these versions. Since ALL of them except the AV 1611 King James Version have their perverted roots in ALEXANDRIA, and ONLY the King James Bible has its roots in ANTIOCH, it isn't difficult for a person with a nominal amount of intelligence to figure out which version is GOD'S!

However . . . as my reader can see, the ALEXANDRIANS have a really hard time accepting the fact that God only inspired ONE Bible, so that there can only be ONE translation in ANY language that is the pure, perfect, uncontaminated, inerrant, incorruptible, inspired Word of God. This is true of the ENGLISH language. The ALEXANDRIANS butt their heads against it because this gives the BOOK the authority over THEM. They can't take this, so they attack the "God who wrote only ONE Bible" doctrine. If they admit to that fact, it takes away their "authority" over the BOOK. The Alexandrians who USE the King James Bible but don't BELIEVE it, love to stand in their pulpits and say, "A better translation of this verse is . . ." or "The Greek says . . ." or "The King James translators made an error here, and I will show you what God REALLY said . . ."

With this approach, the Alexandrians can gloat in their magnificent education and glory in their vast intelligence. Whenever they find a passage, verse, or word in the King James Bible that they don't understand or don't believe, they feel free to mangle it, manipulate it, or wrest it so that it agrees with their own ideas and concepts. This is why the Alexandrians hate the "God wrote only ONE Bible" fact and say that such reasoning and logic is "rather asinine." Poor little jerkos. They've just GOT to be in the limelight by asserting their authority over the BOOK.

Let's see just how asinine it is to reason that God wrote only ONE Bible. In the Word of God, there is only

CAN I TRUST MY BIBLE?

ONE Pearl of Great Price (Matt. 13:46)
ONE Master (Matt. 23:8)
ONE God (Rom. 3:30; I Cor. 8:6)
ONE Father (Matt. 23:9; I Cor. 8:6)
ONE Lord Jesus Christ (I Cor. 8:6)
ONE Holy Spirit (Eph. 2:18; 4:4)
ONE Way of Salvation (John 14:6)
ONE Gospel (Gal. 1:8-9)
ONE Bread (John 6:48; I Cor. 10:17)
ONE Body (Eph. 4:4)
ONE Hope (Eph. 4:4)
ONE Lord (Eph. 4:5)
ONE Faith (Eph. 4:5)
ONE Baptism (Eph. 4:5)
ONE Mediator (I Tim. 2:5)
ONE Lawgiver (James 4:12)
ONE Sacrifice for sins forever (Heb. 10:12)
ONE Offering to perfect the saints (Heb. 10:14)
ONE Heaven where saved people go (Matt. 6:9; I Pet. 1:4)
ONE Hell where lost people go (Isa. 14:9; Luke 16:23)
ONE Lamb of God (John 1:29)
ONE Lamb's Book of Life (Rev. 21:27)
ONE Book of Life (Rev. 20:15)

Then is it asinine to believe and teach that the same God who was so singular in all of these inspired more than ONE Bible? Seems to me it is VERY ASININE to say God inspired more than

CAN I TRUST MY BIBLE'S TRANSLATION?

ONE Bible, which would cause nothing but total CONFUSION. God is NOT the Author of CONFUSION!

But the ALEXANDRIANS cry, "God DID inspire only ONE Bible . . . the ORIGINAL AUTOGRAPHS! And since they are gone forever, WE HAVE NO INSPIRED WORD OF GOD TODAY!"

Talk about asinine. If there is no inspired Word of God on earth TODAY, *nobody on the face of God's green earth can get saved!!!*

All the Alexandrians will agree that "inspiration" means GOD-BREATHED. Well, friend of mine, if God is not STILL breathing on His holy, perfect, inerrant, incorruptible Word TODAY, it will KILL us! Paul wrote,

. . . God . . . hath made us able ministers of the new testament; not of the LETTER, but of the SPIRIT: for the LETTER KILLETH, but the SPIRIT GIVETH LIFE (II Cor. 3:5-6).

The letter by *itself* KILLS if the Spirit is not there to breathe on it and give it LIFE. Jesus said,

It is the SPIRIT that quickeneth . . . (John 6:63).

To "quicken" something is to put LIFE into it. Something that is "quick" is ALIVE. Paul compared the "quick" and the "dead" in II Timothy 4:1. The "quick" are opposite of the "dead," which, in this sense of the word, means ALIVE. In the BOOK of Ephesians, Paul compares the "quick" with the "dead" again.

And you hath he (God) QUICKENED, who were DEAD in trespasses and sins; (Eph. 2:1).

But God . . . even when we were DEAD in sins, hath QUICKENED us together with Christ (Eph. 2:4-5).

We are told of the Word of God,

For the word of God is QUICK, and powerful . . .

CAN I TRUST MY BIBLE?

(Heb. 4:12).

This makes it clear that the Word of God is ALIVE. In Philippians 2:16, it is called the "word of LIFE." Well, WHO is it that gives the Bible LIFE? Jesus told us in John 6:63, *"It is the SPIRIT that quickeneth"!*

Peter wrote,

> *For the prophecy came not in old time by the will of man: but holy men of God spake as they were moved by the HOLY GHOST* (II Pet. 1:21).

I am going to deal with the *inspiration* of the King James Bible at length in the next chapter, but I must establish in THIS chapter (since we are answering the question: CAN I TRUST MY BIBLE'S TRANSLATION?) that if a TRANSLATION is not inspired, then there is no breath of the Holy Spirit on it, and it will KILL you! Remember . . . the letter KILLETH, but the SPIRIT giveth LIFE.

Let me point out again that when God gave the Great Commission, He knew that His Word would have to be TRANSLATED in order for souls to be quickened from spiritual death. If there were not going to be TRANSLATIONS upon which the Spirit of God would breathe . . . NOBODY COULD GET SAVED! It is the Holy Spirit that "quickeneth" the Word of God so that it can give you LIFE!

Is it not clear that if the Spirit of LIFE (Rom. 8:2) does not breathe LIFE into a translation, that translation CANNOT GIVE YOU SPIRITUAL LIFE? The letter KILLETH!

Look what Paul wrote to Timothy under the inspiration of the Holy Spirit . . .

> *. . . From a child thou hast known the HOLY SCRIPTURES, which are able to make thee WISE UNTO SALVATION through faith which is in Christ Jesus. ALL SCRIPTURE is given by inspiration of*

CAN I TRUST MY BIBLE'S TRANSLATION?

God, and is profitable for doctrine, for reproof, for correction, for instruction in righteousness: That the man of God may be perfect, throughly furnished unto all good works (II Tim. 3:15-17).

QUESTION: Did Timothy have the "original autographs" in his possession?

ANSWER: Absolutely NOT! The original parchments of the Old Testament were long gone when Timothy was born. When Timothy was a child, NOT ONE PAGE of the New Testament had been written. So WHAT did Timothy have? Paul said he had the HOLY SCRIPTURES! But how could that be possible if the Alexandrians are correct in saying the ONLY Holy Scriptures were the "original autographs"?

It is quite doubtful that Timothy could read Masoretic Hebrew since he was neither a rabbi, a scribe, a priest, or a Pharisee. I will demonstrate shortly that the common people among the Jews in Jesus' day and in Paul's day DID NOT SPEAK THE HEBREW LANGUAGE OF THE OLD TESTAMENT. The language died two hundred years BEFORE the Lord Jesus left Heaven to come to earth in human flesh. The Jews in His day and in Paul's day spoke *Aramaic*.

According to Acts 16:1, Timothy's mother was a Jewess who had put her faith in the Lord Jesus Christ. His father was a Greek, and no doubt, an unsaved man. As Paul opens his second letter to Timothy, he calls to remembrance the unfeigned faith that is in Timothy, which had dwelt first in his grandmother Lois, and his mother, Eunice. It would seem, then, that the HOLY SCRIPTURES that Timothy had in his hands as a child were the Aramaic Scriptures. This would make the "HOLY SCRIPTURES" that Timothy read as a child a TRANSLATION!

Note that Paul said from a child Timothy had known the HOLY SCRIPTURES which were able to make him *"wise unto*

CAN I TRUST MY BIBLE?

salvation through faith which is in Christ Jesus." Interesting, wouldn't you say? This means that the Old Testament is so full of Christ Jesus and salvation by grace through faith that a person can get saved by hearing or reading the OLD Testament! This does away with the heresy that is believed by some today that people in the Old Testament days got saved by faith and WORKS. Baloney! Paul labors in the early part of Romans 4 to show that both Abraham and David were saved by faith WITHOUT WORKS! That makes it GRACE! Then Paul whacks the "faith and works" heresy in the head by stating in Romans 4:16, *"Therefore it is of FAITH, that it might BE by GRACE!"*

That's plain enough for a country boy like me. If salvation is by FAITH, it is automatically by GRACE. If some people who get to Heaven are saved by faith and WORKS, then THEY will get the glory, and NOT the Lord Jesus Christ! No way, Jose!

No one HAS EVER been saved by works, nor will anyone EVER be saved by works... Not on OLD TESTAMENT ground, not on NEW TESTAMENT ground, not on TRIBULATION PERIOD ground, and not on MILLENNIUM ground! God said in the OLD Testament,

> *... Let not the wise man glory in his wisdom, neither let the mighty man glory in his might, let not the rich man glory in his riches: But let him that glorieth glory in this, that he understandeth and KNOWETH ME* (Jer. 9:23-24).

God said through Paul's pen in the NEW Testament,

> *That NO flesh should glory in HIS presence. But of HIM are ye in Christ Jesus, who OF GOD is made unto us wisdom, and righteousness, and sanctification, and REDEMPTION: That, according as it is written, He that glorieth, let him glory IN THE LORD* (I Cor. 1:29-31).

CAN I TRUST MY BIBLE'S TRANSLATION?

God's presence is concentrated in Heaven. Therefore, there will not be ANYONE in Heaven who would or COULD glory in themselves, or their WORKS! They can glory in only ONE direction . . . IN THE LORD! Of God the Father, Jesus Christ is made unto us (saved people) REDEMPTION . . . Not just on THIS side of the cross, but also on the OTHER side of the cross. Jesus is the Lamb slain FROM THE FOUNDATION of the world (Rev. 13:8), so He could be the Redeemer of ALL mankind (I Tim. 4:10), from Adam to the last person who ever draws breath on this earth. As the LAMB was slain, He shed His precious BLOOD, and it is by the BLOOD that EVERY person who ever escapes Hell will be redeemed.

NO ONE is redeemed partially by the BLOOD and partially by their WORKS . . . EVER! That would take glory from the Lord Jesus Christ, and God will NEVER let that happen! In Revelation chapter 5, we see ALL the Old Testament saints, ALL of the New Testament saints, and no doubt some who were saved in the Tribulation period, standing around the throne of the Lamb. Listen to them!

And they sung a new song, saying, THOU art worthy . . . for THOU wast slain, and hast redeemed us to God BY THY BLOOD out of every kindred, and tongue, and people, and nation (Rev. 5:9).

Not ONE of the Old Testament saints says, "Thou hast redeemed us PARTIALLY by Thy blood, and we did the rest by faith and works!" ALL the glory FOREVER will go to the LORD JESUS CHRIST because in ALL ages HE has done ALL the redeeming ALL BY HIMSELF!

So we can readily see that the Holy Spirit knew that Timothy ONLY had the OLD Testament in his hands, yet He caused Paul to write to Timothy . . .

. . . From a child thou hast known the HOLY SCRIPTURES, which are able to make thee wise

CAN I TRUST MY BIBLE?

unto SALVATION through faith which is in CHRIST JESUS (II Tim. 3:15).

It is a fact, then, that whether Timothy somehow had learned to read classic Hebrew . . . or whether he read it in the Aramaic . . . he HAD the Holy Scriptures in his hands! This blows the Alexandrian idea that the ONLY inerrant, inspired Word of God that ever existed was the "original manuscripts"!!!

Since it is VERY doubtful that Timothy could read the classic Hebrew in which the Old Testament had been written, we must assume that what he had in his hands to read and study was an Aramaic TRANSLATION. Isn't that something? The Holy Spirit told Paul to call a TRANSLATION the "Holy Scriptures"! I'll guarantee you this . . . the Holy Spirit of God is NOT going to call a Bible with errors in it HOLY SCRIPTURES! And even if you Alexandrians argue that Timothy was reading the Old Testament HEBREW . . . you have to admit that what he had was a copy of a copy of a copy of a copy of a copy of a copy! Yet it had to be *without error* because the Holy Spirit called it "HOLY SCRIPTURES"! If what Timothy was reading had even ONE error, that error would be UNTRUTH. If it is not TRUTH, it is FALSE. The Holy Spirit of God would not be guilty of calling something that was false "holy." Therefore, we know that what Timothy HELD IN HIS HANDS and READ was the pure, incorruptible, inerrant, inspired Word of God!

I, for one, believe that what Timothy was reading was an Aramaic TRANSLATION of the Holy Scriptures . . . and you will see why as you read on. Of course, such belief gives ulcers and nervous breakdowns to the ALEXANDRIANS! Their little wimp of a god can't even keep COPIES of his original manuscripts correct . . . much less ever get his words TRANSLATED into another language. However, since the puny little god of the Alexandrians is NOT the God of the Bible, we won't waste time on him.

Let us consider the God of the BIBLE. Did He use mortal

CAN I TRUST MY BIBLE'S TRANSLATION?

men to give us the original manuscripts? MOST ASSUREDLY. Then can't He preserve His words, letters, jots, and tittles EVEN THOUGH THEY ARE COPIED BY MORTAL HANDS? *WITHOUT A DOUBT.* Let's take it a step further. Can't He also get His Holy Scriptures TRANSLATED from Hebrew and Greek into OTHER earthly languages by using mortal men? To answer in the negative is to show one's self to be a blatant IGNORAMUS!

Not long ago, I was in conversation with an Alexandrian "Baptist" pastor in California. We were discussing the Bible translation issue. Mocking me for the stand I take on the inerrancy and inspiration of my AV1611 King James Bible, he sneered, laughed, and said, "That is nothing but GROSS IGNORANCE!"

Being as sweet and lovable as I am, I did not bite back. I won't tell you what I WANTED to do! I just walked away in my GROSS IGNORANCE thanking the God of the Bible that He gave me His pure, perfect, inerrant, inspired, incorruptible, powerful Word in MY language, so I could PREACH the WORD as I am told to do in II Timothy 4:2!

I have been mocked and laughed at by many an Alexandrian because I believe my God CAN and HAS given me a PERFECT TRANSLATION. Let 'em laugh. Just because THEY have a weak, mealy-mouthed pansy of a god, doesn't mean I do! The God of the BIBLE said,

Behold, I am the Lord, the God of all flesh: IS THERE ANY THING TOO HARD FOR ME? (Jer. 32:27).

The Alexandrians THINK there is! Or course, it IS for THEIR god! They just THINK their god is the God of the Bible!

The God of the BIBLE told me in His Word to PREACH the Word (II Tim. 4:2), to STUDY and RIGHTLY DIVIDE the Word (II Tim. 2:15), to READ the Word (Rev. 1:3), to HIDE the Word in my heart (Psalm 119:11), and to let the Word LEAD me, KEEP me, and

CAN I TRUST MY BIBLE?

TALK to me (Prov. 6:22) . . . BUT HOW CAN I DO THAT IF I DO NOT HAVE THE WORD??? Go ahead and laugh, Alexandrians, but I have yet to have one of you answer that question! You can laugh NOW, but one day you'll face the GOD OF THE BIBLE! We'll see who laughs THEN! You'll be like Sarah of old. Remember her? Let's read it.

> *And he [GOD] said [to Abraham], I will certainly return unto thee according to the time of life; and, lo, Sarah thy wife shall have a son. And Sarah heard it in the tent door, which was behind him. Now Abraham and Sarah were old and well stricken in age; and it ceased to be with Sarah after the manner of women. Therefore Sarah LAUGHED within herself, saying, After I am waxed old shall I have pleasure, my lord being old also?*
>
> *And the Lord said unto Abraham, Wherefore did Sarah LAUGH, saying, Shall I of a surety bear a child, which am old? IS ANY THING TOO HARD FOR THE LORD? At the time appointed I will return unto thee, according to the time of life, and Sarah shall have a son. Then Sarah DENIED, saying, I LAUGHED NOT; for she was AFRAID. And he [GOD] said, Nay; but thou DIDST laugh* (Gen. 18:10-15).

Well, let me ask you Alexandrians . . . IS anything too hard for the Lord? Huh? What's that? SPEAK UP; I can't hear you! Do you feel a LAUGH coming on? Go ahead. Let it out, but the day will come when YOU WILL FACE THE SAME GOD SARAH DID! I can just hear you now when the God of the BIBLE looks you straight in the eye and says, "Why did you LAUGH when I said in My Word that I would PRESERVE EVERY WORD OF MY BIBLE FOREVER? HMM? WHY DID YOU LAUGH, SAYING

CAN I TRUST MY BIBLE'S TRANSLATION?

THERE WAS NO SUCH THING AS A PERFECT TRANSLATION WHEN I SHOWED YOU RIGHT IN MY BIBLE THAT I COULD PRODUCE A PERFECT TRANSLATION EVEN USING MORTAL MEN?"

And you ignoramus Alexandrians will look into His burning eyes and lie weakly saying, "I laughed not." Then the God of the BIBLE will retort, "Nay, but thou DIDST laugh!" I want to see your faces at that moment.

As for me, I HAVE a perfect translation in English so I can PREACH it, STUDY it, RIGHTLY DIVIDE it, READ it, HIDE it in my heart; and I can let it LEAD me, KEEP me, and TALK to me. The God of the BIBLE would not TELL me to do all of this, then let me stand there empty-handed, wondering how I was going to obey Him. I BELIEVE the God of the BIBLE has given me His Bible as He said He would. So I say with Jeremiah, *"Ah Lord God! behold, thou hast made the heaven and the earth by thy great power and stretched out arm, and THERE IS NOTHING TOO HARD FOR THEE"* (Jer. 32:17)!!!

But the poor "intelligent" Alexandrians (bless their scholarship) just can't bring themselves to believe that the God who made this universe could watch over His Word so carefully that He would preserve perfect copies in Hebrew and Greek so that we could have a perfect translation in English.

Gleason Archer, in his *Encyclopedia of Bible Difficulties* has a section headed: "The Remarkable Trustworthiness of the Received Text of Holy Scripture." Why he uplifts the Received Text and uses the NIV as his bible, I will never figure out. Anyway, in spite of the "remarkable trustworthiness of the Received Text," Mr. Archer says it has errors. He then asks the question, "Why do we not now possess infallible copies of those infallible original autographs?"

Now, check out his ridiculous answer: "Because the production of even one perfect copy of one BOOK is so far beyond

CAN I TRUST MY BIBLE?

the capacity of a human scribe as to render it necessary FOR GOD TO PERFORM A MIRACLE IN ORDER TO PRODUCE IT."

Tsk, tsk. Mr. Archer . . . REALLY! Are you so blind that you can't see that that is EXACTLY what God did? This perfect, infallible, inspired, inerrant BOOK that lies on my desk before me IS a miracle! But is that such a surprise? *"Ah Lord God! behold, thou hast made the heaven and the earth by thy great power and stretched out arm, and THERE IS NOTHING TOO HARD FOR THEE"* (Jer. 32:17).

Archer goes on to say, "No reasonable person can expect even the most conscientious copyist to achieve technical infallibility in transcribing his original document into a fresh copy. No matter how earnest he maybe, he will commit at least an occasional slip."

What he says would be true IF God were not hovering over the copyist and performing His miracle of keeping it perfect EVEN AS HE HAD DONE WHEN HE GAVE THE "ORIGINALS"! And there is no question in my mind that He did the SAME THING when the King James translators were doing their magnificent work! If He did NOT . . . then the King James Bible is no better than all those English translations which came from the rotten ALEXANDRIAN manuscripts.

Of course, the Alexandrians don't think the Lord really CARED that much about giving a perfect translation. I have a book before me written by an Alexandrian named James Montgomery Boice. It is entitled *Does Inerrancy Matter?* In keeping with his Alexandrian brethren, he works hard in the book to establish his unwavering belief that the "original autographs" were indeed inerrant. Ho-hum . . . Same old thing.

On the first page of the book, Mr. Boice declares, "All Scripture quotations are taken from the New International Version of the Bible." So, really, we know the rules of the game before the whistle blows.

CAN I TRUST MY BIBLE'S TRANSLATION?

Anyway, there's something on page 14 that I've just got to show you. Under the heading, "Copies and Translations," Boice makes it clear that he believes no TRANSLATION can be perfect since no copy of the original manuscripts is perfect. Now get this . . . and I quote, "There are people who say, 'Since translations of the Bible differ and since all of them cannot be right, inerrancy is a mistaken notion.' The misunderstanding here is to suppose that inerrancy applies to the COPIES of the original documents or to TRANSLATIONS of these documents. Actually, it applies ONLY to the ORIGINAL MANUSCRIPTS, called autographs."

The capitals in the quotation are mine, so you can get the impact of his words. Now, here comes the *zinger*. Mr. Boice goes on. Pointing to these same inquiring people, he says, "They ask, 'But why didn't God see to it that we have error-free copies?' This question is a bit more substantial. It may be that in the final analysis we have to say that WE SIMPLY DO NOT KNOW WHY GOD HAS SEEN FIT TO ACT AS HE DID."

How do you like THAT one, reader? This educated Alexandrian figures God is a strange One. In not seeing to it that we have error-free copies of the "originals," God has acted in a weird manner. Why, if we only had error-free COPIES, we might also have error-free TRANSLATIONS! Well, Mr. Boice, I guess God just DIDN'T CARE! Or at least this seems to be the opinion you have. Well, let me tell you, pal . . .YOUR little Alexandrian god may not care, BUT THE GOD OF THE BIBLE DOES!!! He not only kept us error-free COPIES in the Masoretic manuscripts of the Hebrew and the Received Text of the Greek . . . But HE ALSO GAVE US AN ERROR-FREE TRANSLATION IN ENGLISH, even as He had done in other languages long before!

Let me guide your mind, dear reader, to some historical facts which tie in with Bible truth.

As you probably know, Babylon of old was the capital city

CAN I TRUST MY BIBLE?

of Chaldea. The language they spoke was "Chaldean," also known as "Syriac." Later it became known as "Aramaic."

The word "Hebrew" is used in the Bible to depict Abraham and his descendants in both the Old and New Testaments (see for instance Gen. 14:13; 43:32; Acts 6:1; Phil. 3:5). The *tongue* of the Hebrews is not called "Hebrew" in the Old Testament, but is referred to as "the language of Canaan" (Isa. 19:18), or as "the Jews' language" (II Kings 18:26, 28; Neh. 13:24).

In the New Testament, the tongue of the Jews is called "Hebrew" in such passages as Luke 23:38; John 5:2; 19:13, 17, 20; Acts 21:40; 22:2; 26:14; Rev. 9:11; 16:16.

In 605 B.C., Nebuchadnezzar King of Chaldea besieged Jerusalem and carried off to Babylon the vessels of the house of God and members of the nobility of Judah. Among them was Daniel the prophet (II Chron. 36:2-7; Dan. 1:1-3). Later, Nebuchadnezzar destroyed Jerusalem and carried thousands more of the Jews to Babylon. Notice what we read in the book of Daniel.

> *And the king spake unto Ashpenaz the master of his eunuchs, that he should bring certain of the children of Israel, and of the king's seed, and of the princes; Children in whom was no blemish, but well favoured, and skilful in all wisdom, and cunning in knowledge, and understanding science, and such as had ability in them to stand in the king's palace, and whom they might teach the learning and the TONGUE OF THE CHALDEANS* (Dan. 1:3-4).

You will note that immediately after taking them captive, Nebuchadnezzar began teaching the Jews the language of the Chaldeans, known as "Syriac" (Dan. 2:4; II Kings 18:26). Some seventy years later (Jer. 25:1, 11, 12), Babylon was conquered by Cyrus king of Persia. Cyrus issued a decree permitting the Jews to return to Jerusalem to rebuild the temple (Ezra 1:1-4). But after

CAN I TRUST MY BIBLE'S TRANSLATION?

seventy years as captives of the Chaldeans, the people of Israel returned home with a new vernacular . . . the Syrian language known as "Aramaic."

The old Hebrew language slowly died. By 200 B.C. it was dead, and the only men of Israel who could read it were the scribes and the priests. Not long before Jesus was born in Bethlehem, the term "rabbi" came about, depicting the teachers (or "masters") in Israel. About that same time, the sect of the Pharisees came into being. In Jesus' day, the rabbis knew the dead Hebrew language, as did most of the Pharisees. Up until that time, the SCRIBES were the teachers.

When the Lord Jesus arrived on the scene some two hundred years after the Hebrew language died, the common people spoke and read ONLY the Aramaic language. The highly-educated men of Israel also knew Greek, but even these did not know Hebrew. This knowledge was still confined to the scribes, priest, rabbis, and the majority of the Pharisees.

It is interesting to note that there are three sections of the Old Testament that were NOT written in Hebrew, but were written in *Aramaic*. They are Jeremiah 10:11, Daniel 2:4-7:28, and Ezra 4:8-6:18. Each of these passages is linked to Israel's captivity in Babylon. If you will read them, I believe you will see that the Holy Spirit wanted to make the messages in those sections REAL CLEAR to the Chaldeans, so He put them in THEIR language.

I have already pointed out that the people of Israel had been in captivity in Babylon for SEVENTY years. By this time in man's history, the average age allotted to human beings was SEVENTY YEARS (Psalm 90:10). So when the Israelites were sent back to their homeland after the Babylonian captivity, only those who had lived *past* the average age had ever BEEN in Judaea. Besides the elderly people, only the scribes and priests knew the Hebrew language.

I point this out because I want you to see something very

significant. Early in the history of the Hebrew nation, the office of the scribe was established so that copies of the Scriptures could be made to PRESERVE them. Of course, the scribes also served as public writers, secretaries, composers of legal documents, jurists, and legal experts (II Sam. 8:17; 20:25; I Kings 4:3; II Kings 12:10; Jer. 8:8; 32:12; 36:4, 18, etc.).

As time passed, the scribes became a class of learned men who made the systematic study of the Scriptures and the teaching of them their professional occupation. During the Babylonian captivity, it was the SCRIBES who labored at TRANSLATING the Scriptures from the COPIES of the Hebrew language into Aramaic. During that time, the scribes became the zealous defenders of the Scriptures against the heathen Chaldeans, and they taught the Scriptures to the people of Israel so that the pagan doctrines of the Chaldeans would not corrupt their minds.

When the people of Israel had come into Judaea after the captivity, they gathered in Jerusalem.

> *And all the people gathered themselves together as one man into the street that was before the water gate; And they spake unto Ezra the Scribe to bring the BOOK of the law of Moses, which the Lord had commanded to Israel. And Ezra the priest (he was BOTH a scribe and a priest) brought the law before the congregation both of men and women, and all that could hear with understanding, upon the first day of the seventh month. And he read therein . . . and the ears of all the people were attentive unto the BOOK of the law. . . . And Ezra blessed the Lord, the great God. And all the people answered, Amen, Amen, with lifting up their hands: and they bowed their heads, and worshipped the Lord with their faces to the ground* (Neh. 8:1-3, 6).

CAN I TRUST MY BIBLE'S TRANSLATION?

Now get the picture. Except for those Israelites over seventy years of age, there was no one among the common people in this crowd who knew the Hebrew language. So when Ezra read from the Scriptures, there is no doubt that he was reading from an *Aramaic* TRANSLATION. It HAD to be so that ALL could hear with understanding. And since the ears of ALL the people were attentive, and ALL the people shouted "Amen! Amen!" . . . we know they ALL understood. In this passage, what Ezra read from is called "the BOOK of the law of Moses." Even though it was a TRANSLATION from Hebrew into Aramaic so that all the Jews who had been born and brought up in Chaldea on the Chaldean language could understand, the Holy Spirit calls it the "book of the law of Moses."

Think about it. The translation had come from COPIES of what Moses had written some nine hundred years previously. Yet, the Holy Spirit (knowing He had kept the COPIES pure and perfect) called the TRANSLATION "the book of the law of Moses." This tells me that even though it was a TRANSLATION, it was perfect, infallible, and inerrant! Not only did the blessed Holy Spirit know that . . . SO DID EZRA! Not ONE time while reading the BOOK of the law of Moses to the people do we hear Ezra saying, "Now, folks, I must remind you that the only perfect Scriptures were the 'original autographs' penned by Moses, so this translation came from imperfect COPIES, you understand. Therefore, this TRANSLATION is not perfect, infallible, inspired, and inerrant. However, we will just have to sort of pick our way through here and see if we can try to figure out what God wanted to say to us."

NO SIR! Ezra was not an ALEXANDRIAN!!! Though he did NOT have the "original parchments" in his hands . . . and though what he read from was a TRANSLATION . . . Ezra knew and believed that he was reading the VERY WORD OF GOD to the people! And the people were not ALEXANDRIANS, either! They listened attentively BECAUSE THEY KNEW WHAT EZRA

CAN I TRUST MY BIBLE?

WAS READING TO THEM WAS THE PERFECT, INFALLIBLE, INSPIRED, INERRANT WORD OF GOD!!!!!!!!!!!

This will not set well with you Alexandrians, but I'm not trying to be in your good graces, anyhow. Just face the TRUTH, straighten up, and BELIEVE IT!

I would also have you to notice that Ezra did not read to the people from six or seven different versions. He didn't get up and say, "Now folks, in order to get as much of the true meaning of this Scripture as possible, I will read to you from the NIV (New Israeli Version), the ASV (Artaxerxes Standard Version), the NASV (New Artaxerxes Standard Version), the NKJV (New King Jehoiakim Version), the NCV (Nebuchadnezzar Confusion Version), the JFCSJMCSJDV (Jerry Falwell, Chuck Swindoll, John MacArthur, Charles Stanley, James Dobson Version), and the RSVNCC (Rotten Standard Version of the National Council of Churches)."

Nope. He just got up and read to them from the OOAV (One and Only Aramaic Version). Since God wrote only ONE Bible, there could only be ONE version of that Bible in ANY language! Let me point out that the Scripture says, *"They spake unto Ezra the scribe to bring THE BOOK of the law of Moses . . . and the ears of all the people were attentive unto THE BOOK of the law"* (Neh. 8:1, 3).

Did you get that? *The* BOOK. THE BOOK. *THE* BOOK! If there had been more than ONE version in the Aramaic language, their WORDS would have been different. If the Holy Spirit was behind any of the translations, He could only be behind ONE, or He would be the Author of CONFUSION! The same is true in the ENGLISH language. The Holy Spirit is not behind all of these English versions. He is behind only ONE! Otherwise, He is the Author of CONFUSION, and if He is not behind ANY English version, WE DO NOT HAVE THE PERFECT, INFALLIBLE, INERRANT, INSPIRED WORD OF GOD IN ENGLISH! And if this is true, the only thing we have is a mass of confusion and a bunch of perverted

CAN I TRUST MY BIBLE'S TRANSLATION?

versions that are jam-packed with errors. Therefore, NOT ONE of them is the Word of TRUTH, and we are cast on a "subjective sea of perplexity, uncertainty, hopelessness, doubt, and confusion . . . and might as well eat, drink, and be merry, for tomorrow we die.

However . . . we who believe our God was ready, willing, and ABLE to give us His Holy Scriptures in ENGLISH are not on this "subjective sea." We're not on the SEA at all. We're standing on the solid ROCK and shouting,

How firm a foundation,

    Ye saints of the Lord;

Is laid for your faith

    In His excellent WORD!

We HAVE the ONE and ONLY BOOK in the English language that the Holy Spirit authorized . . . the AV1611 King James Bible!!! I repeat . . . God only inspired ONE Bible. Therefore, there can only be ONE real Bible in ANY language.

Look again at what Jesus said.

For verily I say unto you, Till heaven and earth pass, ONE jot or ONE tittle shall in no wise pass from THE law, till all be fulfilled (Matt. 5:18).

Since neither ONE jot nor ONE tittle shall ever pass from THE law, how could God's ONE law (Bible) ever pass away? Hallelujah, it CAN'T!!! In the English language, that ONE BOOK is the KING JAMES BIBLE! It is indestructible, and all of its enemies . . . be they modernists, cults, liberals, evangelicals, or "fundamentalists" WILL NEVER BE ABLE TO DESTROY IT!

Not long ago, a man came to me after a service in which I preached one of my sermons on the King James Bible. He said, "Brother Lacy, I don't understand why you are so sure the KING JAMES Bible is the one that GOD has given the English speaking

CAN I TRUST MY BIBLE?

people. Aren't you aware that there were THREE complete English bibles before 1611?"

Nodding with my sweet smile, I replied, "Yes. I'm aware of that. There were several New Testaments in English before 1611, and there were a great number of gospels of John and other singular books of the New Testament in English before 1611. The three English versions you refer to are John Wycliffe's translation published in 1382, William Tyndale's translation published in 1536, and the Puritans' Geneva bible published in 1550."

"Correct," he said. "What makes you think one of THEM cannot be the English Bible that God wanted us to have?"

I responded, "I'll answer that question by asking you two questions. Number one . . . did God say His Word would never pass away?"

"Yes, He did," came the reply.

"Okay," I proceeded. "Next question . . . where ARE the 1382 Wycliffe, the 1536 Tyndale, and the 1550 Geneva 'bibles'?"

"They're gone," he said.

"Right," I replied. "If you can find one at all, it's gathering dust in a museum somewhere or in some rare collection of old books where it is not being used to win souls, nor is anyone preaching from it. All three of those versions are GONE. The King James Bible has been with us for nearly four hundred years and is still going strong. Does that answer your question?"

Smiling warmly, he gripped my hand and said, "It sure does. Thank you!"

It didn't take that dear man long to see that the English Bible GOD gave us is the time-honored, rough, tough, two-fisted, double-edged, indestructible KING JAMES BIBLE! The first version that came out in the English language after 1611 was the Westcott and

CAN I TRUST MY BIBLE'S TRANSLATION?

Hort ALEXANDRIAN mess in 1881. WHERE IS IT TODAY? Gone. Another ALEXANDRIAN perversion came out in 1901 . . . the American Standard version. WHERE IS IT TODAY? Gone. As hard as the Federal Council of Churches (now the National Council) tried to keep it from dying, it finally gasped its last breath about 1956 and DIED.

Since that time, we've seen one after another English version appear for a few years, then DIE. It will keep on being that way . . . but I guarantee you . . . as long as God's people are in this world, His ONE and ONLY English Bible will be right here with us!

On the subject of the Aramaic language being the language of the Jews in Jesus' day, I have read many historians, both Biblical and secular. They are ALL in agreement that when Jesus was on the earth, the standard vernacular of the Jews was Aramaic. Therefore, in order for the people to learn and know the Word of God, it had to have been translated from the Hebrew to Aramaic. But the Alexandrians tell us repeatedly that there is no such thing as a perfect TRANSLATION, nor has there EVER been. After all, they reason, how can there be a perfect translation when the only perfect Word of God was the "original manuscripts" . . . and those manuscripts are out of existence, so the manuscripts we translate from have numerous errors.

It is TRUE that the manuscripts the ALEXANDRIANS translate from have numerous errors . . . but those manuscripts are not the PRESERVED WORD OF GOD. The Masoretic Hebrew and the Textus Receptus Greek manuscripts ARE the PRESERVED Word of God. These are the manuscripts the translators used under the guidance of the Holy Spirit to produce the King James Bible. The reason that it has never happened SINCE is quite simple. God only wrote ONE Bible . . . therefore there can only be ONE true translation of the Bible in ANY language.

Historians tell us that Aramaic continued as the vernacular

CAN I TRUST MY BIBLE?

for the Jews until about A.D. 1300. At that time, it was replaced by the Arabic language, which was closely related to both the Hebrew and Aramaic languages. Arabic continued as the Jews' vernacular until late in the eighteenth century, when it was replaced by Yiddish, which had its birth in medieval Germany. "Yiddish," which means *Jewish*, is still the language of the Jews today.

One historian points out that the Galileans of Jesus' day spoke Aramaic with a decided accent, and that it was easily recognizable in other parts of Palestine . . . just as Bostonian would be recognized by his speech in Atlanta or Dallas, even though he spoke English.

You recall that on the day of Pentecost when Peter and the other apostles were preaching to the crowd which was made up of people from fifteen different lands of fifteen languages, the people said one to another, *"Behold, are not all these which speak Galilaeans?"* (Acts 2:7). Though they did not understand the language spoken by the Galilaeans, they recognized it as Aramaic.

The night Peter stood with the enemies of Christ while his Lord was in the high priest's palace, his northern Aramaic accent gave him away as a Galilaean.

> *Now Peter sat without in the palace: and a damsel came unto him, saying, Thou also wast with Jesus of Galilee. But he denied before them all, saying, I know not what thou sayest . . . And after a while came unto him they that stood by, and said to Peter, Surely thou also art one of them; for thy SPEECH bewrayeth thee* (Matt. 26:69-70, 73).

And so it is clear that even though the people of Galilee spoke Aramaic—as did ALL Jews of that day—they spoke it with an accent.

I make my point again that since the Jews all spoke Aramaic, their Scriptures were ALSO in Aramaic, which means the scribes

CAN I TRUST MY BIBLE'S TRANSLATION?

had TRANSLATED the Word of God from Hebrew into Aramaic. They did not have several VERSIONS in Aramaic. Just ONE. So any time the common people heard the word "Scriptures," they immediately thought of the TRANSLATION of the Scriptures in Aramaic that they could HOLD IN THEIR HANDS and read.

The Alexandrians, of course, tell us that only the "original autographs" were the Scriptures. Since the "original autographs" are gone, and all we have are error-filled manuscripts of Hebrew and Greek, we have no Scriptures. And certainly we have no TRANSLATION that is Scripture, so according to the Alexandrians it is impossible for anyone on the face of the earth today to hold the Scriptures IN THEIR HANDS. *Let's see just how utterly mistaken they are.*

In Jesus' day, when the Jews congregated in the synagogue for their worship services, they followed several customs. The congregation were divided, the men and boys on one side and the women and girls on the other. The service began with the recitation of the Jewish confession of faith, known as the *Shema*. It is found in Deuteronomy 6:4-5. After the *Shema,* came the prayer, called the *Tefillah.* The ruler (or "minister") of the synagogue would then call upon any adult male of the congregation to offer the prayer.

The Scripture lesson which followed the prayer would be read by another male of the congregation, sometimes even young boys. The only exception was that at the Feast of Purim; a minor was not allowed to read the book of Esther. The readers always stood while reading. Let us follow the Lord Jesus into Galilee after being baptized by John the Baptist and then defeating the devil in the wilderness.

> *And he came to Nazareth, where he had been brought up: and, as his custom was, he went into the synagogue on the sabbath day, and stood up for to read. And there was delivered unto him the book of the prophet*

CAN I TRUST MY BIBLE?

> *Esaias. And when he had opened the book, he found the place where it was written (Luke 4:16-17).*

Please notice that the book of Esaias (Old Testament "Isaiah") was "delivered unto Him." I would say He was holding the book IN HIS HANDS, wouldn't you? Then with His HANDS, he turned the scroll until it came up to what we know as Isaiah chapter 61. After He had held it IN HIS HANDS and read it to the congregation, *"And He closed the book, and he gave it again to the minister, and sat down . . ."* (Luke 4:20).

Yes, sir. With His HANDS, Jesus closed the book and placed it into the minister's HANDS. The book of Isaiah is part of the Bible, is it not? That makes it SCRIPTURE, right? Only an imbecile would answer in the negative.

It is an historical fact that to the Jews, the "SCRIPTURE" or "SCRIPTURES" were the "sacred writings" that had come from Jehovah God. They regarded them as perfect, infallible, inerrant, and inspired; so whenever the words "SCRIPTURE" or "SCRIPTURES" were used, everyone understood what was meant . . . the perfect, infallible, inerrant, inspired sacred writings that had come from Jehovah God.

Now let's see what the Lord Jesus Christ called what He had just read to the congregation.

> *And he began to say unto them, This day is this SCRIPTURE fulfilled in your ears* (Luke 4:21).

Since Jesus called it "Scripture," He was saying that what He had just read to them was perfect, infallible, inerrant, and inspired. Please note three things. (1) What He read from could not possibly have been the VERY PARCHMENTS upon which Isaiah had written. They had crumbled to dust at least six hundred years previously. (2) What He read from was the Aramaic TRANSLATION, since that was the language the common people knew. (3) What Jesus read

CAN I TRUST MY BIBLE'S TRANSLATION?

from and HELD IN HIS HANDS, He called "Scripture," meaning that it was perfect, infallible, inerrant, and inspired.

So there goes the asinine philosophy of the Alexandrians up in Scriptural smoke! I have quoted them as saying that the only perfect, infallible, inerrant, inspired Scriptures were the "original autographs." The Lord Jesus Christ, who is the Author of the Scriptures (Matt 24:35; John 12:47-48), did NOT have the "original autographs," yet He called what He had "Scripture!"

Who are you going to believe, reader friend of mine . . . the lame-brain Alexandrians . . . or the AUTHOR OF THE BOOK?

I have quoted Alexandrians in this book saying that there cannot be a perfect translation. Well, the Lord Jesus read from a TRANSLATION and called it "Scripture." Who are you going to believe . . . the humanist Alexandrians . . . or the AUTHOR OF THE BOOK?

The Alexandrians, by their very man-made philosophy, are saying that ever since the "original manuscripts" went out of existence . . . it is impossible to HOLD THE VERY WORD OF GOD IN YOUR HAND. I've had 'em tell me that to my face time and again. Who's right? The cloudy-minded Alexandrians . . . or JESUS CHRIST? Who are you going to believe? As for me, I believe the AUTHOR OF THE BIBLE!

Not long ago, I was accosted after a service when I had preached that the King James Bible was THE perfect, inspired, inerrant Word of God in the English language. Carrying a New American Standard perversion, a man in his forties approached me and said in a sugary tone, "Brother Lacy, may I say something to you in l-o-o-ove?" I knew right now I had me a "live one." Trying to smile, I said, "Sure. Shoot."

He pointed to the Book that I had in my hand and said, "Don't call that King James Bible the Word of God. It is NOT the Word of

CAN I TRUST MY BIBLE?

God."

I felt my collar heat up, but being of a passive nature (ahem), I looked at the NASV he was holding and said, "I suppose you are going to tell me THAT thing is the Word of God."

"No, it's not," he replied quickly, "but it's better than the King James."

Because of the stand of the church that I was in takes on the AV1611, I knew this dude wasn't a member. Squinting at him, I asked, "Where are you from?"

Knowing what I was after, he responded, "I'm a graduate of Tennessee Temple University."

I said, "I thought Tennessee Temple was a Fundamentalist school."

"Oh, it IS," he assured me. "We are Fundamentalist to the core!"

I already knew that his school was ALEXANDRIAN, but I played dumb (which is VERY difficult for someone as smart as me!) and said, "I always thought Fundamentalists believed in the verbally, plenarily, inerrant, inspired Word of God."

"Oh, we DO!" he responded.

"Well, let me ask you something," I said, "Can you place a copy of the verbally, plenarily, inerrant, inspired Word of God IN MY HANDS?"

I knew I had him because ALL Alexandrians believe that the ONLY verbally, plenarily, inerrant, inspired Word of God that ever existed was the "original manuscripts" (which were never EVER collected together in one book). A dill-pickle look framed his features as he pulled his lips tight over his teeth and snorted, "An intelligent person cannot argue with a fool!"

I chuckled and said, "Yea, I just figured that out."

CAN I TRUST MY BIBLE'S TRANSLATION?

This is not an isolated incident. I've had students, graduates, and professors from many "Fundamentalist" schools accost me numerous times, intending to straighten me out on my "King James only" foolishness. I have faced 'em from Pensacola Christian College, Bob Jones, Maranatha, Cedarville, Liberty University, Baptist Bible College, Springfield, Missouri, Pillsbury, Denver's Conservative Baptist Seminary, and many other citadels of Alexandrianism. None of those students, graduates, and professors who have "jumped" me believe that there is ANY BOOK that we can HOLD IN OUR HAND today and say, "THIS IS THE INFALLIBLE, INERRANT, INSPIRED, UNCORRECTABLE, INCORRUPTIBLE, WORD OF GOD."

I have already shown you that the Lord Jesus Himself held a Book IN HIS HANDS and called it "Scripture." It was a TRANSLATION, yet He called it "Scripture." Though what He held IN HIS HANDS was not the "original manuscripts," He called it "Scripture." If God could preserve His Word even though the "originals" went back to dust, and even though it was TRANSLATED into another language as late as A.D. 30 . . . is He so weak and/or unconcerned about His Word that He could not do it TODAY???

Well, as I have said before . . . the god of the Alexandrians could not do it, but the God of the Bible CAN and DID!!! If the people could hold the Word of God IN THEIR HANDS in Jesus' day, they can do it TODAY! Let's look at some more proof that they could hold the Scriptures IN THEIR HANDS in New Testament days.

> *Jesus said unto them (the chief priests and the elders), Did ye never read in the scriptures, The stone which the builders rejected, the same is become the head of the corner: this is the Lord's doing, and it is marvelous in our eyes? (Matt. 21:42).*

Now I ask . . . how could the chief priests and elders READ

CAN I TRUST MY BIBLE?

the Scriptures unless the Scriptures were in physical form and they could hold them IN THEIR HANDS? Certainly, if (as the Alexandrians say) the only Scriptures were the "original autographs," the chief priests and elders could not READ them because they were not available to hold them IN THEIR HANDS! If Jesus took the Alexandrian view, He would know these men did not have access to the Scriptures . . . because the only real Scriptures were the "original autographs" . . . and the chief priests and elders DID NOT HAVE THE ORIGINALS!

Since Jesus Christ is not an Alexandrian, I don't want to be one either.

We have a similar situation on the day of our Lord's glorious resurrection. You will recall that two disciples from Emmaus were headed home from Jerusalem where they had heard about the women who saw the angels and the empty tomb. As yet, they had not realized that Jesus had risen from the dead. Suddenly, the Lord drew near the two men as they walked toward Emmaus and discussed the situation. Jesus fixed their eyes, so they could not recognize Him.

> *Then he said unto them, O fools, and slow of heart to believe ALL that the prophets have spoken: Ought not Christ to have suffered these things, and to enter into his glory? And beginning at Moses and all the prophets, he expounded unto them in all the scriptures the things concerning himself* (Luke 24:25-27).

Now, wouldn't it have been unkind and inconsiderate of the Lord to upbraid these two men for not believing ALL that the prophets had spoken (which they also WROTE) if they did not have ALL that the prophets had spoken available so that they could hold it IN THEIR HANDS and read it? Of course. But our Lord is NOT unkind and inconsiderate. He upbraided them for their unbelief because in spite of the fact that they HAD the Scriptures in the Aramaic language and they could HOLD THE SCRIPTURES IN

CAN I TRUST MY BIBLE'S TRANSLATION?

THEIR HANDS, they either had not read them, or even if they had read them, they had not BELIEVED them. He had a right to scold them.

To refresh your memory, let me once again quote Alexandrian J.H. Melton's words. I remind you that HE put all of these words in capitals when he typed them. "THERE NEVER HAS BEEN, THERE IS NOT NOW, THERE NEVER WILL BE BUT ONE INERRANT, INFALLIBLE, VERBALLY INSPIRED WRITING- THE ORIGINAL MANUSCRIPTS OF THE SIXTY-SIX BOOKS COMPRISING THE ONE BOOK, THE BIBLE, THE WORD OF GOD!"

One thing is for sure . . . The Lord Jesus Christ and Mr. J.H. Melton ARE IN TOTAL DISAGREEMENT! Jesus would not call ANYTHING "Scripture" unless it is inerrant, infallible, and verbally inspired.

Let's look at some more Bible. In John chapter 5, the Lord is surrounded by a crowd of Jews. These are the common people. They could not read the Hebrew of the Old Testament. Yet Jesus said to them, *"Search the SCRIPTURES"* (John 5:39).

Come on, now, Alexandrians . . . are you going to tell me that Jesus told them to search something they DID NOT HAVE? YOU say that the only inerrant, infallible, verbally inspired writing was the "original manuscripts." JESUS says different. The people to whom He spoke DID NOT have the original manuscripts. Neither did they have the Scriptures in the Hebrew language. What they had and could HOLD IN THEIR HANDS was a TRANSLATION into Aramaic, yet the Author of the Bible called what they had "Scriptures"!!!

The Alexandrian philosophy is not only ridiculous . . . it is downright blasphemous! Time and again the Alexandrians come on with "only the original manuscripts were inerrant, infallible, and inspired" . . . and "there is no such thing as a perfect translation"

CAN I TRUST MY BIBLE?

IN THE FACE OF THE FACT THAT JESUS CHRIST TOLD THE JEWS TO SEARCH THE SCRIPTURES, KNOWING THEY DID NOT HAVE THE ORIGINAL MANUSCRIPTS...AND KNOWING THAT WHAT THEY HAD WAS A TRANSLATION!!!

Listen to Jesus again in the same chapter, speaking to the same people.

Do not think that I will accuse you to the Father: there is one that accuseth you, even Moses, in whom ye trust. For had ye believed Moses, ye would have believed me: for he WROTE of me. But if ye believe not his WRITINGS, how shall ye believe my words? (John 5:45-47).

Can anything be plainer? Jesus blasts them for not believing what Moses WROTE of Him. Then certainly, though they DID NOT have the original parchments on which Moses wrote . . . and though what they had was a TRANSLATION that had been translated from a COPY of what Moses had written . . . Jesus still held them responsible for not believing what Moses had WRITTEN!

Pray tell . . . how could He hold them responsible for not believing what Moses had WRITTEN unless they could hold what Moses had written IN THEIR HANDS so that they could READ what Moses had written? Unless the Holy Spirit had seen to it that the COPIES had been kept inerrant so the TRANSLATION could be inerrant, the people did NOT have what Moses had WRITTEN! To say that only the "original manuscripts" were the inerrant Word of God, and that there is no such thing as a perfect translation IS TO MAKE JESUS OUT TO BE A FOOL AND A LIAR!

Like I keep saying . . . I wouldn't want to be in YOUR sneakers when you face him, Alexandrians!

Let's move on and see some more Scripture that shows us how ignorant the Alexandrians really are. We have already seen the

CAN I TRUST MY BIBLE'S TRANSLATION?

Lord Jesus standing in the synagogue at Nazareth, reading from the book of Isaiah and calling it "Scripture." I remind you that although Jesus did NOT have the "original manuscripts" that Isaiah wrote, and although what He had was a TRANSLATION, He called it "Scripture." Do you suppose the Holy Spirit feels the same way about the book of Isaiah?

In Acts chapter 8, Philip the evangelist comes upon the Ethiopian eunuch in the Gaza desert, reading the book of Isaiah. I remind you that what the eunuch was holding IN HIS HAND was NOT the "original autographs." What he had IN HIS HAND was probably an Aramaic TRANSLATION, but even if it were in old Hebrew, it was definitely NOT the original parchment upon which Isaiah had written. Yet, look what the Holy Spirit did.

Then the Spirit said unto Philip, Go near, and join thyself to this chariot. And Philip ran thither to him, and heard him read the prophet Esaias, and said, Understandest thou what thou readest? And he said, How can I, except some man should guide me? And he desired Philip that he would come up and sit with him. The place of the SCRIPTURE which he read was this, He was led as a sheep to the slaughter; and like a lamb dumb before his shearer, so opened he not his mouth: In his humiliation his judgment was taken away: and who shall declare his generation? for his life is taken from the earth. And the eunuch answered Philip, and said, I pray thee, of whom speaketh the prophet this? of himself, or of some other man? Then Philip opened his mouth, and began at the same SCRIPTURE, and preached unto him Jesus (Acts 8:29-35).

You will note that the Holy Spirit TOLD Philip to join himself to the chariot. He wanted Philip to lead the eunuch to Christ.

CAN I TRUST MY BIBLE?

In guiding Luke as he wrote the book of Acts, the Holy Spirit called what the eunuch HELD IN HIS HAND "Scripture"!!! If what the eunuch held in his hand was NOT Scripture, the Holy Spirit would not have expected Philip to use it to lead the man to Christ! But since the Holy Spirit called it "Scripture," it HAD to have been inerrant, infallible, and inspired!

This is directly the OPPOSITE from what Mr. Melton said. Mr. Melton said, "THERE NEVER HAS BEEN, THERE IS NOT NOW, THERE NEVER WILL BE BUT ONE INERRANT, INFALLIBLE, VERBALLY INSPIRED WRITING-THE ORIGINAL MANUSCRIPTS OF THE SIXTY-SIX BOOKS COMPRISING THE ONE BOOK, THE BIBLE, THE WORD OF GOD!" Well pardon me, but the Holy Spirit called what the eunuch held IN HIS HAND "Scripture." He called it that TWICE!

I don't know about you, dear reader . . . but I'll believe the Holy Spirit ANY DAY before I'll believe an ALEXANDRIAN!!! More? Okay.

> *Now when they had passed through Amphipolis and Apollonia, they came to Thessalonica, where was a synagogue of the Jews: And Paul, as his manner was, went in unto them, and three sabbath days reasoned with them OUT OF THE SCRIPTURES, OPENING and alleging, that Christ must needs have suffered, and risen again from the dead; and that this Jesus, whom I preach unto you, is Christ* (Acts 17:1-3).

The only "Scriptures" that Paul had were the thirty-nine books of the Old Testament. He had absolutely NO "original manuscripts." If he spoke to them in Hebrew, all he had were COPIES of COPIES of COPIES of COPIES. If he spoke to them in Aramaic, he had a TRANSLATION that was made from a COPY of a COPY of a COPY of a COPY. Since Paul OPENED the Scriptures, he most certainly held them in his HAND. Away with this Alexandrian "only

CAN I TRUST MY BIBLE'S TRANSLATION?

the original manuscripts were inspired" baloney!

If we were to go on reading in Acts 17, we would find that when Paul opened the Scriptures and reasoned with the crowd in the synagogue, there were GREEKS there who got saved. Isn't that interesting? Unless those Greeks knew Hebrew or Aramaic, Paul had to TRANSLATE what he was reading from the Scriptures into GREEK!

Ah, but the Alexandrians tell us there is no such thing as a perfect TRANSLATION! Poor Paul. Too bad he didn't know Greek well enough to translate it correctly.

Some "learned" one might say, "Well, Paul must have reasoned with them out of the Septuagint, which was a Greek translation of the Old Testament, produced in Alexandria, Egypt, in 250 B.C."

Nope. There is absolutely NO HISTORICAL EVIDENCE that such a thing as the "Septuagint" ever existed. So-called "scholars" will quickly point to one of the six "versions" in Adamantius Origen's "Hexapla" and say that the Septuagint was one of those six translations. Baloney. Origen's Greek version was HIS OWN translation.

Look up the word "Septuagint" in any good dictionary. This is what you will find: *Septuagint:* tradition; a legendary translation into Greek of the Old Testament.

My reader is smart enough to know what *tradition* is . . . and what a *legend* is. There are absolutely NO Greek Old Testament manuscripts in existence that date back to 250 B.C. Jewish history has absolutely NO record of any such translation ever existing; and even if there WERE a Septuagint, Paul would never have used it! The supposed translation is said to have been done in ALEXANDRIA, EGYPT! Paul was ANYTHING BUT an Alexandrian! When he opened and reasoned from the Scriptures . . . he DID NOT have

CAN I TRUST MY BIBLE?

the "originals," but he sure preached soulwinning sermons from the COPY and/or TRANSLATION that he HELD IN HIS HAND!

Even though he did not have the "original manuscripts," Paul kept on preaching the Word of God.

> *And the brethren immediately sent away Paul and Silas by night unto Berea: who coming thither went into the synagogue of the Jews. These were more noble than those in Thessalonica, in that they received the WORD with all readiness of mind, and searched the SCRIPTURES daily, whether those things were so* (Acts 17:10-11).

You will notice that through Luke's pen the Holy Spirit calls the "Word" the *Scriptures* . . . and says the Bereans SEARCHED the Scriptures! Now tell me, you Alexandrians . . . how could the Bereans SEARCH the Scriptures unless they could hold them IN THEIR HANDS??? Hmm???

After Apollos got his doctrine straightened out by Priscilla and Aquila (Acts 18:26), he went to Achaia. There . . .

> *For he mightily convinced the Jews, and that publickly, SHEWING BY THE SCRIPTURES that Jesus was Christ* (Acts 18:28).

All right, let's use our craniums. How could Apollos SHOW BY THE SCRIPTURES that Jesus is Christ unless he had the Scriptures IN HIS HAND? Unless you're a cross-eyed, buck-toothed, retarded gorilla . . . or an ALEXANDRIAN (and I'd rather be the GORILLA!), the answer is obvious. And WHAT SCRIPTURES did Apollos HAVE in his hand? The "original autographs"? Hardly. Yet the Holy Spirit calls what Apollos used to show the Jews in Achaia that Jesus was Christ . . . the "SCRIPTURES"!!!

Let's see now . . . what is it the Alexandrians tell us? "There NEVER HAS BEEN, THERE IS NOT NOW, THERE NEVER

CAN I TRUST MY BIBLE'S TRANSLATION?

WILL BE BUT ONE INERRANT, INFALLIBLE, VERBALLY INSPIRED WRITING-THE *ORIGINAL MANUSCRIPTS* OF THE SIXTY-SIX BOOKS COMPRISING THE ONE BOOK, THE BIBLE, THE WORD OF GOD."

Well, well. Then what Apollos HELD IN HIS HAND and used to show the Jews that Jesus is Christ HAD to have been the original manuscripts! The "Scriptures," the "Word of God," and the "Bible" are all exactly the SAME BOOK, aren't they? Of course.

QUESTION: DID Apollos have the "original manuscripts"?

ANSWER; Not on your life. They were long-gone before Apollos was kicking the slats out of his cradle.

FACT: Apollos did NOT have the "original manuscripts." What he had IN HIS HAND was a TRANSLATION that came from a COPY of a COPY of a COPY of a COPY of a COPY of a COPY of the "original manuscripts," yet the Holy Spirit called what he had in his hand "SCRIPTURES."

This brings us to one conclusion . . . either the Holy Spirit does not know what He is talking about . . . OR . . . the craniums of the Alexandrians are chocked plumb full of SAWDUST AND SAP. The cross-eyed, buck-toothed, retarded gorilla could tell you which is so. Can my reader keep up with the gorilla?

According to Mr. J.H. Melton and all of his Alexandrian buddies, "THERE NEVER HAS BEEN, THERE IS NOT NOW, THERE NEVER WILL BE BUT ONE INERRANT, INFALLIBLE, VERBALLY INSPIRED WRITING-THE ORIGINAL MANUSCRIPTS OF THE SIXTY-SIX BOOKS COMPRISING THE ONE BOOK, THE BIBLE, THE WORD OF GOD." Do you see that? According to Melton and his pals, there does not NOW exist an inerrant, infallible, verbally inspired BOOK that is known as the Bible, which is called the Word of God . . . and no such Book will EVER exist. Hence, there is not NOW, nor will there EVER be

CAN I TRUST MY BIBLE?

a BOOK you can HOLD IN YOUR HAND and say, "I have in my grasp the Bible, the Scripture, the Word of God."

I have already demonstrated RIGHT IN THE BOOK that though the "original manuscripts" were out of existence in New Testament days, the Lord Jesus Christ, His preachers, and His followers HELD THE WORD OF GOD, THE SCRIPTURE, IN THEIR HANDS and *read* it, *studied* it, *searched* it, and *preached* it. I guarantee you . . . if God could maintain His Word until New Testament days, keeping it pure, infallible, and inspired even though all they had were Hebrew COPIES and Aramaic TRANSLATIONS . . . He can STILL do it today!

He not only CAN . . . but He HAS! I have the perfect, inspired, infallible, inerrant Word of God, the Bible, the Scripture TRANSLATED from Hebrew and Greek copies of copies of copies of copies into English right here on the desk as I pound this typewriter. It is the precious old Antiochan 1611 King James Bible!

Mr. Melton and his Alexandrian cronies say there never WILL BE an inerrant, infallible, verbally inspired Book you can HOLD IN YOUR HAND and say, "I am holding the Bible, the Scripture, the Word of God." More African baloney.

Daniel's prophetical seventieth week (Dan. 9:24-27) is often called the Seven Years of Tribulation. Jesus called the first 3 1/2 years the "beginning of sorrows" (Matt. 24:8); and the last 3 1/2 years, He called "great tribulation" (Matt. 24:21). This seven-year period is yet FUTURE. The Alexandrians say there never WILL BE a BOOK known as the Word of God. Let's take a look into the future and reveal once again that the Alexandrians have their heads, jam-packed full of SAWDUST AND SAP. Revelation chapter 6 opens up, revealing the antichrist on the back of a white horse going forth conquering and to conquer. This happens at the VERY BEGINNING of the seven year period, bringing about the "beginning of sorrows." As you read on, you see three other riders following the antichrist,

CAN I TRUST MY BIBLE'S TRANSLATION?

bringing war, bloodshed, famine, and death.

During this time, there will be people getting saved on the earth. Under the antichrist's reign of terror, they will be martyred for their faith in Christ. Watch how it is worded, keeping in mind that this is yet FUTURE.

And when he had opened the fifth seal, I saw under the altar the souls of them that were slain for the WORD OF GOD, and for the testimony which they held: (Rev. 6:9).

Now isn't that somethin'? I have already demonstrated in this book that no one can get saved without the Word of God. These people most definitely are saved, for we find them under the altar in Heaven (see also Rev. 14:17-18) after their martyrdom. While on earth, they had the Word of God IN THEIR HANDS so they could get saved . . . and afterward they had the Word of God IN THEIR HANDS because it was for this VERY BOOK that they were slain. Certainly, no one is going to tell me that they were slain for the "original manuscripts"! NO! NO! They were slain for a BOOK they could HOLD IN THEIR HANDS and preach!

Remember . . . this takes place yet in the FUTURE. The Alexandrians say the only Book you could call the Word of God is the "originals," which have been out of existence for centuries, yet the Holy Spirit tells us here that the martyrs will be slain in the tribulation period for the WORD OF GOD. Will these martyrs have the originals? Hardly. Then WHAT will they have? Simple. They will have the WORD OF GOD! The Holy Spirit SAYS SO! The martyrs will NOT have the originals, nor will they even have COPIES of the originals. These people will not be Hebrew and Greek scholars. They will have the Word of God IN THEIR OWN LANGUAGES! They will die for TRANSLATIONS! Are they fools for dying for TRANSLATIONS? Absolutely not! God always has been and is still able to get His inerrant, infallible, inspired Word TRANSLATED

CAN I TRUST MY BIBLE?

from Hebrew and Greek into other languages!

No matter what the Alexandrians say . . . GOD tells us that IN THE FUTURE, His faithful saints will HAVE the Word of God in their language, and that they will DIE for it! The Alexandrians do not believe there is any Book that we can call the Word of God on earth RIGHT NOW. Neither do they believe there will be a Book on earth that is known as the Word of God IN THE FUTURE. Poor kiddies. THE HOLY SPIRIT SAYS THERE WILL BE. If God's saints will have the Word of God IN THE FUTURE . . . I guarantee you, we have it NOW!

Let's look at some more Tribulation martyrs,

And I saw thrones, and they sat upon them, and judgment was given unto them: and I saw the souls of them that were beheaded for the witness of Jesus, and for the WORD OF GOD . . . (Rev. 20:4).

One thing is for sure . . . these martyrs are NOT Alexandrians. According to their own mouths, THE ALEXANDRIANS HAVE NO WORD OF GOD TO DIE FOR. Only a fool would die for something that doesn't even exist! Will these martyrs die as fools for a Book that does not exist? It would take a REAL fool to answer in the affirmative. These gallant martyrs will die for the Word of God . . . for the Book they can HOLD IN THEIR HANDS, read, study, believe, love, teach, and preach! They will have it THEN . . . and we have it NOW!

Let me ask you Alexandrians something. You say you are saved. You say that you are children of God and that you are "in the faith." God told His people to "earnestly contend for the FAITH" (Jude 3). Can you obey that command? If you say yes, I ask . . . HOW? How do you earnestly contend for the faith? Can you show me or an enemy of God what your faith is built upon? Could you hold a BOOK in your hand and show me or anyone else the basis of your faith? Huh? Could you?

CAN I TRUST MY BIBLE'S TRANSLATION?

The answer is as obvious as a black wart on the face of an albino Norwegian. Oh, I know you would tell me that your faith is based on the Word of God. Can you OPEN this Word of God that your faith is based on and show me what your faith IS? Can you put your finger on the pages and say, "See? Right there. Written on the pages of the Word of God is what I believe, stand for, and contend for." Can you? Of course not. Your faith is based on papyrus parchment that DOES NOT EXIST! How in the name of Fenton John Anthony Hort can you build your faith on writings YOU HAVE NEVER SEEN? How can you earnestly contend for a faith that has absolutely NO FOUNDATION? You have NEVER LAID EYES on the "original manuscripts." You have NOTHING to contend for, NOTHING to defend, NOTHING to stand on, NOTHING to preach to a lost and dying human race, and NOTHING to die for.

Well, I DO have a foundation upon which I have built MY faith. I DO have something to contend for. I DO have something to defend. I DO have something to stand on. I DO have something to preach to a lost and dying world. I have the inerrant, infallible, inspired, perfect, incorruptible, uncorrectable WORD OF GOD IN MY HAND!!!

How about it, Alexandrians? If wicked, atheistic, God-hating infidels were to back you and me up against a wall and say, "We're going to kill you for the Word of God that you believe, preach, teach, promote, and love" . . . they could jerk the Word of God OUT OF MY HAND and say, "You'll die for THIS!" When they turned to you and asked you to SHOW THEM the Word of God for which YOU could die . . . *what would you show them?*

You'd be perfectly SAFE, wouldn't you? You've NEVER SEEN your Bible. You couldn't SHOW it to them. You would have NOTHING to stand for and DIE for.

The tribulation saints will have the Word of God IN THEIR HANDS, just as we Antiochans do. They will die for the Word of

CAN I TRUST MY BIBLE?

God that is IN THEIR HANDS and hold it up and SHOW it to the world while the deadly blade of the guillotine is falling toward their naked necks.

I have demonstrated over and over again that IN THE BIBLE the Holy Spirit calls COPIES and TRANSLATIONS of the Word of God "SCRIPTURE." Let's look at one more clear-cut example. In II Peter chapter 3, Peter is writing of the Day of the Lord when God is going to melt down the heavens and the earth. He says,

> *Wherefore, beloved, seeing that ye look for such things, be diligent that ye maybe found of him in peace, without spot, and blameless. And account that the longsuffering of our Lord is salvation; even as our beloved brother Paul also according to the wisdom given unto him hath written unto you; As also in all his epistles, speaking in them of these things; in which are some things hard to be understood, which they that are unlearned and unstable WREST, as they do also the OTHER SCRIPTURES, unto their own destruction* (II Pet. 3:14-16).

You will note that Paul's epistles are called SCRIPTURE. That makes them THE WORD OF GOD. You will also note that in that day there were unlearned and unstable men who WRESTED the Scriptures . . . PAUL'S and "OTHER SCRIPTURES."

The OTHER Scriptures were no doubt OLD TESTAMENT Scriptures. Now let's use the brains God gave us, along with a little logic. If the Alexandrians are correct when they say that the ONLY inerrant, inspired Scriptures were the "original manuscripts" . . . how could the unlearned and unstable men WREST the *Scriptures?* They most certainly did not have the ORIGINALS to wrest! What they were wresting were COPIES which were made from COPIES which were made from COPIES which were made from COPIES of the "originals." OR . . . they were wresting TRANSLATIONS which

CAN I TRUST MY BIBLE'S TRANSLATION?

were produced from COPIES of COPIES of COPIES of COPIES of COPIES of the "originals." Yet the Holy Spirit through Peter's pen calls what they wrested "Scriptures." That makes them the inerrant, inspired, infallible WORD OF GOD!

And another thing . . . in order to wrest the Scriptures, they had to be able to HOLD THE SCRIPTURES IN THEIR HANDS! You can't wrest something unless you can HOLD IT IN YOUR HANDS and read it so you know WHAT to wrest! Since they were wresting the SCRIPTURES, it is without doubt they were wresting the perfect, infallible, inspired, inerrant Word of God . . . which they were READING.

According to what Peter wrote, unlearned and unstable men were wresting the very epistles that Paul had written. The Alexandrians tell us that ONLY the original parchments were the Word of God. Are they going to tell us that these unlearned and unstable men ACTUALLY HAD PAUL'S ORIGINAL PARCHMENTS IN THEIR HANDS??? Come on, kiddies. Let's not be foolish. Paul's "originals" most certainly were already being COPIED. I mean, really . . . how would these Bible perverters get their dirty hands on the very parchments upon which Paul had written?

They didn't. What they had were COPIES. Yet the Holy Spirit, through Peter's pen, called what they wrested "SCRIPTURES"!!! Now for a person with any sense at all, it would be perfectly clear that God was able to keep His Word intact even though it was COPIED . . . and that He was able to keep it intact even when it was TRANSLATED. This being the case, the Holy Spirit calls COPIES and TRANSLATIONS "Scripture," which means what these men were wresting was inspired, inerrant, perfect, and incorruptible . . . even though they did not have the "originals"!!! So let me say right here . . . the ONE AND ONLY English Bible that is the perfect, inspired, inerrant, incorruptible Word of God is the ANTIOCHAN AV1611 King James Bible. When the unlearned and unstable

CAN I TRUST MY BIBLE?

ALEXANDRIANS attack or correct the King James Bible, they are wresting the SCRIPTURES! What was it that Peter said . . . ? Oh, yes . . . "to their own DESTRUCTION."

God has only ONE Bible in any language. The AV1611 is God's Bible in English. Go ahead, Alexandrians. Wrest the precious old BOOK to your heart's content . . . but just remember the solemn warning pronounced on you by its Author in Revelation 22:18-19!!! But, of course, you will ignore what I am saying. You don't believe there is only ONE BOOK. You can't stand the idea that there is ONE BOOK. This is why you will tear away at my King James Bible without the least bit of concern. You will wield your scholarly penknife just like Jehoiakim did, and boast of your deed.

You say you are not Bible correctors, but TRANSLATION correctors. You believe the only Bible that has ever existed was the "original autographs," so you are free to "correct" any TRANSLATION you please. You deny that there is ONE true Bible in the English language in existence today, so you hack away at the King James Bible without one pang of guilt in your Alexandrian conscience.

If you do not believe there is only ONE BOOK which is the very Word of God in English today . . . why is it that you only work at correcting ONE BOOK? I never hear you guys correcting the New American Standard perversion, or the New International perversion, or the "Living (Ha! Ha!) Bible," or the "New" King James perversion. Why is it your penknives slash ONLY at the King James Bible and the perversions remain unmolested? You won't admit it, but I'll tell you why . . . because down deep inside, you KNOW there is only ONE BOOK, but you don't want that ONE BOOK to have authority over you . . . so you attack it by pointing out its "spurious" passages and the places where it is not translated correctly (according to you).

Well, whether you like it or not, God has ALWAYS had only

CAN I TRUST MY BIBLE'S TRANSLATION?

ONE BOOK, and He will NEVER have more than ONE BOOK. He is not the Author of confusion. ONE BOOK? Yes. ONE BOOK.

> THE Lord gave THE word: great was THE company of those that published it (Psalm 68:11).

That's plain enough—ONE Lord, ONE Word, ONE company that published it. Who was that ONE company that published the Hebrew Old Testament? The men whom God used to WRITE the Old Testament, of course. WHO was that ONE company that published the Greek New Testament? The men whom God used to WRITE the New Testament, of course. We have already established that the Old Testament was translated into Aramaic by the scribes so the post-captivity Jews could have the Word of God in their hands. Thus, there was ONE BOOK of God in Aramaic. Who was that ONE company that published it? The company of scribes who did the translating, of course.

Since God has only ONE BOOK in any language (so He will not be the Author of confusion), . . . what is the ONE BOOK in the English language? For sure it would not have its roots in Alexandria, Egypt. That leaves only ONE . . . the God-blessed AV1611 King James Bible! WHO was that ONE company that published it? Why, the team of translators who PRODUCED the King James Bible, of course!

I have already pointed out that when Ezra the scribe stood up to read the Scriptures to the people from a pulpit, he read from only ONE BOOK. God did not inspire TWO. That would be confusing. God gave us only ONE Bible. God says,

> Seek ye out of THE book of the Lord, and read . . . (Isa. 34:16).

Let me ask you Alexandrians . . . can YOU obey that command? Not with what YOU believe. You HAVE no BOOK of the Lord. *I* can. I have the ONE BOOK of the Lord in the English

CAN I TRUST MY BIBLE?

language right here before me.

Please note that it says THE Book of the Lord. Yes . . . He has only ONE Book. Listen to the Lord Jesus say so as He speaks to His Father,

> *Then said I, Lo, I come [in the volume of THE book it is written of me,] to do thy will, O God* (Heb. 10:7).

Did you get that? *The* Book. THE Book. *THE* Book. God HAS only ONE Book. Look what the Author of THE Book put on the very last page of His Book.

> *Behold, I come quickly: blessed is he that keepeth the sayings of the prophecy of THIS BOOK . . . keep the sayings of THIS BOOK . . . Seal not the sayings of the prophecy of THIS BOOK . . . For I testify unto every man that heareth the words of the prophecy of THIS BOOK, If any man shall add unto these things, God shall add unto him the plagues that are written in THIS BOOK: And if any man shall take away from the words of THE BOOK of this prophecy, God shall take away his part out of the book of life, and out of the holy city, and from the things which are written in THIS BOOK* (Rev. 22:7, 9, 10, 18-19).

Did you count 'em? On the last page of His Bible, the Lord tells us SEVEN times that He has only ONE BOOK!!! Seven, as you know, is God's number of PERFECTION. SEVEN times, He confirms for us on the last page of the Bible that He has only ONE BOOK . . . and, of course, that BOOK is PERFECT! (Psalm 19:7; I Cor. 13:10; James 1:25). God's ONE BOOK was PERFECT when it came from the mouths of the prophets (II Pet. 1:21). God's ONE BOOK was PERFECT when it was written down for the first time on parchment (John 5:46-47). God's ONE BOOK was *maintained* PERFECT when it was copied over and over again (Psalm 12:6-7).

CAN I TRUST MY BIBLE'S TRANSLATION?

God's ONE BOOK has been translated into several languages from the PERFECT copies, thus giving PERFECT translations.

I have demonstrated my last statement over and over again. As a reminder . . . we have seen that the Jews of Jesus' day did not know the classic Hebrew in which the Old Testament was written. Their language was Aramaic. Therefore, when Jesus spoke of the Scriptures to them, He was referring to the Scriptures they HELD IN THEIR HANDS, which was a TRANSLATION from Hebrew into Aramaic. If I should have a reader who has come this far in the book and STILL is not convinced that the Jews of Jesus' day did not know Hebrew, let me give you one more opportunity to see that I am telling you the truth.

While the three hours of darkness blanketed the earth on the day of the cross, a cry was wrenched from the lips of the Crucified One that pierced that darkness.

> *And about the ninth hour Jesus cried with a loud voice, saying, Eli, Eli, lama sabachthani? that is to say, My God, my God, why hast thou forsaken me? Some of them that stood there, when they heard that, said, This man calleth for Elias. And straightway one of them ran, and took a sponge, and filled it with vinegar, and put it on a reed, and gave him to drink. The rest said, Let be, let us see whether Elias will come to save him* (Matt. 27:46-49).

Eli, Eli lama sabachthani is CLASSIC HEBREW . . . the language in which the Old Testament was written. You will notice that the Jews who stood near the cross DID NOT UNDERSTAND WHAT JESUS SAID! They heard Him cry "Eli, Eli," and thought He was calling for Elias! If they had known Hebrew, they would have understood what He said!

This backs up again what I have said repeatedly . . . when Jesus READ from the Scriptures to the Jews or when He

CAN I TRUST MY BIBLE?

REFERRED to the Scriptures, He was reading from or referring to a TRANSLATION! Since He called the translation "Scripture," we know it was PERFECT. If the Author of the Scriptures could get His Word translated from Hebrew into Aramaic and keep it PERFECT, He can also do it from Hebrew and Greek into ENGLISH!!!

Let me take you back to the twelfth Psalm once more.

The words of the Lord are pure words: as silver tried in a furnace of earth, purified SEVEN times. Thou shalt keep them, O Lord, thou shalt preserve them from this generation for ever (Psalm 12:6-7).

Please note that God's words are as silver tried in a furnace of earth, purified SEVEN times. Now let me give you some historical facts. If you don't believe me, you'll have some fun checking it out for yourself . . . then you'll believe me.

Let me list for you the first SEVEN languages into which God put His Word. I will give it to you in the chronological order in which it was done.

1. Hebrew
2. Aramaic
3. Greek
4. Old Syriac
5. Old Latin
6. German
7. ENGLISH

God's Word in ENGLISH is the AV1611 King James Bible . . . and isn't it interesting that number *seven* is ENGLISH!!!

There is something else that is fascinating. The King James Bible was first published in 1611, a time when there was no set way to spell English words . . . and no guidelines for punctuation. Shortly

CAN I TRUST MY BIBLE'S TRANSLATION?

thereafter, effort was made among the English-speaking people to set down some rules for punctuation and establish fixed spellings for words. During the next 158 years, the English language, therefore, underwent rapid changes. Each time there was a plateau established, a new edition of the King James Bible was published to bring the spelling and punctuation in line with it. I hasten to point out that these were EDITIONS . . . *not* REVISIONS. I pointed out the difference between editions and revisions earlier.

Let me now give you the chronological order of the editions:

1. 1611
2. 1613
3. 1617
4. 1629
5. 1638
6. 1743
7. 1769

The King James Bible that we have today is the 1769 edition. Please note that it is number SEVEN! There has never been another edition since. Of course not! SEVEN is the number of PERFECTION! There will never be an eighth edition. You cannot improve on PERFECTION! God has the spelling and punctuation EXACTLY as He wants it.

When Jerry Falwell and Thomas Nelson came out with their so-called New King James version, Mr. Falwell advertised it as the "Fifth Edition" of the King James Bible. This was to make people who didn't know better think it was just another edition. Baloney. For one thing, the fifth edition came out in 1638. And for another, the "New" King James version is NOT an edition. . .it is a PERVERSION.

CAN I TRUST MY BIBLE?

The 1769 edition of the 1611 King James Bible is PERFECT. It has 31,175 verses. I believe God has every chapter and every verse EXACTLY as He wants them in His BOOK. The middle verse of the King James Bible is Psalm 118:8. Look at it.

It is better to trust in THE LORD than to put confidence in man (Psalm 118:8).

Count the words in the middle verse of God's English Bible. FOURTEEN! That's twice SEVEN. SEVEN for the first half . . . and SEVEN for the last half. Fourteen is an even number. Therefore to find the very center of the middle verse in God's English Bible, you would have TWO words. Please note that the middle two words in the middle verse of God's Book are "THE LORD"!!! Praiselluiah! The VERY CENTER of God's BOOK is THE LORD Himself!!!

Check out the other versions and see what they've done to it. They've messed it up. Sure. The other versions are PERversions. They are NOT God's books. He has only ONE BOOK . . . and He is at the VERY CENTER of the middle verse in HIS BOOK.

Take a look at the New International perversion, for instance. Its translators have TAKEN OUT many verses, so Psalm 118:8 is NOT the middle verse of their perversion. And even if it were, the Lord is NOT the center of it. It reads: "It is better to take refuge in the Lord than to trust in man." The WORDS have been changed (Rev. 22:18-19) . . . and the middle words are "IN THE." The NIV is NOT God's book. Check out the "Living (Ha! Ha!) Bible," the NASV, etc. They've messed it up, too. Verses are missing and/or the words have been changed.

Of course the "New" King James boys were careful to keep Psalm 118:8 intact. You will find it exactly as it reads in the REAL King James. They knew about "THE LORD" being the center of the verse in the REAL King James Bible, so they did not dare make a change there. However, if my reader can get your hands on a "New" King James "bible," read the seven verses in Psalm 118 PRIOR

CAN I TRUST MY BIBLE'S TRANSLATION?

to verse 8. You will find that they have changed EVERY ONE OF THEM! Sneaky, eh? Well, don't let 'em fool you. The "New" King James is no more God's BOOK than Aesop's Fables. GOD'S Book is PERFECT.

You ask, "CAN I TRUST MY BIBLE'S TRANSLATION?" Absolutely . . . IF you have an AV1611 King James Bible!!! We will deal with the most popular ''bible'' perversions in the last chapter of this book, and show them to be just THAT . . .*perversions*. Suffice it to say at this point . . . God only has ONE Bible in the English language . . . the good old AV1611 King James! The Lord has it translated EXACTLY the way He wants it.

Of course, the ALEXANDRIANS argue with that truth and attack God's Bible, pointing out its "errors." Let me show you some of the "errors" that they work on most frequently . . . and we shall see that God's Book is ALWAYS right, and the Alexandrians are DEAD WRONG when they attack it.

Let's take the word "devils," as found in both the Old and New Testaments in the King James Bible. I have had sneering Alexandrians approach me and declare that where the King James Bible translates the Greek word *daimonion* as "devil," it is wrong . . . that *daimonion* should be translated "demon." They then proceed to inform me in my ignorance that only the Greek word *diabolos* can be properly translated "devil" . . . and that the King James translators were ignorant also, because they even went so far as to translate *daimonion* in the PLURAL as "devils." Curling their sneer even tighter, they say, "Don't you know that there is only ONE devil? Your King James Bible is in error when it says there are devils."

Oh, really?

Seems our Alexandrian "friends" should do a little study on the word "demon." They just might learn that the word was not in common usage in 1611, and had they translated it as such, most people would not have known what a "demon" was. However, they

CAN I TRUST MY BIBLE?

DID know what a DEVIL was. They understood a devil to be an evil or an unclean SPIRIT. For instance, in the King James Bible in Mark chapter 5, the word "devil" is also being called an "unclean spirit." In Luke 8:2, "devils" are called "evil spirits." In John 13:27, even Satan, himself, is seen as an evil SPIRIT, entering into a human body. Though he is the devil, he is also a SPIRIT (see Ephesians 2:2).

Now let us see just how far off the King James translators were when they translated *daimonion* as "devil." I have before me Webster's New World Dictionary of the English Language. Let's look at a couple of definitions.

Demon - 1. a DEVIL; evil spirit

2. a person or thing regarded as evil, cruel, etc.

Do you see that? According to the dictionary, a "demon" is a DEVIL. Now tell me, Alexandrians that the King James translators were in error when they translated *daimonion* "devil."

Devil - 1. (a) the chief EVIL SPIRIT; Satan (b) any DEMON of hell

2. a very wicked person

3. a reckless person

Looks to me like the King James translators were RIGHT ON TARGET since a "devil" can be ANY DEMON OF HELL. So the "evil spirits" in the King James Bible ARE *devils*!

But the Alexandrians are persistent in their hatred for God's ONLY Book. Like tenacious bulldogs, they grit their teeth, hang onto their unscriptural philosophy, and growl, "But there is only ONE devil! The King James Bible is WRONG to ever put the word 'devil' in plural because only ONE being in Scripture is ever called a *diabolos*, and that's Satan!"

You're SURE about that?

CAN I TRUST MY BIBLE'S TRANSLATION?

"Yes! We are great Greek scholars! WE know the King James Bible is wrong to ever use the word 'devils' because there is only ONE devil! There is only ONE *diabolos!*"

My reader may wonder why I am so sure just how the Alexandrians would handle this subject. Simple. I've gone nose-to-nose with them on this very subject . . . that's why.

Now let's have all of you Alexandrian Greek scholars take a look in the King James Bible at what Jesus said about Judas Iscariot.

> *Jesus answered them, Have not I chosen you twelve, and one of you is a DEVIL? He spake of Judas Iscariot the son of Simon: for he it was that should betray him, being one of the twelve* (John 6:70-71).

Since you boys are so adept in Greek, look in your Greek New Testament and tell me what Greek word is used in the aforegoing passage for "devil." Find it? Please tell me what Greek word is used. What's that you say? SPEAK UP! I can't hear you! You say the Greek word for "devil" there is *diabolos?* You are quite correct. Now what was that you were saying about only ONE being in Scripture ever called a *diabolos?*

Chalk one up for the good old AV1611! It is ALWAYS correct! When it says there are devils . . . there are *DEVILS!!!*

Let us now address another "error" (as per the Alexandrians). They pull out their Jehoiakim penknives and slash away at the King James Bible for calling the Holy Spirit an "it" in Romans chapter 8. It reads,

> *The Spirit ITSELF beareth witness with our spirit, that we are the children of God: . . . the Spirit ITSELF maketh intercession for us with groanings which cannot be uttered* (Rom. 8:16, 26).

The "godly" Alexandrians are appalled at the utter insolence of the King James translators in daring to call the Holy Spirit an "it." They boast that the wonderful New International version and the glorious "New" King James version both translate it correctly as "himself." They both translate it "himself," all right, but not CORRECTLY. Even the corrupt Westcott and Hort manuscripts from which both of those versions were translated have it ITSELF in the Greek! In trying to appear to be so "godly," they have been DISHONEST (What's new?) in their translating!

Does my reader know what a pneumatic tool is? Of course. It is a tool that is AIR-OPERATED. The word "pneumatic" has its roots in the Greek language, from the word *pneuma,* which means "air," "breath," "wind," or "spirit." The Greek word used for "Spirit" in Romans 8:16 and 26 is *pneuma,* which is NEUTER. Any language student knows that means it is neither masculine nor feminine. Therefore, it would be INCORRECT to translate it the "Spirit HIMSELF." It MUST be translated in the NEUTER to be correct. The King James translators were EXACTLY ON TARGET when they translated it the "Spirit ITSELF," even as they honestly kept it neuter in I Peter 1:11 . . .

> *Searching what, or what manner of time the Spirit of Christ which was in them did signify, when IT testified beforehand the sufferings of Christ, and the glory that should follow.*

The Alexandrian perversions have been noble once again in trying to "correct" the King James by putting in HE in place of IT. Aren't they sweet? Sweet . . . but DISHONEST. It is NEUTER in ALL the Greek manuscripts. If the Holy Spirit wants to speak of Himself in the neuter, who are WE to correct Him? After all, both the Father and the Son are ALSO spoken of in the neuter in Scripture. Watch Jesus speak of the FATHER in the neuter.

> *Jesus saith unto her, Woman, believe me, the hour cometh, when ye shall neither in this mountain, nor*

CAN I TRUST MY BIBLE'S TRANSLATION?

yet at Jerusalem, worship the Father. Ye worship ye know not what: we know WHAT we worship: for salvation is of the Jews. But the hour cometh, and now is, when the true worshippers shall worship THE FATHER in spirit and in truth: for THE FATHER seeketh such to worship him (John 4:21-23).

How about that? Jesus says, *"We know WHAT we worship . . . true worshippers . . . worship THE FATHER."* Jesus calls His Father "WHAT." That's NEUTER.

What grinds my gizzard is that the Alexandrians get so upset at the King James Bible for calling the Holy Spirit "IT," but raise no fuss at all at the Father being called "WHAT." One's as neuter as the other. In fact, in THEIR OWN "BIBLES," THE ALEXANDRIANS CALL THE FATHER *"WHAT"* !!!!

I'm not going to bother to quote much in this book from the Living (Ha! Ha!) Bible or the New American Standard perversion. Both of these are slipping fast. The main Alexandrian "bibles" have become the New International perversion and the "New" King James perversion. The NIV is fast pulling ahead of the NKJV because of its ONE WORLD (international) scope, but I'll punch them both really hard as we go along. Look at this same passage in the NIV:

> Jesus declared, "Believe me, woman, a time is coming when you will worship the Father neither on this mountain nor in Jerusalem. You Samaritans worship what you do not know; we worship WHAT we do know, for salvation is from the Jews. Yet a time is coming and has now come when the true worshipers will worship THE FATHER in spirit and in truth, for they are the kind of worshipers THE FATHER seeks" (John 4:21-23).

Tch. Tch. You Alexandrians did the same thing; you attack the King James translators for doing . . . speaking of deity in the

CAN I TRUST MY BIBLE?

NEUTER! Look at the same passage in the NKJV.

> Jesus said to her, "Woman, believe Me, the hour is coming when you will neither on this mountain, nor in Jerusalem, worship the Father. You worship what you do not know; we know WHAT we worship, for salvation is of the Jews. But the hour is coming, and now is, when the true worshipers will worship THE FATHER in spirit and truth; for THE FATHER is seeking such to worship Him" (John 4:21-23).

Both of these leading Alexandrian "bibles" call God the Father "WHAT" . . . but the Alexandrians will scream vehemently at the King James Bible for calling the Holy Spirit "IT." Sounds like two-faced, double-tongued hypocrisy to me. By the way . . . take a close look at the wording and sentence structure of the NKJV. They CLAIM they translated their New Testament from the Received Text. If so, WHY DOES IT RESEMBLE THE NIV SO CLOSELY???

Let's look at a couple of places where the SON is spoken of in the neuter.

> *Then said Mary unto the angel, How shall this be, seeing I know not a man? And the angel answered and said unto her, The Holy Ghost shall come upon thee, and the power of the Highest shall overshadow thee: therefore also that holy THING which shall be born of thee shall be called the Son of God* (Luke 1:34-35).

Yes sir . . . Gabriel called God's Son a THING! I wonder if he got his mouth washed out with soap when he got back to Heaven. Probably not. For one thing, they don't HAVE soap in Heaven. No need. No dirt. And for another . . . Gabriel had been sent directly from the throne of God to make this announcement to Mary. I have no doubt at all that he used the very words the Father had TOLD him to use. Yes . . . Scripture speaks of the Lord Jesus in the neuter as

CAN I TRUST MY BIBLE'S TRANSLATION?

that holy THING.

Of course the NIV and the NKJV had to smooth Gabriel's words over and "correct" him a bit. They both have Gabriel calling Jesus the "holy one." But it's still neuter, no matter what they do with it.

Another place where we have God's Son being spoken of in the neuter is when He appears as the Lamb of God in the book of Revelation.

> *And I beheld, and, lo, in the midst of the throne and of the four beasts, and in the midst of the elders, stood a Lamb as IT had been slain . . .* (Rev. 5:6).

Once again, the King James Bible speaks of the Lord Jesus in the neuter. The reason, of course, is because the Received Text calls Him "IT," here. So what did the gallant, noble, and "godly" translators of the NIV and NKJV do with Him here? See for yourself.

> NIV - Then I saw a Lamb, looking as if IT had been slain, standing in the center of the throne, encircled by the four living creatures and the elders.

> NKJV - And I looked, and behold, in the midst of the throne and of the four living creatures, and in the midst of the elders, stood a Lamb as though IT had been slain . . .

Tch. Tch. You naughty boys. You called Jesus an "IT." Again we see the two-faced, double-tongued hypocrisy of the Alexandrians. They get up on their soap boxes and scream at the King James Bible for referring to the Holy Spirit as "ITSELF" in Romans 8:16 and 26 . . . then speak of God the Father and God the Son in their own "bibles" IN THE SAME MANNER! Hypocrites.

Recently, a rank modernist Southern Baptist named Clayton Sullivan authored a nefarious book entitled *Toward A Mature Faith:*

CAN I TRUST MY BIBLE?

Does Biblical Inerrancy Make Sense? Sullivan is an associate professor of philosophy and religion at the University of Southern Mississippi at Hattiesburg. By what he says in his book, he makes it clear that he thinks Biblical inerrancy is ridiculous. He says the Bible has all kinds of errors. He throws out two hundred questions, attacking Bible passages he believes are in error.

The modernist Alexandrian professor writes, "Evangelical clergymen have proclaimed biblical inerrancy . . . have repeatedly expressed to parishioners the view that the Bible is a Book void of limitations, mistakes, contradictions, or puzzles. To support this position, scholars have quoted II Timothy 3:16, which asserts: 'All scripture is given by inspiration of God, and is profitable for doctrine, for reproof, for correction, for instruction in righteousness.' Believing what they are told, well-intended Christians have come to view biblical inerrancy as a vital component of the Christian faith."

Well pardon me, professor, but Biblical inerrancy MOST CERTAINLY IS a vital component of the Christian faith . . . the REAL Christian faith, that is! What YOU have, sir, is as false as a set of dentures!

My reader will note that the professor's quotation of II Timothy 3:16 is from the KING JAMES BIBLE. He continues to attack the REAL Bible throughout his book . . . and his hatred for it comes through time and again. Striking, isn't it? Modernist Alexandrians and "fundamentalist" Alexandrians agree in their scheme to rip up God's Book with their Jehoiakim-style penknives. Seems to me that birds of a feather really DO flock together! Modernist Alexandrians and "fundamentalist" Alexandrians are nothing but *kissin' cousins*.

Professor Sullivan explains that he has joined the Bible critics who study it like they study any piece of literature. He and his "scholar" buddies study the Bible to examine carefully its books as to their historical background and their text, composition, and character. He says, "When some people hear about scholars studying

CAN I TRUST MY BIBLE'S TRANSLATION?

the Bible critically, they quite understandably conclude that scholars are 'picking' on the Bible, searching for faults."

While picking on God's Book, the professor throws out two hundred questions designed to prove it is very much in error. Let's look at a few.

1. When sending out his disciples, did Jesus instruct them to *wear* sandals as reported in Mark 6:9 or did he instruct them *not* to wear sandals as reported in Matthew 10:10?

Sullivan is joining all his Alexandrian pals in attempting to show that the King James Bible is in error. I'm going to SHOW you where ERROR is! Let's look at the two passages.

> *And [Jesus] commanded them that they should take nothing for their journey, save a staff only; no scrip, no bread, no money in their purse: But be shod with sandals; and not put on two coats* (Mark 6:8-9).

> *Provide neither gold, nor silver, nor brass in your purses, Nor scrip for your journey, neither two coats, neither shoes, nor yet staves: for the workman is worthy of his meat* (Matt. 10:9-10).

Does my reader see any error here? Not unless you are as BLIND as Professor Sullivan! In Mark 6:8, Jesus told them to TAKE nothing for their journey except a staff. Now, what do you do with a staff? Do you WEAR it? Of course not. You CARRY it. What do you do with scrip, bread, money, or an extra coat? You CARRY them. In Mark, Jesus tells them to be SHOD with sandals. In the Matthew passage, He is telling them not to CARRY an extra pair of shoes. Good grief, Charlie Brown! How dumb can an Alexandrian get? We can plainly see that the ERROR is not in the Book . . . but rather, it is in the professor's brain. Let's consider his next question.

2. Assuming the Bible is inerrant, why did Jesus think that Deuteronomy 24:1 needed to be corrected and superceded by

CAN I TRUST MY BIBLE?

Genesis 1:27 and 2:24 as reported in Matthew 19:3-9?

Can you believe this bird . . . saying that Jesus was thinking WRONG? Jesus neither corrected NOR superceded Deuteronomy 24:1 with Genesis 1:27 and 2:24. He flat SAID in the Matthew passage that FROM THE BEGINNING God intended for a husband and wife to STAY MARRIED. It was because of the HARDNESS OF MEN'S HEARTS that Moses allowed men to put away their wives. Where is any CORRECTING or SUPERCEDING? What needs correcting is the twisted thinking of the professor! . . . *hath not God made foolish the wisdom of this world* (I Cor. 1:20)?

Here's the professor's next foolish question.

3. Luke 3:23 states that Jesus' grandfather was named Heli, but Matthew 1:15 states that Jesus' grandfather was named Jacob. Was Jesus' grandfather named Jacob or Heli?

This is the typical Alexandrian way to approach a Bible passage that completely stumps 'em. Make it look like the translators boo-booed . . . OR that Matthew and Luke had just forgotten to "get together" on their stories. I would like to ask Professor Sullivan how many grandfathers he had. If he's like the rest of us, he had TWO. My grandfathers' names were Frank and Ben. Frank was my mother's dad, and Ben was my father's dad. My reader could quickly tell me the names of YOUR grandfathers, right? Of course.

Though Joseph of Nazareth was only Jesus' STEP-father, I'm sure Jacob looked on the child as his grandson. Heli, being Mary's father, was also Jesus' grandfather. This modernist Alexandrian doesn't know much Bible (Again, what's new?). If he did, he would know that "the son of" in Scripture does not ALWAYS mean the man's LITERAL son. Luke's account reads like this:

> *And Jesus himself began to be about thirty years of age, being (as was supposed) the son of Joseph, which was the son of Heli, Which was the son of*

CAN I TRUST MY BIBLE'S TRANSLATION?

Matthat, which was the son of Levi, which was the son Melchi, which was the son of Janna, which was the son of Joseph, (Luke 3:23-24).

Matthew's account reads like this:

And Eliud begat Eleazar; and Eleazar begat Matthan; and Matthan begat Jacob; And Jacob begat Joseph the husband of Mary, of whom was born Jesus, who is called Christ (Matt. 1:15-16).

I said a moment ago that in Scripture "the son of" does not ALWAYS mean the man's LITERAL son. Look how the book of Matthew starts out.

The book of the generation of Jesus Christ, the son of David, the son of Abraham (Matt. 1:1).

Certainly, Jesus is not David's LITERAL Son. He was only in the LINEAGE of David, and David was not LITERALLY the son of Abraham. He was in the LINEAGE of Abraham, but Jesse was David's literal father, even as GOD is literally Jesus' Father.

Sometimes when Scripture uses "the son of," it is speaking of a SON-IN-LAW. There are TWO such cases in the lineage listed in Luke chapter 3. Let me show you. First let us go back to Genesis.

And Arphaxad begat Salah; and Salah begat Eber. And Arphaxad lived after he begat Salah four hundred and three years, and begat sons and daughters (Genesis 10:24; 11:13).

Now let's look at how it is recorded in the genealogy according to Dr. Luke.

. . . which was the son of Sala, Which was the son of Cainan, which was the son of Arphaxad . . . (Luke 3:35-36)

You will note that CAINAN was not mentioned at all in the

CAN I TRUST MY BIBLE?

Genesis account. Moses plainly stated twice that Arphaxad begat Salah (Sala in Luke). Yet here in Luke 3:35 and 36, we read, *"Cainan, which was the son of Arphaxad..."* Is this an error? Hardly. We have solid evidence from Genesis that Salah was begotten by Arphaxed. Then WHO was Cainan? Quite simply, he was tucked in there by Luke (under the guidance of the Holy Spirit) because he had married one of Arphaxad's daughters. He was a SON-IN-LAW. That's easy for me to grasp. I have TWO sons-in-law, and I often call them my "sons."

So we have it EARLIER in Luke chapter 3. Joseph of Nazareth was Heli's SON-IN-LAW . . . because he was married to Heli's daughter, Mary. If you will check out the two genealogies in Matthew and Luke, you will find that none of the names of the fathers is the same UNTIL YOU GET TO DAVID. Then, they are exactly the same until you get back to Abraham. Matthew's genealogy goes no further back than Abraham, but Luke's goes all the way back to Adam.

Thus, we have it on Scriptural authority that through His step-father's lineage AND through His mother's lineage, Jesus is the ONLY King who has the right to sit on the throne of David forever . . . that He is the ultimate One to rule over the house of Israel forever, according to God's oath to Abraham . . . and that His virgin birth makes Him literally Mary's Son wherein He received His humanity (declaring so by Mary's lineage being traced solidly all the way back to the FIRST human being, Adam) . . . so that He is rightfully the LAST Adam and the Head of a Heavenly race . . . the blood-washed, born-again family of God (Luke 1:32-33, 73; I Cor. 15:45).

So to answer Mr. Sullivan's question, "Was Jesus' grandfather named Jacob or Heli?" . . . His step-paternal grandfather was named Jacob, and His maternal grandfather was named Heli. Somebody needs to order this Alexandrian a white cane. He's blind.

4. Did Jesus say to Peter that before the cock crows you will

deny me three times (Matt. 26:34), or did He say that before the cock crows *twice,* you will deny me three times (Mark 14:30)?

Talk about straining at a gnat and swallowing a camel! Even a casual reading of the two passages will show a sensible person that Mark simply gives MORE DETAIL in his story than Matthew. Mercy Maude! What lengths will an Alexandrian go to in order to discredit the Book he hates?

5. On Easter morning, did *one* woman (John 20:1) or did *three* women (Mark 16:1) discover Jesus' empty tomb?

Here we go again. Somebody get this man a seeing-eye dog! How blind do you have to be to see that THREE women went to the tomb as recorded in Mark 16:1 . . . but that in John's account, the Holy Spirit saw fit to concentrate ONLY on Mary Magdalene. This is often done in the writings of the four Gospels. We must BLEND all four to get the full story. God WROTE it that way because He WANTED it that way! He wanted us to do more than READ the Gospels . . . He wanted us to *STUDY* them (II Tim. 2:15)!

It is evident that Professor Sullivan has not STUDIED the Bible. Of course, he just might have the problem that is written by Paul in I Corinthians 2:14!

Let us move on to some more alleged errors in the AV 1611. We have heard from a modernist "Baptist" Alexandrian . . . now we will hear from a "fundamental Baptist" Alexandrian. I have quoted from Evangelist J.H. Melton's "Public Forum" already in this book. I find so much standard Alexandrianism in the "forum" that it gives an abundant supply of their humanistic doctrine on which to draw a bead.

The "forum" is embodied in three letters. On page 1 of letter #1, Mr. Melton says, "I have preached in all fifty states in over fifteen hundred churches and do not recall one in which the KJV was or became an issue. However, the KJV is the most divisive

CAN I TRUST MY BIBLE?

issue among independent Baptists today. Because there is so much propaganda on one side of the issue, I feel I should address the other side. I use only the King James Version in my meetings . . . The King *James* Version! How can Baptist preachers believe the King James Version to be without error? King James was a homosexual."

Mr. Melton then lists two books (one written in 1975 and the other in 1976) and three encyclopedias as his source of proof. As for the encyclopedias, they prove NOTHING. These same encyclopedias also teach the devil's doctrine of evolution as a fact. They also teach that Jesus Christ was a religious leader on the same level with Buddha, Mohammed, and Confucius. Scrap the humanistic encyclopedias.

As for the books . . . James I died in 1625. These people wrote their books after King James had been dead for 350 years. What was their source of proof? A "document" written by a man named Anthony Weldon TWENTY-FIVE YEARS *after* James had died. Sour grapes was what it was.

The truth is that Weldon once served in the king's court. The two had a falling out, and James fired him. Weldon swore revenge. If he raised a finger against the king, however, he would be in real trouble. The people of Great Britain loved their king, so Weldon waited until James was long dead; then he produced his "document" claiming the king had been a homosexual. Sorta hard for a fella to defend himself when he's dead, wouldn't you agree? The common decent people of England abhorred homosexuality just like the common decent people of America abhor it today. Yet the British people loved and adored King James (who is on record as a monarch who fought immorality in his domain during his entire reign) and highly respected him.

But let's say, for argument's sake, that the accusation is true. It wasn't JAMES who did the translating anyhow. What he was wouldn't affect the great work the translators did. But since such accusation is totally unfounded, we'll discount Mr. Melton's words on the subject.

Did my reader catch that in one breath Mr. Melton says, "I use only the King James Version in my meetings" . . . then in the next breath begins a tirade on the same Book by saying, "How can Baptist preachers believe the King James Version to be without error?" Talk about being double-minded! If the KJV is so bad, WHY DOES HE USE IT?

On page 2 of letter #1, Mr. Melton lists five "errors" in the King James Bible. They are, as I said, the STANDARD points the Alexandrians use to "prove" the KJV has errors. Let's take them in the order Mr. Melton lists them.

1. "There are errors in the King James Version. Most of these errors reflect the beliefs of the Church of England. The first, and one of the most grievous, is the use of the word 'church' to translate 'ekklesia' . . . The word 'church' has associations and connotations utterly foreign to the 'ekklesia' of the New Testament."

My first reaction is to ask if the places where Evangelist Melton preaches have any connection to the New Testament. He also states in the forum that "The translators were ordered by King James not to use 'assembly' or 'congregation,' but to use a word with a more universal meaning." Mr. Melton says he is a Baptist. I wonder if he has ever preached in a church called the First Baptist Assembly or the Bible Baptist Congregation. To take the words of his own mouth, he says on page one of letter #1, "I have preached in all fifty states in over fifteen hundred CHURCHES." If the word "church" is so bad . . . why does he preach in "CHURCHES"??? And why does he use the word "church," himself, rather than assembly or congregation?

On page 4 of letter #3, he says, "I always address my correspondence to the pastor in care of the CHURCH." On the same page, he says, "I had never been inside a CHURCH in my life until

CAN I TRUST MY BIBLE?

my thirteenth year." On page 4 of the same letter, he says of his son David's ministry, "The ministry will be sponsored by the CHURCH of which he is a member."

Seems to me that Mr. Melton makes use of a bad word that is found in the King James Bible to denote the living organism for which Christ died and shed His blood (Acts 20:28; Eph.5:25). Well, I'll tell you what . . . if the word "church" is good enough for the Holy Spirit AND the Baptist Alexandrians . . . it's GOOD ENOUGH FOR ME! I'll still go to CHURCH on Sunday. It seems easier than going to "assembly." That's where I used to go to when I was in public school. "Assembly" sure didn't have anything to do with God. And . . . I think I'll stick with going to CHURCH. Going to "congregation" doesn't even sound sensible. It is quite evident that the Holy Spirit guided the King James translators to use the word "church" in the New Testament when *ekklesia* had something to do with God.

"Church" may have a universal meaning to Mr. Melton, but it sure doesn't for ME. It means the SAME THING to me that it does to the Holy Spirit . . . a local, visible collection of God's born-again, blood-washed, Scripturally-baptized people who are the body of Christ and are not ashamed to be called BAPTISTS.

2. "The KJV translators did not translate 'baptidzo.' They transliterated it and left the reader to give it whatever meaning he desired. In Matthew3:11, the KJV reads, 'I indeed baptize you with water.' The KJV translators used 'with' instead of 'in' because the church of England sprinkles."

Mr. Melton needs to read a little history before he makes such statements. I agree that the church of England sprinkles TODAY . . . but the practice of sprinkling in the church of England did not begin until 1644! (see *History of English Baptists* by Thomas Crosby; *An Essay to Restore the Dipping of Infants* by Sir John Floyer; *History of the Baptists* by John T. Christian).

CAN I TRUST MY BIBLE'S TRANSLATION?

When the King James Bible was translated, the church of England BAPTIZED people . . . it did not sprinkle them! The truth is, the Greek word *en* can be translated 'with' or 'in.' Since the church of England immersed people at the time the King James Bible was being translated, WHY WOULD THE TRANSLATORS USE "WITH WATER" TO TRY TO STEER BIBLE READERS TOWARD SPRINKLING AS A SUBSTITUTE??? Nonsense.

Since the translators thoroughly understood *baptidzo* to mean "dip" or "immerse," they used "with" to denote what element the person was being baptized IN. Was it milk? Grape juice? Lemonade? No! They were being baptized with WATER!

The Holy Spirit had a good reason for guiding the King James translators to transliterate *baptidzo*. What if they had translated it instead, and everywhere you read "baptize" or "baptized" in Scripture you found "dip" or "immerse"? When you hear "dip," do you automatically associate it with something to do with GOD? Hmm? When I was a kid growing up in the country, we used to dip our sheep in sheep-dip come spring every year. It had nothing to do with anything spiritual. When we spoke of what we were doing, we always used the word "dip."

When you hear the word "immerse," do you automatically think of something that has to do with GOD? Hmm? For years, we have watched a gal named Madge in Palmolive commercials immersed her hands in dishwater gleaming with Palmolive dishwashing liquid. Did you instantly think of something spiritual? Nope.

This is why the Holy Spirit had the King James translators transliterate *baptidzo* instead of translate it. Whenever you hear the word "baptize," you immediately connect it with God, church, and spiritual matters. Sure, the devil has taken it and twisted it so that in the minds of multitudes "baptism" means sprinkle. Sure, the old dragon has prostituted the truth of baptism into a rite that is

CAN I TRUST MY BIBLE?

supposed to cleanse sin and save the soul . . . but are we to allow the devil and his crowd to change how we talk of the things of the Lord just because they are wrong in the way *they* talk of spiritual things?

It is unjust to accuse the King James Bible of misleading people because you don't agree with the way it was translated. Every rock solid Baptist I know learned his doctrine from the AV1611 King James Bible!

3. "In Romans 8:1, the words 'who walk not after the flesh but after the Spirit' are not in the best Greek manuscripts. The addition of these words by the translators denies the saving efficacy of the blood of Jesus. 'There is therefore now no condemnation [judgment] to them which are in Christ Jesus.' PERIOD. Our freedom from judgment for sin is not dependent on us. It is eternally settled the instant we put saving faith in Jesus Christ. In this regard, the Savior died to make it possible for every man, woman, boy and girl to be saved. Calvinism is a Satanic Protestant teaching. The claim of inerrancy for the KJV is in the same category."

My reader will note that Mr. Melton refuses to spell the word "Saviour" the way it is spelled in the King James Bible. S-A-V-I-O-R is the way it is spelled in the PERversions. I agree completely with Mr. Melton that Jesus died to make it possible for EVERYONE to be saved . . . and that Calvinism is a Satanic Protestant teaching. But I deeply resent his linking the claim for my Bible's inerrancy with Calvinistic heresy!!!

I also deeply resent Mr. Melton's attack on the translation of Romans 8:1 in my King James Bible. If he would read the rest of the chapter instead of getting hung up on verse 1, he would see the error of his attack. Let's get the verse in front of our eyes.

There is therefore now no condemnation to them which are in Christ Jesus, who walk not after the flesh, but after the Spirit (Rom. 8:1).

CAN I TRUST MY BIBLE'S TRANSLATION?

Mr. Melton's statement "the words 'who walk not after the flesh but after the Spirit' are not in the best Greek manuscripts" simply reveals the Alexandrian blood in his veins. The Received Text HAS the words "who walk not after the flesh, but after the Spirit." So he is siding with Adamantius Origen and all the other Alexandrians in his vicious attack on God's English Bible. I am in perfect agreement with his statement, "Our freedom from judgment for sin is not dependent on us. It is eternally settled the instant we put saving faith in Jesus Christ." But I am in TOTAL disagreement with him when he says, "The addition of these words by the translators denies the saving efficacy of the blood of Jesus!" THAT IS GROSS ERROR!!! Mr. Melton is saying that the "added" words are teaching that we have to STAY SAVED by not walking after the flesh but after the Spirit. Hogwash. People who are in Christ Jesus DO walk after the Spirit . . . and do NOT walk after the flesh!

For proof that Mr. Melton has read no further than verse 1, look at verse 4.

That the righteousness of the law might be fulfilled in us, WHO WALK NOT AFTER THE FLESH, BUT AFTER THE SPIRIT.

The EXACT SAME WORDS are found in verse 4 as in verse 1. Why hasn't Mr. Melton pointed THEM out? Are THEY found in the "best" manuscripts? He hasn't told us. Like I said . . . he hasn't read past verse 1. I repeat: People who are in Christ Jesus DO walk after the Spirit . . . and do NOT walk after the flesh. Verse 5 SAYS SO!

For they that are after the flesh DO mind the THINGS OF THE FLESH; but they that are after the Spirit the THINGS OF THE SPIRIT (Romans 8:5).

Mr. Melton's alleged "added" words were not added at all. They ARE in the genuine manuscripts and therefore are found in the genuine English Bible. They fit perfectly with the context of

CAN I TRUST MY BIBLE?

the entire chapter. What a blatant insult to the translators to say they added those ten words to verse 1 in order to teach salvation by works! The simple truth is that those who are in Christ Jesus are NOT in the flesh but in the Spirit. Therefore, saved people walk after the Spirit. Lost people walk after the flesh. Follow the theme in the same chapter.

> So then they that are IN THE FLESH, cannot please God. But ye are NOT IN THE FLESH but IN THE SPIRIT, if so be that the Spirit of God dwell in you (Rom. 8:8-9).

Only a self-blinded Alexandrian could read that and say the words "who walk not after the flesh, but after the Spirit" were ADDED by the translators. Ridiculous! Pure-dee Alexandrian dribble.

4. Mr. Melton says in his forum, *"By one Spirit are we all baptized into one body* (I Cor. 12:13) is an inexcusable translation responsible for the heretical universal church and Holy Spirit baptism teachings. The Scripture should be translated, '*In* one spirit *were* we all baptized into one body.'"

Again, Mr. Melton has neglected to bone up on his history. He says the mistranslation of I Corinthians 12:13 by the King James translators is "responsible for the heretical universal church teachings." If he would do a little reading, he would find that *Martin Luther* invented the universal church heresy NINETY YEARS before the King James Bible was translated and published!!! Only his historical ignorance would supply him with the unmitigated gall to accuse the King James Bible of being responsible for the universal church heresy! And as for Holy Spirit baptism . . . the word "by" in I Corinthians 12:13 isn't going to bother anyone who knows the rest of the Bible. On the same page of his forum, Mr. Melton says, "The Holy Spirit never baptized anyone." I agree. But the use of the word "by" in I Corinthians 12:13 does NOT have to mean that the Holy

CAN I TRUST MY BIBLE'S TRANSLATION?

Spirit DID THE BAPTIZING. A little knowledge of the English language clears it right up.

The preposition "by" can be used as instrumental or locative. Mr. Melton has insisted on "in" when "by" can just as easily mean BY one Spirit *in the sense of the LEADERSHIP of the Holy Spirit.* Every born-again member of a true New Testament church has been led BY the Holy Spirit after conversion to be baptized into that local church, which is the body of Christ.

The Greek word *en* can be translated "with," "by," "in" and "among" . . . and is translated such throughout the New Testament. To insist on "in" instead of "by" in I Corinthians 12:13 is forcing something that cannot be done honestly.

Mr. Melton's insistence that "are" in the verse should be translated "were" is utter nonsense. If I ever *was* baptized, I am STILL baptized! I didn't USE TO BE . . . I *AM* a baptized believer! On page 4 of letter #3, Mr. Melton says, "You did not get your local church belief from the King James Version. Thousands of so-called Baptist men got their universal church doctrine from the King James translation. The King James mistranslation of I Corinthians 12:13 is responsible for most of the interdenominationalism rampant in the world today."

I can only speak for myself, but I can tell Mr. Melton that I most certainly DID get my local church belief from the King James Bible!!! I'm sure there have been many people who have MISUNDERSTOOD I Corinthians 12:13 as teaching a universal "body of Christ" . . . but anyone who studies that verse in the light of the rest of I Corinthians and the rest of the New Testament could NEVER get mixed up on it. Let me show my reader what I mean. We have already established that the Greek word *ekklesia,* which is translated "church" in the New Testament MANY TIMES MORE than it is translated "assembly" or "congregation," can mean nothing but a LOCAL collection of people. By no means can it be universal.

CAN I TRUST MY BIBLE?

The church and the body are EXACTLY one in the same thing.

And hath put all things under his feet, and gave him to be the head over all things to the CHURCH, Which is his BODY, the fulness of him that filleth all in all (Eph. 1:22-23).

And he is the head of the BODY, THE CHURCH: . . . (Col. 1:18).

Thus we read in I Corinthians 12:13 . . .

For by one Spirit are we all baptized into one body, . . .

Paul uses the word "body" in the abstract sense, even as Jesus used the word "church" in Matthew 16:18. Those who misunderstand the use of abstract and concrete in language get all mixed up and think there is some kind of universal, spasmodic, ectoplasmic, ghostly, invisible SPOOK CHURCH floating around somewhere that ALL Christians have been baptized into by the Holy Spirit. They mistakenly assume that since the church and the body are the same thing, there exists a mystical, ethereal "body of Christ" to which ALL Christians belong, since they were baptized into it by the Holy Spirit at conversion. NO! NO! NO! When Jesus said, "I will build My church" . . . and Paul said, "We are all baptized into one body," they were using ABSTRACT terms for a CONCRETE item.

Let me give you an example. I could say, "The jury is being tampered with in the United States today." Is there a GREAT BIG UNIVERSAL INVISIBLE MYSTICAL JURY somewhere? Hardly. We find the abstract "jury" localized and visible *in the concrete* as we see the individual JURIES all over America. The only way you can see the "jury" is to find it in a local jury box!

Another example . . . I hear people all over this country saying, "I'm so sick of the way the post office keeps raising its rates and giving less service!" What do they mean "the post office"? Is

CAN I TRUST MY BIBLE'S TRANSLATION?

there ONE GREAT BIG UNIVERSAL, INVISIBLE MYSTICAL POST OFFICE floating around somewhere? Of course not. When they say "the post office" in the abstract, you FIND "the post office" in the concrete when you go to the LOCAL post office down on the Corner.

Ephesians 4:4 says, "There is ONE body . . ." Does this mean there is one BIG, UNIVERSAL, INVISIBLE, MYSTICAL BODY OF CHRIST to which all Christians belong? NO! I can say to you, "There is ONE Book." Does this mean there is one BIG UNIVERSAL, INVISIBLE, MYSTICAL Bible? Of course not. The ONE Book in the abstract appears in thousands of LOCAL, INDIVIDUAL King James Bibles in the concrete. Just so . . . each New Testament church is the concrete of the abstract "church" or "body." Look at this.

For THE HUSBAND is the head of THE WIFE, even as Christ is head of THE CHURCH . . . (Eph. 5:23).

Now, tell me . . . is there ONE GREAT BIG UNIVERSAL, INVISIBLE, MYSTICAL *husband*? Hmm? Is there ONE GREAT BIG UNIVERSAL, INVISIBLE, MYSTICAL *wife*? Of course not. NEITHER IS THERE ONE GREAT BIG UNIVERSAL, INVISIBLE MYSTICAL *church*! Here Paul speaks of "the husband," "the wife," and "the church" in the ABSTRACT, but we can only FIND them in the CONCRETE! It is a LOCAL husband . . . a LOCAL wife . . . a LOCAL church. A few verses later, Paul says,

For *we are members of his BODY . . .* (Eph. 5:30).

Just as sure as there is no such thing as a UNIVERSAL, INVISIBLE, MYSTICAL *husband, wife,* or *church* . . . neither is there a UNIVERSAL, INVISIBLE, MYSTICAL *body of Christ!!!*

Writing to the local church in Corinth, Paul said, *"Now ye ARE the body of Christ, and members in particular."* He did not say, "Ye are PART of the body of Christ." He said, "Ye ARE the body of

CAN I TRUST MY BIBLE?

Christ." Every local New Testament church IS the body of Christ. So when we are baptized by water, we are baptized into the body of Christ. Ephesians 4:5 says there is ONE baptism. According to Matthew 28:19, Acts 8:38, Romans 6:4, and a multitude of other New Testament Scriptures, the ONE baptism is WATER baptism. Therefore, I Corinthians 12:13 CANNOT be Spirit baptism in the way the "universal church" people take it. It is WATER baptism which places the convert into the body of Christ. The body is LOCAL . . . not universal. The church is LOCAL . . . not universal. *Ekklesia* DEMANDS that it be LOCAL. You can no more have a universal church than you can have a universal jury, post office, husband, wife, Bible, or body. The Bible knows no more of a universal church than it does of a heavenly devil. NEITHER exist. The idea of a universal church is ROMAN CATHOLIC. The very word "catholic" MEANS universal. The pope will tell you that his church is a universal, VISIBLE church. Martin Luther disagreed with the pope and declared that the "true" church (Shades of C.I. Scofield!) was an INVISIBLE church and that the body of Christ was a universal, mystical body, Catholic and Protestant BALONEY!!!

The only way into the body of Christ is by BAPTISM IN WATER. At baptism, the convert BECOMES a member of the body, the church. This is why I get so puzzled when a person gets saved and baptized; and then the church "votes" them in as a member. This is downright insidious. According to God, they are ALREADY a member of the church when they come up out of the water!

For by one Spirit are we all baptized INTO ONE BODY . . . (I Cor. 12:13). Each believer has been baptized INTO that local body by whose authority they were baptized. There is NO OTHER BODY into which you can be baptized. The Holy Spirit doesn't baptize anybody into ANYTHING. By the LEADERSHIP of the Holy Spirit, we are baptized by WATER into a local, visible New Testament Baptist church.

CAN I TRUST MY BIBLE'S TRANSLATION?

On the day of Pentecost, three thousand people responded to Peter's invitation to repent. When you repent Bible-style, you put your faith in the Lord Jesus Christ for salvation (Acts 20:21). Those three thousand people got saved. What did they do next?

Then they that gladly received his word WERE BAPTIZED: and the same day there were ADDED unto them about three thousand souls (Acts 2:41).

Yes sir, they got baptized and were ADDED unto something. What were they ADDED TO?

And the Lord ADDED TO THE CHURCH daily such as should be saved (Acts 2:47).

You will note that those new converts were added to the church UPON THEIR BAPTISM. This coincides perfectly with I Corinthians 12:13. The church and the body are EXACTLY the same thing. After a person is saved through the ministry of a New Testament church, they are COMMANDED to be baptized (Matthew 28:19-20; Acts 10:48). The church, in the Great Commission, is COMMANDED to baptize the converts . . . and the converts are COMMANDED to be baptized. Therefore, by the leadership of the Holy Spirit, they OBEY Him and GET BAPTIZED.

Which brings up another thing that puzzles me. Most Baptist churches that I've been in take a "vote" to baptize people who have received Christ. The pastor will stand up and say, "Everyone in favor of receiving these new converts into our membership by baptism say 'Amen.' Opposed, like sign." The people say "Amen!" . . . and no one ever opposes it . . . so the converts get baptized.

WHY VOTE? The church is COMMANDED to baptize their converts. Is the church voting to OBEY God? We certainly shouldn't have to VOTE whether or not to obey God! Don't VOTE! *DO IT!!!*

When it's done, the newly-saved person is in the body of

CAN I TRUST MY BIBLE?

Christ. *"By one Spirit are we all baptized into one body."* People who get saved but do not get baptized into a New Testament church are NOT in the body of Christ.

"Oh, dear!" cry those who have allowed Catholic and Protestant heresy to permeate their thinking. "You mean if they don't get baptized into a New Testament church they will go to Hell? We thought they were baptized into the mystical body of Christ by the Holy Spirit and made a member of the universal, invisible church the moment they received Christ!"

When you get the Catholicism and the Protestantism out of your thinking, you will see that you have to be saved BEFORE you can be in the body of Christ and a member of a New Testament church. Saved people are called the family of God (Eph. 3:15), the "children of God" (Gal. 3:26), and "saints" (Rom. 1:7)... but in order to be OBEDIENT children and saints, they must be BAPTIZED into a local New Testament Baptist church, which is the body of Christ (I Cor. 12:27).

Such a thing as a universal, mystical, invisible BODY cannot exist. In order for it to be a body, it must be FITLY JOINED TOGETHER. Scattered fragments do NOT make up a body. All Christians cannot possibly make up the body of Christ. All Christians have never been assembled together in one place and FITLY JOINED TOGETHER. Most of the saved people are in Heaven... and the rest are scattered all over the face of the earth, which its circumference is 25,600 miles. To the local, visible New Testament church at Ephesus, Paul wrote under the inspiration of the Holy Spirit.

> *And [YE] are built upon the foundation of the apostles and prophets, Jesus Christ himself being the chief corner stone; In whom all the building FITLY FRAMED TOGETHER groweth unto an holy temple in the Lord: In whom YE [in the local church at Ephesus] also are BUILDED TOGETHER for an*

CAN I TRUST MY BIBLE'S TRANSLATION?

habitation of God through the Spirit (Eph. 2:20-22).

Speaking to the same church, Paul called Christ their Head, and referring to Him said,

From whom the whole body FITLY JOINED TOGETHER AND COMPACTED by that which every joint supplieth, according to the effectual working in the measure of EVERY PART, maketh increase of the body unto the edifying of itself in love (Eph. 4:16).

In order to have EVERY PART of the body of Christ FITLY FRAMED *together,* BUILDED *together,* FITLY JOINED *together* and COMPACTED, it MUST be all in ONE place! It HAS to be local! The idea of a universal body is ridiculous.

Picture yourself walking down the local railroad tracks. Suddenly, you look down and see blood all over the place. Your eye falls on a hand. You say, "That looks like Humphrey's left hand." Twenty yards down the tracks, you find another hand. You say, "Hmm. That looks like Humphrey's right hand." Continuing on, you walk another twenty yards and see a leg. You say, "That looks like Humphrey's left leg."

Another thirty yards, you spy a second leg, saying, "Sure enough, that looks like Humphrey's right leg." You proceed a little further . . . let's say twenty-three yards, and you find a torso. You say, "That looks like Humphrey's torso." Hurrying onward, you walk another forty yards and find Humphrey's head. Quickly, you run, pick up the head, and say, "Humphrey! Are you hurt?"

Now I ask you . . . is that a BODY? Of course not. Scattered parts DO NOT MAKE UP A BODY! . . . neither do Christians who are scattered all over the universe! In I Corinthians chapter 12, Paul says the church is like a human body. He speaks of the hands, the feet, the eyes, the ears, the nose . . . and says,

. . . but God hath TEMPERED THE BODY

CAN I TRUST MY BIBLE?

> *TOGETHER . . . that the members should have the same care one for another. And whether one member suffer, ALL THE MEMBERS suffer with it; or one member be honored, ALL THE MEMBERS rejoice with it. Now YE ARE THE BODY OF CHRIST, and members in particular. And God hath set some in the CHURCH, first apostles, secondarily prophets, thirdly teachers . . .* (I Cor. 12:24-28).

Now THINK, dear reader . . . Nothing can be a "body" unless it is TEMPERED TOGETHER. That MAKES it local. The idea of it being universal is absurd. Please notice that Paul said when one member suffers, ALL THE MEMBERS suffer with him, or when one member is honored ALL THE MEMBERS rejoice with him. There is NO WAY this can be true except in a LOCAL church. If there is such a thing as a universal body or church (which would be made up of ALL Christians) . . . will you please tell me how ALL THE MEMBERS would KNOW about all the other Christians on earth suffering . . . or being honored???

I'm telling you . . . the Catholic church has done a real SNOW-JOB on a lot of Baptists . . . and what it didn't accomplish, the ex-Catholic monk who never got the Catholicism out of his system did accomplish. Good ol' Martin Luther! Universal church? Invisible body? HOGWASH!

Paul said God had set apostles, prophets, and teachers in the CHURCH. Were the apostles universal and invisible? Of course not. Were the prophets universal and invisible? Of course not. Were the teachers universal and invisible? Only an idiot would answer in the affirmative. Of course they weren't . . . NEITHER IS THE CHURCH! So, of course, NEITHER IS THE BODY!!!

In Ephesians 4:11-12, Paul says the Lord gave evangelists and pastors for the edifying of the BODY OF CHRIST. Are the evangelists universal and invisible? I'll guarantee you I'M NOT! Are

CAN I TRUST MY BIBLE'S TRANSLATION?

the pastors universal and invisible? Hmm? Hardly. THE BODY OF CHRIST IS NOT UNIVERSAL AND INVISIBLE EITHER! I hope you pastors and evangelists who believe in an INVISIBLE church GET THAT KIND OF PAYCHECK!!!

Till the day I leave this world, I will fight, kick, scratch and claw at the Alexandrians who say I Corinthians 12:13 is translated WRONG in the King James Bible. God has it translated EXACTLY as He wants it, but let us KEEP IT IN ITS CONTEXT and understand it EXACTLY as He wants us to understand it. *"By one Spirit are we all baptized into one body"* is the obedient child of God following the leadership of the Holy Spirit in being baptized with water into a local New Testament Baptist church, which is the BODY OF CHRIST. There is nothing universal or invisible about it.

I said let us KEEP IT IN ITS CONTEXT. I want to show you what I mean. To say that the "body" in I Corinthians 12:13 is invisible and universal is to say that the Holy Spirit PULLED A TRICK ON US. The Greek word *soma* is translated "body" in the book of I Corinthians forty-five times. When it is used in I Corinthians 12:13, it could not be closer to the MIDDLE of the forty-five. It is number twenty-two. Keep in mind what I said about keeping "body" in that verse IN ITS CONTEXT.

Every Greek lexicon I can find gives a similar definition of *soma*. It is as follows:

SOMA: 1. The body of both men and animals
2. The corpse of both men and animals
3. The bodies of plants
4. Heavenly bodies (stars, etc.)
5. A large or small number of men closely united into one society
6. An object, a person, or thing having a bodily

CAN I TRUST MY BIBLE?

form which casts a shadow

Notice definition #6 . . . an object, person, or thing having a bodily form WHICH CASTS A SHADOW!!! Whooee! There goes the INVISIBLE body! An invisible body CANNOT CAST A SHADOW!!!

Let's examine the twenty-one "bodies" which come BEFORE I Corinthians 12:13, then examine the twenty-three "bodies" that FOLLOW. Do they all cast a SHADOW?

1. 5:3 . . . *"absent in BODY but present in spirit."* The human body most certainly casts a shadow.

2. 6:13 . . . *"the BODY is not for fornication."* The human body casts a shadow.

3. 6:13 . . . *"the Lord for the BODY."* The human body casts a shadow.

4. 6:15 . . . *"your BODIES are the members of Christ."* The human body casts a shadow.

5. 6:16 . . . *"he which is joined to an harlot is one BODY."* The human body casts a shadow.

6. 6:18 . . . *"Every sin that a man doeth is without the BODY."* The human body casts a shadow.

7. 6:18 . . . *"he that committeth fornication sinneth against his own BODY."* The human body casts a shadow.

8. 6:19 . . . *"your BODY is the temple of the Holy Ghost."* The human body casts a shadow.

9. 6:20 . . . *"glorify God in your body."* The human body casts a shadow.

10. 7:4 . . . *"power of her own BODY."* The wife's body casts a shadow.

11. 7:4 . . . *"power of his own BODY."* The husband's body

casts a shadow.

    12. 7:34 . . . *"that she may be holy both in BODY and spirit."* A woman's body casts a shadow.

    13. 9:27 . . . *"I keep under my BODY."* Paul's body cast a shadow.

    14. 10:16 . . . *"The cup of blessing which we bless, is it not the communion of the blood Christ? The bread which we break, is it not the communion of the BODY of Christ?"* Our Lord's BLOOD cast a shadow . . . and so did His BODY that was nailed to the cross.

    15. 10:17 . . . *"We being many are one bread, and one BODY."* Each New Testament church is the BODY of Christ (I Cor. 12:27). A loaf of bread casts a shadow, and so does the congregation of a New Testament church.

    16. 11:24 . . . *"the Lord Jesus . . . took bread: And when he had given thanks, he brake it, and said, Take, eat: this is my BODY, which is broken for you."* The bread in His hand cast a shadow, and so did His body that was broken on the cross.

    17. 11:27 . . . *"guilty of the BODY and blood of the Lord."* The BLOOD He shed at Calvary cast a shadow, and so did the BODY that hung on the tree.

    18. 11:29 . . . *"not discerning the Lord's BODY."* The Lord's body that was crucified and broken cast a shadow.

    19. 12:12 . . . *"the BODY is one, and hath many members."* The human body casts a shadow.

    20. 12:12 . . . *"all the members of that one BODY."* The human body casts a shadow.

    21. 12:12 . . . *"being many, are one BODY."* The human body casts a shadow.

CAN I TRUST MY BIBLE?

22. 12:13 . . . *"all baptized into one BODY."* Does this "BODY" cast a shadow? Think on it while we continue . . .

23. 12:14 . . . *"the BODY is not one member, but many."* The human body casts a shadow.

24. 12:15 . . . *"If the foot shall say, Because I am not the hand, I am not of the BODY."* The human body's hands and feet cast a shadow.

25. 12:15 . . . *"is it therefore not of the BODY?"* The human body casts a shadow.

26. 12:16 . . . *"And if the ear shall say, Because I am not the eye, I am not of the BODY."* Eyeballs and ears cast a shadow, and so does the human body.

27. 12:16 . . . *"is it therefore not of the BODY?"* The human body casts a shadow.

28. 12:17 . . . *"If the whole BODY were an eye."* The human body casts a shadow.

29. 12:18 . . . *"But now hath God set the members every one of them in the BODY."* When the Lord added to the church daily in Jerusalem (Acts 2:41,47), those new members cast a shadow . . . as do ALL church members. The human body casts a shadow . . . whether it is alone or in a congregation. Even the COLLECTIVE bodies of the congregation cast a shadow.

30. 12:19 . . . *"where were the BODY?"* The human body casts a shadow.

31. 12:20 . . . *"they are many members, yet but one BODY."* The human body casts a shadow.

32. 12:22 . . . *"members of the BODY."* The human body casts a shadow.

33. 12:23 . . . *"those members of the BODY."* The human body casts a shadow.

CAN I TRUST MY BIBLE'S TRANSLATION?

34. 12:24 . . . *"For our comely parts have no need: but God hath tempered the BODY together."* The human body casts a shadow.

35. 12:25 . . . *"That there should be no schism in the BODY; but that the members should have the same care one for another."* Church members cast a shadow. If they can care for one another, they can SEE one another. Anybody you can SEE casts a shadow.

36. 12:27 . . . *"Now ye are the BODY of Christ, and members in particular."* The members of the church in Corinth cast a shadow . . . as do the members of ANY New Testament church.

37. 13:3 . . . *"though I give my BODY to be burned."* Paul's body casts a shadow.

38. 15:35 . . . *"How are the dead raised up? and with what BODY do they come?"* Jesus' resurrected body casts a shadow, and so will ours. The human body casts a shadow.

39. 15:37 . . . *"And that which thou sowest, thou sowest not that BODY which shall be, but bare grain, it may chance of wheat, or of some other grain."* The body of a grain of wheat casts a shadow.

40. 15:38 . . . *"God giveth it a BODY as it has pleased him."* The body of a grain of wheat casts a shadow.

41. 15:38 . . . *"and to every seed his own BODY."* The body of a seed casts a shadow.

42. 15:40 . . . *"There are also celestial BODIES."* Those bodies that ride through the heavens above all cast shadows. They are solid and can be SEEN.

43. 15:40 . . . *"BODIES terrestrial."* Anything terrestrial belongs on the earth (Latin: *terra*) and casts a shadow. The earth casts a shadow, and so does every body on it.

44. 15:44 . . . *"It is sown a natural BODY."* When a human body dies, becoming a corpse, it still casts a shadow . . . even as it is

being placed in a coffin for burial.

45. 15:44 . . . *"it is raised a spiritual BODY."* When Jesus was raised from the grave, He had a spiritual body, but it was solid even though it passed through walls, for He could be touched and embraced (John 20:17, 19, 27; Matt. 28:9). His spiritual body cast a shadow, as will ours (Philippians 3:21).

Note: In actuality, the word *soma* is found forty-seven times in I Corinthians. I Corinthians 15:44 has it FOUR times, though I showed only two. The reason for this is that "natural body" and "spiritual body" are each used twice, the second for each being an exact repeat.

Now let us look once more at the definition of *soma* in the lexicons.

SOMA: 1. The body of both men and animals

2. The corpse of both men and animals

3. The bodies of plants

4. Heavenly bodies (stars, etc.)

5. A large or small number of men closely united into one society

6. An object, person, or thing having bodily form which casts a shadow

Numbers one through five all are a description of number six. They all have bodily form, and they all cast a shadow. Therefore . . . when the Holy Spirit uses *soma*, He is speaking of an object, person or thing that has a BODILY FORM WHICH CASTS A SHADOW.

Remember what I said about keeping I Corinthians 12:13 IN ITS CONTEXT? Think about it. TWENTY-ONE times *before* the Holy Spirit used *soma* in I Corinthians 12:13, He used it to depict something that had BODILY FORM and would CAST A SHADOW . . . something that was SOLID that you could see. TWENTY-

CAN I TRUST MY BIBLE'S TRANSLATION?

THREE times *after* the Holy Spirit used *soma* in I Corinthians 12:13, He used it to depict something that had BODILY FORM and would CAST A SHADOW . . . something that was SOLID that you could SEE.

Has the Holy Spirit TRICKED us in I Corinthians 12:13? Did He go right into the MIDDLE of all these BODIES and throw us a curve by making the BODY in I Corinthians 12:13 something that does NOT have BODILY FORM . . . something that does NOT CAST A SHADOW . . . something that is NOT SOLID . . . something that you CANNOT SEE? To believe that the BODY in I Corinthians 12:13 is INVISIBLE, MYSTICAL, and UNIVERSAL is to go against every established rule of rightly dividing the Word of God!

FORTY-FIVE times in I Corinthians the Holy Spirit guided Paul to use the word *soma*. FORTY-FIVE times the Holy Spirit used a word that can ONLY mean that which has BODILY FORM, casts a SHADOW, is SOLID, and can be SEEN with the physical eye. It falls under definitions #5 and #6. The BODY in I Corinthians 12:13 is the LOCAL, VISIBLE, New Testament church. It is "a large or small number of men closely united into one society." It is "a thing having bodily form which casts a shadow."

When Paul wrote, *"By one Spirit are we all baptized into one body,"* he was speaking of WATER baptism into the BODY of Christ which is the LOCAL, VISIBLE, body of believers which make up a New Testament church.

Therefore, I say to Mr. J.H. Melton and all who would declare that I Corinthians 12:13 in the King James Bible is "an inexcusable translation responsible for the heretical universal church and Holy Spirit baptism teachings" . . . YOU ARE DEAD WRONG! Just because a great number of Catholic-brain-washed-Protestants have WRONGLY divided the Word of Truth in I Corinthians 12:13 (as they have many other passages) DOES NOT MEAN THE VERSE

CAN I TRUST MY BIBLE?

IS TRANSLATED INCORRECTLY!!! The AV1611 King James Bible is the perfect, infallible, inerrant, inspired, uncorrectable, incorruptible WORD OF GOD!!!

Let us move on to the fifth "error" Mr. Melton wants us to see in the translating of the King James Bible.

5. "Another error or mistranslation [take your choice]. In Acts 1 2:4, the Greek word translated 'passover' elsewhere in the New Testament is mistranslated 'Easter'."

Mr. Melton once again displays his lack of Bible study. He is not alone. I have had this same accusation thrown in my face by many an Alexandrian. They love to give me a crooked grin and point to the word "Easter" in Acts 12:4 and say, "Well, King James nut. There is a BIG error! The King James translators really boo-booed here! Any Greek scholar knows that *pasha* is ALWAYS translated 'passover'!"

Mm-hmm. ANY Greek scholar knows that, eh? Well twinkies, the truth is that if YOU GREAT GREEK SCHOLARS were as smart as you think you are, you would know that if the King James translators HAD translated the Greek word *pascha* as 'passover' in Acts 12:4, it would be WRONG! If you twinkies would spend less time bragging about your great educational qualifications and MORE TIME studying the inerrant, inspired, infallible King James Bible, you wouldn't stick your big feet in your mouths so often!

Let's look at the passage in question. You will see that arriving at the truth of this "Easter" business is all a matter of TIMING.

> Now about that time Herod the king stretched forth his hands to vex certain of the church. And he killed James the brother of John with the sword. And because he saw it pleased the Jews, he proceeded further to take Peter also. (Then were the days of unleavened

CAN I TRUST MY BIBLE'S TRANSLATION?

bread.) And when he had apprehended him, he put him in prison, and delivered him to four quaternions of soldiers to keep him; intending after Easter to bring him forth to the people (Acts 12:1-4).

I said that understanding this passage is all a matter of TIMING. The reason Mr. Melton and his Alexandrian buddies can't see the truth here is that they are so eager to prove the AV1611 wrong that they open their mouths when the gears in their brains are not meshing . . . and are out of sync with the Book. I would have my reader to notice two statements in the aforegoing passage.

1. *Then were the DAYS of unleavened bread.*

2. *. . . intending AFTER EASTER to bring him [Peter] forth to the people.*

Any book on ancient mid-eastern history will reveal that Easter has nothing to do with the resurrection of the Lord Jesus Christ, but rather was a pagan holiday *season* LONG before our Lord even came into this world by the virgin birth. For many centuries, the worshippers of the goddess Ishtar held a heathen festival in her honor the last few days of April. Ishtar was the goddess of REPRODUCTION. When spring came to that part of the world in late April, the followers of Ishtar held the festival in celebration of the end of winter when the earth was being regenerated by the power of Ishtar. They attributed the appearance of flowers and green grass, along with the spring rains, to the hand of Ishtar.

In the spring . . . not only was the earth "reproducing" again, but in the forests, mountains, and fields, the animals were giving birth to their young. It was a joyful time of REPRODUCTION. This is why *today* the familiar symbols for Easter are the RABBIT and the EGG. Both are well-known for their outstanding REPRODUCTIVE abilities. Hence we have an "EASTER BUNNY" who lays colored EGGS!

CAN I TRUST MY BIBLE?

The Alexandrians tell us that the Greek word *pascha* should ALWAYS be translated "passover." Not so. *Pascha* is found twenty-nine times in the *Textus Receptus* of the New Testament. The Holy Spirit led His New Testament writers to put down the word *pascha* twenty-eight times, referring to the historic night when the Lord went into Egypt with a great slaughter, thus setting the people of Israel free after four hundred years of bondage (Exodus Chapter 12) . . . but He led Luke to put down the word *pascha* in Acts 12:4, giving it an entirely different meaning. The King James translators picked up on it because the Holy Spirit was guiding them to give us a perfect, infallible, inerrant TRANSLATION in English. (I have already pointed out earlier WHY the English-speaking people HAD to have the perfect of Word of God).

If my reader will read Exodus 12, he will find that God told the people of Israel to kill the passover lamb on the evening of the FOURTEENTH day of the FIRST month of the year. He told them to apply the blood of the lamb on the two side posts and the upper door post of their houses (this made the form of a CROSS!). Then He said,

> *And the blood shall be to you for a token upon the houses where ye are: and when I see the blood, I will PASS OVER you, and the plague shall not be upon you to destroy you, when I smite the land of Egypt* (Ex. 12:13).

Thus, we have the term "PASSOVER." The first month on the Jewish calendar is Abib (April). The Passover is observed, then, by the people of Israel on the 14th of April every year . . . even as it was in King Herod's day. The Passover and its single feast is only ONE day. God did the delivering from Egyptian bondage in ONE day; thus the Passover is ONE day. Following the Passover comes a week of celebration called the "days of unleavened bread." God told the people of Israel AFTER their passover deliverance,

CAN I TRUST MY BIBLE'S TRANSLATION?

Observe the month of Abib, and keep the passover unto the Lord thy God: for in the month of Abib the Lord thy God brought thee forth out Egypt by night. Thou shalt therefore sacrifice the passover unto the Lord thy God, of the flock and the herd, in the place which the Lord shall choose to place his name there. Thou shalt eat no leavened bread with it; SEVEN DAYS shalt thou eat unleavened bread therewith . . . (Deut. 16:1-3).

And in the FOURTEENTH day of the FIRST month is the passover of the Lord. And in the FIFTEENTH day of this month is the feast: SEVEN days shall unleavened bread be eaten (Num. 28:16-17).

In the FOURTEENTH day of the FIRST month at even is the Lord's passover. And on the FIFTEENTH day of the same month is the feast of unleavened bread unto the Lord: SEVEN DAYS ye must eat unleavened bread (Lev. 23:5- 6).

Thus we learn that the Passover feast was ONE day . . . and the "days of unleavened bread" were SEVEN. The "days of unleavened bread" always FOLLOWED the day of the Passover. Scripture makes it clear that the Israelites were faithful in keeping the Passover and the days of unleavened bread.

And the people came up out of Jordan on the tenth day of the FIRST month, and encamped in Gilgal, in the east border of Jericho . . . and kept the passover on the FOURTEENTH day of the month at even in the plains of Jericho. And they did eat of the old corn of the land ON THE MORROW AFTER the passover, unleavened cakes . . . (Joshua 4:19; 5:10-11).

And the children of the captivity kept the passover upon the FOURTEENTH day of the FIRST month . . .

CAN I TRUST MY BIBLE?

> *And kept the feast of unleavened bread SEVEN DAYS with joy* . . . (Ezra 6:19, 22)

We see then, that according to Scripture (even though we don't have the "originals") the Passover is ALWAYS the meal (or feast) eaten on ONE day, the fourteenth of April. The Feast of Unleavened Bread (also known as "days of unleavened bread") FOLLOWS on the fifteenth and lasts for SEVEN DAYS. The Passover DAY is *never* part of the days of unleavened bread. The TIMING of what we read in Acts Chapter 12 gives us the truth about Herod waiting till AFTER *Easter* to bring Peter before the people for execution.

Acts 12:3 makes it clear that Peter was arrested DURING the days of unleavened bread. Of Herod we read, *"And because he saw it pleased the Jews, he proceeded further to take Peter also. (THEN were the days of unleavened bread.)"*

Now WHAT have we learned in Scripture about the TIMING of the Passover and the days of unleavened bread? Remember? The Passover ALWAYS was observed on April 14th. The days of unleavened bread ALWAYS started on the 15th and ran for SEVEN days. Peter, then, was arrested by Herod's magistrates sometime between April 15th and the 21st . . . which were the "days of unleavened bread." The passover HAD ALREADY PASSED!!! Yet we read,

> *And when he [Herod] had apprehended him [Peter], he put him in prison, and delivered him to four quaternions of soldiers to keep him; intending AFTER EASTER to bring him forth to the people* (Acts 12:4).

Herod was a heathen Roman. He worshipped the goddess Ishtar which is "Easter" in English. The pagan festival, honoring Ishtar, always took place the last few days of April. EASTER, then, was only a few days away! When Herod referred to "EASTER,"

CAN I TRUST MY BIBLE'S TRANSLATION?

he had no reference WHATSOEVER to the Passover! Easter was a SEASON of several days. The Passover was ONE day. Herod's plan was to execute Peter AFTER the heathen holiday, known as "Easter," was over. Again, I say, Herod's use of the word "Easter" HAD NOTHING TO DO WITH THE PASSOVER! Hence, the King James translators were RIGHT ON TARGET when they translated *pascha* "Easter" in Acts 12:4!!!!!!!!!!!!!!!!!!!!!!

HALLELUJAH! Ring the bells for the God of the King James Bible, and play a dirge for the Alexandrians and their puny little god who can't seem to producer an inerrant, infallible, inspired TRANSLATION!!!

CAN I TRUST MY BIBLE'S TRANSLATION? If you have an AV1611 King James Bible you can! You sure can't trust an ALEXANDRIAN "bible"! Look what the NIV says:

> It was about this time that King Herod arrested some who belonged to the church, intending to persecute them. He had James, the brother of John, put to death with the sword. When he saw that this pleased the Jews, he proceeded to seize Peter also. This happened during the Feast of Unleavened Bread. After arresting him, he put him in prison, handing him over to be guarded by four squads of four soldiers each. Herod intended to bring him out for public trial after the PASSOVER (Acts 12:1-4).

One can readily see that the NIV translators have the Passover coming AFTER the SEVEN-DAY feast of unleavened bread! THIS IS A LIE! It is easy to see that the Holy Spirit had NOTHING TO DO WITH THE TRANSLATING OF THE NEW INTERNATIONAL PERVERSION!!!

How about the NKJV? Look at it.

Now about that time Herod the king stretched out

his hand to harass some from the church. Then he killed James the brother of John with the sword. And because he saw that it pleased the Jews, he proceeded further to seize Peter also. Now it was during the Days of Unleavened Bread. So when he had apprehended him, he put him in prison, and delivered him to four squads of soldiers to keep him, intending to bring him before the people after PASSOVER (Acts 12:1-4).

Hmpf! If the translators of the "New" King James version did their translating from the *Textus Receptus* (as they tell us), HOW COME THEY KEEP COMING UP WITH *ALEXANDRIAN* WORDS??? Falwell's boys have made the SAME MISTAKE that the NIV boys did. They have the Passover coming AFTER the days of unleavened bread. THIS IS IN DIRECT OPPOSITION TO WHAT THE WORD OF GOD TELLS US! The SEVEN days of unleavened bread ALWAYS come AFTER the ONE DAY of Passover, as we have seen in the REAL Word of God!

Since the HOLY Spirit had nothing to do with the translation of the "NEW" King James perversion, WHAT spirit did?

The King James Bible is the ONLY one on the bookshelves today that DOES translate *pascha* "Easter" in Acts 12:4. All the rest of them translate it "Passover." Tch. Tch. I'd say it's mighty poor translating when such sloppy work VIOLATES the Scripture. As I've said all along . . . God has only ONE Bible in ANY language. In English, it is the AV1611 King James Bible! You can trust EVERY ONE of its 810,697 words!

Ah, but along come the pesky Alexandrians. They say, "Oh, yeah? How about the *italicized* words? They weren't in the ORIGINALS!"

Well, let me say this about that. Anybody who knows anything at all about translating from one language to another is aware that there ALWAYS has to be words interpolated to make

CAN I TRUST MY BIBLE'S TRANSLATION?

the sentence structure flow freely and to cause it to make sense in the new language that is getting the material. The thing I appreciate about the King James translators is that when they interpolated words, they were honest about it and put them in *italics*. This is not so with the perversions. A few of them have done it SOME of the time, but not honestly and consistently.

Actually, I think we ought to adopt the same approach to the italicized words that the Author of the Bible does. Jesus Christ is the Author. He said so over and over again (see Matt. 24:35, John 8:31; 12:47-48, etc.). If we look at the italicized words EXACTLY as He does, we can't go wrong. Take your AV1611 Bible and turn to Deuteronomy 8:3. You will note that there is only ONE word in the verse that is in italics . . ."word." See it? You know what the italics mean. The word "word" was NOT in the ORIGINALS.

Now turn in your AV1611 King James Bible to Matthew chapter 4 and look at verse 4. Here, Jesus is quoting a portion of Deuteronomy 8:3 to the devil. Please notice that the word "word" is NOT IN ITALICS. That simply means that the word "word" IS in the text of the *Textus Receptus!* Jesus actually *said* the word "WORD"!

When Moses was writing Deuteronomy under the inspiration of the Holy Spirit, it looked like this: ". . . man doth not live by bread only, but by every that proceedeth out of the mouth of the Lord doth man live." To an English-speaking person it does not make sense. Ah, but Moses did not write it in English. He wrote it in Hebrew, and it DID make sense to a Hebrew-speaking person. He would know exactly what Moses was saying.

When the King James translators came to Deuteronomy 8:3, they were led by the Holy Spirit to translate it: " . . . man doth not live by bread only, but by every *word* that proceedeth out of the mouth of the Lord doth man live." In order for it make sense in English, the word "word" had to be inserted.

However, when Jesus quoted this portion of Deuteronomy 8:3

CAN I TRUST MY BIBLE?

to the devil, HE INCLUDED THE ITALICIZED WORD, showing that he APPROVED of the way the King James translators would insert the word "word" in italics when they translated Deuteronomy 8:3? Of course! He is God! The Holy Spirit (who is also God!) would lead the King James translators to put in the word "word" and italicize it.

So . . . as I said, if WE look at the italicized words EXACTLY as Jesus does, we can't go wrong!

My reader will remember the exciting story of young David killing the massive Philistine, Goliath the Gittite. The Bible tells how David brought the big dude down with a stone from his sling, then . . .

David ran, and stood upon the Philistine, and took his sword, and drew it out of the sheath thereof, and SLEW HIM, and cut of his head therewith (I Sam. 17:51).

New dear reader, let me ask you . . . WHO killed Goliath the Gittite? You say, "David did!"

Correct! Now let me show you something about italics in the King James Bible by letting you read something from the New International perversion. "In another battle with the Philistines at Gob, Elhanan, son of Jaare-Oregim the Bethlehemite killed Goliath the Gittite, who had a spear with a shaft like a weaver's rod" (II Sam. 21:19).

How do you like that? The NIV says ELHANAN killed Goliath the Gittite! Yet in I Samuel 17:51, the NIV says, "David ran and stood over him. He took hold of the Philistine's sword and drew it from the scabbard. After he killed him, he cut of his head with the sword."

This Alexandrian "bible" has a glaring CONTRADICTION! First, it says DAVID killed Goliath, then it says ELHANAN killed

CAN I TRUST MY BIBLE'S TRANSLATION?

Goliath. One can easily conclude then that the Holy Spirit had nothing to do with translating the NIV.

We have already seen in I Samuel 17:51 in the REAL Bible that DAVID killed Goliath the Gittite. Now watch really close as we look at II Samuel 21:19 in the REAL Bible. It says, "And there was again a battle in Gob with the Philistines, where Elhanan the son of Jaare-Oregim, a Bethlehemite, slew *the brother of* Goliath the Gittite, the staff of whose spear *was* like a weaver's beam." Did you pick up on the *italics?* The REAL Bible tells us by interpolated words that Elhanan killed the BROTHER of Goliath the Gittite. The Alexandrian NIV translators have made a CONTRADICTION by saying in one passage that DAVID killed Goliath, then in another passage, saying ELHANAN killed Goliath.

The KING JAMES translators, however, were being led by the Holy Spirit when they translated and CORRECTLY put in *italics* that Elhanan killed *THE BROTHER OF* Goliath. This ties with Scripture, for we read,

> *And there was war again with the Philistines; and Elhanan the son of Jair slew Lahmi the brother of Goliath the Gittite, whose spear staff was like a weaver's beam* (I Chron. 20:5).

Looks to me like the Almighty God has EVERY WORD exactly as He wants it in the King James Bible . . . all 810,697 of them . . . INCLUDING the *italicized* ones! Better leave them alone. The italicized words in God's ENGLISH Bible are HIS words!!! Jesus Christ solemnly warned,

> *For I testify unto every man that heareth the WORDS of the prophecy of THIS BOOK, If any man shall ADD unto these things, God shall ADD unto him the plagues that are written in THIS BOOK: And if any man shall TAKE AWAY FROM THE WORDS of the book of this prophecy, God shall TAKE AWAY his*

CAN I TRUST MY BIBLE?

part out of the book of life, and out of the holy city, and from the things which are written in THIS BOOK (Rev. 22:18-19).

Of course the Alexandrians have no fear in ADDING TO or TAKING AWAY FROM the King James Bible because they do not believe it is the Word of God. They think that the warning here applies only to the ORIGINAL AUTOGRAPHS. There are two things DEAD WRONG about this thinking.

1. Since the "original autographs" were doomed to extinction, WHAT DIFFERENCE WOULD IT MAKE IF SOME ALEXANDRIAN ADDED TO OR TOOK AWAY FROM THEIR WORDS?

2. If Jesus was speaking ONLY of the "original autographs" ...WHY SOUND THE WARNING AT ALL? The Alexandrians tell us that the first time a COPY was made of the "original parchments" there were errors of ADDING and SUBTRACTING words anyway. If this were so, certainly Jesus knew it. WHY WASTE HIS BREATH WITH SUCH A SOLEMN WARNING?

The answer to these questions is quite clear. Jesus Christ is no fool, even though the Alexandrians think He is. He well knew that the warning must be sounded because PERFECT COPIES would be produced down through the centuries by the overseeing eye of the Holy Spirit...and PERFECT TRANSLATIONS would be produced in the same way. Therefore, wicked men must be warned to KEEP THEIR DIRTY HANDS OFF HIS WORD till the day all of the Book's enemies have been made His footstool!

Dear reader . . . I sincerely want you to know that you CAN trust your King James Bible's TRANSLATION. Before I close off this chapter on the subject, I want to show you one more precious truth.

The word "translate" in ANY form is only found FIVE times

CAN I TRUST MY BIBLE'S TRANSLATION?

in the Word of God. Three of them are in ONE verse . . . so actually the word is only found in THREE passages. Let's take them in the order they appear in the Book.

The Lord hath sworn to David . . . To TRANSLATE the kingdom from the house of Saul, and to set up the throne of David . . . (II Sam. 3:9-10).

Please notice that GOD is going to TRANSLATE the kingdom from Saul to David. GOD will do the translating. Got that?

Now let's watch the translation:

So Saul died for his transgression which he committed against the Lord, even against the word of the Lord, which he kept not, and also for asking counsel of one that had a familiar spirit, to enquire of it; And enquired not of the Lord: therefore he slew him, and TURNED THE KINGDOM UNTO DAVID the son of Jesse. Therefore came all the elders of Israel to the king to Hebron; and David made a covenant with them in Hebron before the Lord; and THEY anointed David king over Israel, according to the word of the Lord BY SAMUEL (I Chron. 10:13-14; 11:3).

Study it carefully. God said HE would translate the kingdom from Saul to David. When it came to anointing David as King (which would be the moment the kingdom was TRANSLATED to him), THEY (the elders of Israel) presided over the anointing, but it was SAMUEL who actually poured the anointing oil on David to make him king.

You will note that all of this was "according to the word of the Lord." Now, let's put it all together . . . God said HE would translate the kingdom from Saul to David. It was GOD who slew Saul and "turned" the kingdom unto David; so we learn that GOD did the translating; but when He did it, He used HUMAN

CAN I TRUST MY BIBLE?

INSTRUMENTALITY! It is important that you see that.

QUESTION: Did God do a good job of translating even though He used human instrumentality? Well, let's see . . .

The angel Gabriel was dispatched from the very Throne of God in Heaven to bring a message to Mary of Nazareth.

> *And the angel said unto her, Fear not, Mary: for thou hast found favour with God. And, behold, thou shalt conceive in thy womb, and bring forth a son, and shalt call his name JESUS. He shall be great, and shall be called the Son of the Highest: AND THE LORD GOD SHALL GIVE UNTO HIM THE THRONE OF HIS FATHER DAVID: And he shall reign over the house of Jacob FOR EVER; and of his kingdom THERE SHALL BE NO END* (Luke 1:30-33).

Is the Lord Jesus Christ PERFECT? Does He have any flaws? Does HE make mistakes? Of course He is PERFECT! Being perfect, He has NO flaws! Being perfect, He makes NO mistakes. How could He be anything BUT perfect? He is GOD! One day He is going to set up His kingdom here on earth. Will He reign PERFECTLY? Of course he will because HE is perfect and because He will REIGN perfectly; His kingdom will be PERFECT.

Whose throne will Jesus sit on as He rules His earthly kingdom? We just read that He will reign on the throne of His father (ancestor) DAVID. Isn't that something? When the Lord Jesus is given David's throne, David's kingdom IS STILL IN EXISTENCE! Wouldn't you say that God must have done a pretty good job in TRANSLATING the kingdom from Saul to David . . . since David's kingdom is still intact after three thousand years? God made David this promise long, long ago. He sent His prophet Nathan to King David with a divine message.

> *And it came to pass that night, that the word Of the*

CAN I TRUST MY BIBLE'S TRANSLATION?

> *Lord came unto Nathan, saying, Go and tell my servant David, Thus saith the Lord . . . when thy days be fulfilled, and thou shalt sleep with thy fathers, I will set up thy seed after thee, which shall proceed out of thy bowels, and I will establish his kingdom. He shall build an house for my name, and I will stablish the throne of his kingdom FOR EVER. And THINE house and THY kingdom shall be established FOR EVER before thee: thy throne shall be established FOR EVER* (II Sam. 7:4-5, 12-13, 16).

A little Bible study will show that the IMMEDIATE seed that would come from David and sit on his throne was his son, Solomon. However, Solomon, like all men, one day would die. The ULTIMATE seed of David to sit on his throne would be a GREATER than Solomon (Matt. 12:42), David's GREATER "Son," the Lord Jesus Christ . . . who would reign on David's throne FOREVER.

> *I have made a covenant with my chosen, I have sworn unto David my servant, Thy seed will I establish FOR EVER, and build up thy throne to ALL generations* (Psalm 89:3-4).

Thus we read of the Lord Jesus Christ:

> *He shall be great, and shalt be called the Son of the Highest: and the Lord God shall give unto him the throne of his father David: And he shall reign over the house of Jacob FOR EVER; and of his kingdom there shall be NO END* (Luke 1:32-33).

We then learn three important facts about TRANSLATION:

1. GOD does the translating.

2. He uses HUMAN INSTRUMENTALITY.

3. The translation done by God through human instrumentality is PERFECT AND LASTS FOREVER.

CAN I TRUST MY BIBLE?

Let us now go to the second passage where we find the word "translate" in any form in the Word of God.

Giving thanks unto the Father, which hath made us meet to be partakers of the inheritance of the saints in light: Who hath delivered us from the power of darkness, and hath TRANSLATED us into the kingdom of his dear Son: In whom we have redemption through his blood, even the forgiveness of sins: (Col. 1:12-14).

You will notice immediately that it is GOD who does the translating. Does He use HUMAN INSTRUMENTALITY to get people translated into the kingdom of His dear Son? Hmm? Does He use HUMAN INSTRUMENTALITY to get the saving Gospel (Romans 1:16) to the ears of lost people who are held in the power of darkness? Let Scripture answer for us.

For whosoever shall call upon the name of the Lord shall be saved. How then shall they call on him in whom they have not believed? and how shall they believe in him of whom they have not heard? and how shall they hear without a PREACHER? (Rom. 10:13-14).

A "preacher" is human; thus we learn that God uses human instrumentality to get the Gospel to the ears of the lost. God has no other means than HUMAN BEINGS to take the Gospel to a Hell-bound world.

Does God's use of human beings as instruments through which He TRANSLATES those in the power of darkness into the kingdom of His dear Son make the translating imperfect? No! When the Lord redeems us, He does so with the PERFECT blood of His PERFECT Son and gives us PERFECT salvation! HALLELUJAH!!!

This salvation that God gives . . . how long will it last? The

CAN I TRUST MY BIBLE'S TRANSLATION?

"work-your-way-to-Heaven" crowd (Pentecostals, Campbellites, Nazarenes, Seventh Day Adventists, the "holiness" groups, and all others of like ilk) says it will last until you "slip" and lose it. Well, THEY are on probation, but I'M not! I have SALVATION! I have ETERNAL LIFE (I John 5:11-13, John 3:15, Heb. 5:9, etc.). It lasts FOREVER!

We see that the same thing holds true, again, about TRANSLATION.

1. GOD does the translating.
2. He uses HUMAN INSTRUMENTALITY.
3. The translating done by God through human instrumentality is PERFECT AND LASTS FOREVER.

Let us hasten on to the third and final passage where we find the word "translate" in any form in the Word of God.

By faith Enoch was TRANSLATED that he should not see death; and was not found, because God had TRANSLATED him: for before his TRANSLATION he had this testimony, that he pleased God (Heb. 11:5).

You will notice first of all that it says GOD had translated Enoch. Did He use HUMAN INSTRUMENTALITY? Look really close. WHY did Enoch get translated to Heaven? . . . because HE pleased God! IF Enoch had not pleased God, he would NOT have been translated! Hence, we see HUMAN INSTRUMENTALITY in the translation.

Was Enoch's translation PERFECT? Of course. What GOD does, He does PERFECTLY. I seriously doubt that Enoch bumped his head on a star on the way up. His trip was a perfectly smooth one.

How long will Enoch's translation last? Well, it has ALREADY lasted over five thousand years. Do you suppose it will

CAN I TRUST MY BIBLE?

last another five thousand? No question about it. Enoch is a saved man . . . it will last FOREVER!

Once again, we see that the same thing holds true about translation:

    1. GOD does the translating.

    2. He uses HUMAN INSTRUMENTALITY.

    3. The translating done by God through human instrumentality is PERFECT AND LASTS FOREVER.

These same things hold true with the Word of God! If GOD doesn't do the translating, THERE WILL NEVER BE A PERFECT TRANSLATION! Therefore, no one on earth can be saved because it takes the PERFECT, incorruptible Word of God to get us saved (Psalm 19:7; I Pet. 1:23)! However . . . since the Lord Jesus Christ came into the world to save ALL men of ALL centuries (John 12:47; I Tim. 4:10; Heb. 2:9; I John 2:2, etc.), there would HAVE to be TRANSLATIONS of His perfect, incorruptible Word.

In His wisdom, the Lord has chosen to use HUMAN INSTRUMENTALITY to get the translating done. Even though He uses HUMAN BEINGS to do the translating, it will be like He did it when He gave the Word of God to be written in the FIRST place. It will be PERFECT and last FOREVER! If it is the Word of God, it IS perfect . . . and if it is the Word of God, it will last FOREVER! (Psalm 12:6-7; Psalm 19:79; I Pet. 1:23-25).

Thus we see that what holds true about the translating is true when the Bible is TRANSLATED!

    1. GOD does the translating.

    2. He uses HUMAN INSTRUMENTALITY.

    3. The translating done by God through human instrumentality is PERFECT AND LASTS FOREVER!

You ask me, "CAN I TRUST MY BIBLE'S TRANSLATION?

CAN I TRUST MY BIBLE'S TRANSLATION?

Absolutely. . . if you have a good old fashioned, devil-kicking, sin condemning, Christ-exalting, soul-saving, life-changing, perfect, infallible, inerrant, inspired, uncorrectable, incorruptible, double-edged, quick and powerful AV1611 KING JAMES BIBLE!!!

CAN I TRUST MY BIBLE?

IV

CAN I TRUST MY BIBLE'S INSPIRATION?

The Alexandrians tell us that ONLY the "original manuscripts" were inspired. On page 3 of letter #1 in his "Public Forum," J.H. Melton says, "The King James version is the most beautiful and one of the best translations we have—But is NOT inerrant, infallible or INSPIRED." On page 2 of letter #2, he says, "THERE NEVER HAS BEEN, THERE IS NOT NOW, THERE NEVER WILL BE BUT ONE INERRANT, INFALLIBLE, VERBALLY *INSPIRED* WRITING—THE ORIGINAL MANUSCRIPTS OF THE SIXTY-SIX BOOKS COMPRISING THE ONE BOOK, THE BIBLE, THE WORD OF GOD!"

On page 1 of letter #1, Melton says, "To claim the KJV does not have any errors or mistranslations is to claim for it verbal, plenary INSPIRATION."

That is EXACTLY what I claim!

Let's go to the dictionary to learn what "verbal" and "plenary" mean.

verbal: of, in or by means of words

plenary: full; complete

Is not the King James Bible totally made up of WORDS? Then it is VERBAL. We have already seen that the TRANSLATION of the King James Bible was OVERSEEN by the Holy Spirit. Since

CAN I TRUST MY BIBLE?

the King James Bible IS the very Word of God in English, it has EVERY WORD God wants us to have (Matt. 4:4). Therefore, it is FULL of His words and totally COMPLETE, so it is PLENARY. Mr. Melton and his Alexandrian *compadres* now have TWO strikes against them already.

What about strike THREE? What about *inspiration?* The dictionary has five definitions of "inspire." Since only ONE is linked to Scripture, we will not bother to list the others. The third definition is as follows:

inspire: to motivate by divine influence

Since the prophets and the apostles who wrote the Bible were motivated by divine influence as they wrote the "originals," they were INSPIRED. When the apostle John was motivated by the Holy Spirit to write the last word of Revelation, that was the end of men being divinely motivated to write God's Word. BUT! Did God stop motivating His WORD by divine influence when He finished giving the sixty-six books of Scripture? If He DID, when the original parchments faded, crumbled, and went back to the dust, the LIFE went, too.

The root of the English word "inspiration" has in it the idea of LIFE. Notice the letters "S-P-I-R." These are the same letters found in the English word "S-P-I-R-i-t," which is the Greek word *pneuma,* meaning "LIFE," "breath," "wind," or "SPIRIT." If you do not have *breath* or *wind* in your lungs, you are DEAD. If you do not have *life* in your body, you are DEAD.

The Alexandrians make a big to-do about the word "inspiration" meaning GOD-BREATHED. They insist that God BREATHED the words of the ORIGINALS as He "moved" (II Peter 1:21) the holy men to produce Scripture, and I wholeheartedly agree. However, according to the Alexandrians, the "inspiration" stopped when the ORIGINALS disintegrated. Mr. Melton and all of those like him insist that the ONLY inspired writings were the

CAN I TRUST MY BIBLE'S INSPIRATION?

ORIGINALS.

But this foolish idea won't hold Scriptural water! GOD says,

> *The grass withereth, the flower fadeth: but the word of our God shall stand FOR EVER* (Isa. 40:8).

What about THAT, Alexandrians? The Word of our God shall stand FOREVER! The papyrus withereth, the parchment fadeth, but the Word of our God standeth FOREVER!!! God did NOT inspire the fibers of the material upon which the Scriptures were originally written, nor did He inspire the INK! He inspired the WORDS . . . and the Word (comprised of WORDS) of our God shall stand FOREVER!!!

Look what else God said about His Word.

> *For the word of God is QUICK, and powerful, and sharper than any twoedged sword, PIERCING even to the dividing asunder of soul and spirit, and of the joints and marrow, and is a DISCERNER of the thoughts and intents of the heart* (Heb. 4:12).

The word "quick" has many meanings, but in this verse it means ALIVE even as it does in II Timothy 4:1 where Paul speaks of Christ judging the "quick and the dead." The opposite of DEAD is "QUICK" . . . ALIVE. In Hebrews 4:12, God says His Word is QUICK . . . ALIVE! He does not say the Word of God WAS alive until the original parchments disintegrated . . . He says the Word of God IS alive!! The Holy Spirit is STILL breathing on it!

Notice that Hebrews 4:12 says the powerful Word of God which is ALIVE "pierces" to the dividing asunder of soul and spirit. To "pierce," according to the dictionary, is to "FORCE a way into." By its own power, the Word of God PIERCES or FORCES its way into the soul and spirit of men. Only something that is ALIVE can do that! You will also take note that the Word of God is a "discerner."

CAN I TRUST MY BIBLE?

The dictionary says to discern is to "perceive or recognize clearly." To be able to *perceive, recognize,* or *discern,* you must be able to THINK. Only someone who is alive can think!

The Bible speaks of itself as a LIVING PERSON. Take a good look again at Hebrews 4:12. The subject here is THE WORD OF GOD. Now look at the very next verse.

Neither is there any creature that is not manifest in HIS sight: but all things are naked and opened unto the eyes of HIM with whom we have to do (Heb. 4:13).

A careless glance will cause most people to say, "The 'HIS' and 'HIM' in this verse is GOD." NO! NO! NO! To say so is to violate proper English grammar. It is not GOD who is the subject in the previous verse, it is the WORD of God! The Bible is ALIVE, as a PERSON is alive who can SEE and THINK and PERCEIVE and DISCERN and DEAL with men. If the Word of God lost its inspiration when the "original parchments" fell apart, it would not be alive to LOOK at us and DEAL with us today; but Scripture itself says the Word of God IS quick . . . alive. And it will STILL be alive when it comes time to judge Christ rejecters at the White Throne!

And if any man hear my words, and believe not, I judge him not: for I came not to judge the world, but to save the world. He that rejecteth me, and receiveth not my words, hath one that judgeth him: THE WORD that I have spoken, the same shall JUDGE him in the last day (John 12:47-48).

In order to be able to Judge, you must be able to THINK, DISCERN, and PERCEIVE! The Word of God did not DIE when the "original parchments" crumbled back to the dust! It IS quick! It IS alive! And it will STILL be alive at the White Throne Judgment more than a thousand years from now!!! It WAS inspired, and it IS inspired! It has never stopped being inspired! It is ALIVE!

CAN I TRUST MY BIBLE'S INSPIRATION?

Look at this.

Know ye therefore that they which are of faith, the same are the children of Abraham. And the scripture, FORESEEING that God would justify the heathen through faith, PREACHED before the gospel unto Abraham, saying, In thee shall all nations be blessed (Gal. 3:7-8).

Lookee that! The Scripture FORESEES!!! In order to foresee, you must be ALIVE . . . you must be able to THINK, DISCERN and PERCEIVE. Notice further that the Scripture PREACHES! Only a LIVING PERSON can preach! YES SIR! When the living Word of God pierces down to the dividing asunder of my soul and spirit and deals with me, it PREACHES to me! Don't tell me the only inspired writings were the "originals"! My King James Bible PREACHES to me *today*! If it doesn't preach to you Alexandrians, it's because YOU are dead. . .not the Book!

Here's some more.

For the scripture SAITH unto Pharaoh, Even for this same purpose have I raised thee up, that I might shew my power in thee, and that my name might be declared throughout all the earth (Rom. 9:17).

See there? The Scripture SPEAKS! Ah, but I hear some wise guy Alexandrian hiss, "Lacy, you're crazy! It was GOD who said that to Pharaoh in Exodus 9:16! And what's more, it was GOD who said to Abraham in Genesis 12:3, 'In thee shall all nations be blessed'!"

I'm glad you noticed that, pal. This is where INSPIRATION *really* comes ALIVE! Yes, in the Old Testament, it identifies GOD as speaking in those passages. Yet, in the infallible Word of God, when quoting those passages in the New Testament, it says the SCRIPTURE said it!

CAN I TRUST MY BIBLE?

Get the picture?

Jesus Christ is the Author of the Bible. He is also GOD. More than that, He is called the WORD (John 1:1, 14) . . .the WORD OF LIFE (I John 1:1) . . . and the WORD OF GOD (Rev. 19:13)!!!!! And wonder of wonders, the BIBLE is called the WORD (II Tim. 4:2) . . . the WORD OF LIFE (Phil. 2:16) . . . and the WORD OF GOD (Heb. 4:12)!!!!!

It is the Holy Spirit who INSPIRED the written Word in the first place (II Pet. 1:21). Being the "SPIRIT," He IS the breath of God. And wonder of wonders, He is called the Spirit of CHRIST (Rom. 8:9) . . . the Spirit of LIFE (Rom. 8:2) . . . and the Spirit of GOD (Rom. 8:9) !!!!! It was the Holy Spirit who raised Jesus from the dead (Rom. 8:11), and it is the Holy Spirit who LIVES within us and keeps us ALIVE spiritually FOREVER (John 14:16-17).

QUESTION: Is Jesus STILL alive? Yes . . . and will NEVER die again (Rev. 1:18)! The Holy Spirit did a good job in raising Jesus up, didn't He (I Pet. 3:18)?

QUESTION: Can a SAVED person ever die spiritually? No . . . the Spirit of LIFE keeps us spiritually alive FOREVER (Eph. 1:13- 14)! The Holy Spirit is doing His job, isn't He? And He ALWAYS will!

QUESTION: Is the Word of God STILL alive? YES! Hallelujah! The Spirit of LIFE is STILL breathing on His Word! He is still INSPIRING it!!!!!

The letter killeth, but THE SPIRIT GIVETH LIFE (II Cor. 3:6).

If the Holy Spirit is not STILL breathing on the Word, it will KILL you! If He is not STILL inspiring the Word, it CANNOT GIVE YOU SPIRITUAL LIFE! The Alexandrians are full of baloney. The Word of God is as inspired TODAY as it was when it was FIRST breathed out by the Spirit of LIFE!

CAN I TRUST MY BIBLE'S INSPIRATION?

All scripture IS given by INSPIRATION of God, and IS profitable for doctrine, for reproof, for correction, for instruction in righteousness: That the man of God may be perfect, throughly furnished unto all good works (II Tim. 3:16-17).

You will note that all Scripture IS given by inspiration of God . . . not WAS given by inspiration of God. You will note that all Scripture IS profitable . . . not WAS profitable. Of course, at this point, the superbly educated Alexandrians will cry, "Hey, man! Can't you see that both "ISes" are in *italics*? They weren't in the 'originals'!"

I'm not blind, pal. I can see that. So because you believe that ONLY the "original manuscripts" were inspired, you think those "ISes" should be "WASes." Okay, let's do it YOUR way: "All Scripture WAS given by inspiration of God, and WAS profitable for doctrine, WAS profitable for reproof, WAS profitable for correction, WAS profitable for instruction in righteousness: That the man of God might be perfect and throughly furnished unto all good works WHILE HE HAD THE ORIGINALS!!!"

If that makes sense to you, you're a definite candidate for the funny farm.

One of the Alexandrians' biggest problems is that they think the only inspiration of God was in the TRANSMISSION or the WRITING DOWN of the Scriptures. To them, THAT is the sum and substance of inspiration. On page #1 of Mr. J.H. Melton's "Public Forum," he says "I believe verbal, plenary inspiration ceased with the Book of Revelation in the New Testament. There has not been any divinely inspired writing since nor will there be this side of heaven."

This is pure-dee Alexandrian thinking. I will agree that once the book of Revelation was completed, God is not giving any more Scripture, but to say that verbal, plenary inspiration ceased is to say

CAN I TRUST MY BIBLE?

that once the TRANSMISSION was done, the Holy Spirit QUIT INSPIRING it . . . QUIT BREATHING ON IT!

If that were the case, there has not been SINCE any divinely inspired Word of God to GET US SAVED, nor to profit us by teaching us doctrine, reproving us for our wrongs, correcting us where we need it, nor to instruct us in righteousness! No DEAD BOOK can do anything for us in these matters. Our Bible today is a DEAD BOOK unless the Holy Spirit is STILL inspiring it . . . STILL breathing life into it!!!

I have already shown you what the Lord Jesus thinks of the italics in the King James Bible. The only sensible way to translate II Tim. 3:16 is to interpolate "IS" where the verbs are absent in the Greek of the Received Text . . . not "WAS." The Holy Spirit is STILL motivating His Word by His divine influence! He never QUIT!!!

I remind you that II Timothy 3:16 follows on the heels of II Timothy 3:15, which says, *"And that from a child thou hast known the holy scriptures, which ARE able to make thee wise unto salvation through faith which is in Christ Jesus."* Timothy did NOT have the "originals." No sensible person would think he did. Yet, Paul used the PRESENT TENSE . . . *"the holy scriptures which ARE able to make thee wise."*

The chances that Timothy even had a Hebrew COPY are remote. He probably had an Aramaic TRANSLATION. But either way, he did NOT have the "original parchments." Yet the Scriptures that Timothy had were PROFITABLE unto him to bring him to salvation. This would be impossible unless the Scriptures Timothy had were INSPIRED. If they were not INSPIRED, they were DEAD and totally UNPROFITABLE!

But my reader will note that IMMEDIATELY AFTER Paul said Timothy HAD the holy Scriptures, he said ALL scripture (even that in Timothy's hands) IS given by inspiration of God and IS profitable!

CAN I TRUST MY BIBLE'S INSPIRATION?

The Alexandrians must learn that inspiration goes FAR beyond the initial TRANSMISSION of the Word of God onto parchment. The "originals" did not cease to be inspired . . . did not cease to have the breath of God on them after the initial act of transmission was over! And the Word of God did not cease to be inspired when the "original parchments" disintegrated. The COPIES were ALSO inspired!

"Oh, no!" cry the Alexandrians. "That cannot be! Anyone knows that when copies were made, the scribes were only human. They made errors! The copies COULDN'T have been inspired!"

Well, let me ask you kiddies something . . . What if photocopy machines were in existence in Bible days? What if the prophets and apostles had taken their "original autographs" down to the local copy shop and had them PHOTOCOPIED? The photocopies would be absolutely perfect because they were EXACT duplicates of the "originals." What then? Would the PHOTOCOPIES be inspired?

If you say NO, then I repeat what I have said over and over again . . . you believe that the fiber and ink were inspired, NOT the words! Ridiculous.

The Alexandrians are making a LIAR out of God when they say, as does Melton, "THERE NEVER HAS BEEN, THERE IS NOT NOW, THERE NEVER WILL BE BUT ONE INERRANT, INFALLIBLE VERBALLY *INSPIRED* WRITING—THE ORIGINAL MANUSCRIPTS."

Then God LIED when He said,

The grass withereth, the flower fadeth: but the word of our God shall stand FOR EVER (Isa. 40:8).

God LIED when He said,

The word of God IS quick [alive], and powerful, and sharper than any twoedged sword (Heb. 4:12).

CAN I TRUST MY BIBLE?

God LIED when He said the Philippian church was *"Holding forth the word of LIFE"* (Phil. 2:16)! If the inspiration stopped with the "original manuscripts," the Philippians DID NOT HAVE THE WORD OF LIFE! God LIED! Without the BREATH of the Holy Spirit, there is no LIFE. The SPIRIT giveth LIFE (II Cor 3:6)! Inspiration is the life-giving BREATH of Holy Spirit. If there is no inspired Word of God today . . . NOBODY can get saved . . . not even the Alexandrians!

If Mr. Melton and his cronies are correct in saying the only inspired Word of God were original manuscripts, then Jesus Christ LIED when He said,

> . . . *the word that I have spoken, the same shall judge him in the LAST DAY* (John 12:48).

If the Word of God DIED with the "original parchments," it sure won't be around to judge Christ rejecters over a thousand years from now. Jesus LIED. If the Alexandrians are right, then the Holy Spirit LIED when He told Peter to write . . .

> *Being born again, not of corruptible seed, but of incorruptible, by the word of God, which LIVETH and ABIDETH FOR EVER. For all flesh is as grass, and all the glory of man as the flower of grass. The grass withereth, and the flower thereof falleth away. But the word of the Lord endureth FOR EVER* (I Pet. 1:23-25).

DID the Holy Spirit lie? According to Melton and his Alexandrian pals, He did! The Holy Spirit said the Word of God LIVES FOREVER . . . ABIDES FOR EVER . . . and ENDURES FOREVER. The African theologians say the Word of God DIED with the "original manuscripts." Mr. Melton said there is not NOW an inspired writing. He is calling the triune God a LIAR. The Word of God can only LIVE, ABIDE, and ENDURE forever if God BREATHES LIFE INTO IT!!! That IS inspiration.

CAN I TRUST MY BIBLE'S INSPIRATION?

Anything that God BREATHES life into is alive FOREVER. God BREATHED into Adam's nostrils the breath of LIFE, and Adam became a LIVING soul (Genesis 2:7). That LIVING soul will LIVE and ABIDE and ENDURE forever. The soul of Adam will NEVER go out of existence. God will NEVER have to breathe life into Adam's soul again. It is alive permanently. It is a LIVING soul FOREVER.

God has not had to BREATHE a living soul into every descendant of Adam. He did it ONCE in Adam, and it is passed on in procreation. Every child born into this world is a descendant of Adam. . .and every child born into this world is a LIVING soul that will NEVER cease to exist, whether in Heaven or Hell, FOREVER.

God breathed the breath of life into His words when the prophets SPAKE them (Luke 24:25; II Peter 1:21), and He KEPT ON breathing life into them when they were WRITTEN (II Timothy 3:16) . . . and He KEPT ON breathing life into them when they were COPIED under His watchful eye (Nehemiah 8:1-6) . . . and He KEPT ON breathing life into them when they were TRANSLATED into Aramaic (Luke 4:21; John 5:39) . . . and He KEPT ON breathing life into them when they were TRANSLATED under His watchful eye into Old Syriac, Old Latin, and German . . . and He KEPT ON breathing life into them when they were TRANSLATED into English by the King James translators under His watchful eye (I Peter 1:23-25) . . . and He will KEEP ON breathing life into His words whenever they are honestly TRANSLATED into any language from the proper texts or directly from the AV1611 Bible!!!

I have been accused of believing that God re-inspired the King James Bible as He inspired the "originals." NOT SO! God didn't have to re-inspire His Word in English any more than He had to rebreathe the breath of life into all of Adam's descendants. He breathed the breath of life into the human race ONCE and never has

CAN I TRUST MY BIBLE?

to re-do it. Human beings are STILL living souls and always will be. Likewise ... He breathed the breath of life into His Scripture ONCE and never has to re-do it. The Scripture is STILL as inspired as it ever was! It is Alive and always WILL BE!

God's holy Bible is as perfect in ENGLISH as it was in Hebrew and Greek BECAUSE it is just as inspired! If the King James Bible is the word of God (which I have even heard Alexandrians call it!), then it has no errors in it. If, on the other hand, it is NOT fully the Word of God but only contains PORTIONS of the Word of God, then we expect to find errors in those parts that are not the Word of God.

In regard to the first proposition ... my reader should keep in mind that in spite of all its critics, NO ERROR of any kind has ever been proven within the text of the AV1611 King James Bible. This cannot be said of ANY other English "bible"!

The most popular one of all today is the New International version. Let me Quote from its Preface. On page 2 of the Preface, it says, "There is a sense in which the work of translation is never wholly finished. This applies to all great literature and uniquely so to the Bible. In 1973 the New Testament in the New International Version was published. Since then, suggestions for CORRECTIONS and REVISIONS have been received from various sources. The Committee on Bible Translation carefully considered the suggestions and adopted a number of them."

I have capitalized a couple of words in order to draw your attention to them. Do you see what the NIV's own translation committee says about what they have produced and called a "bible"? The New Testament that they put out in 1973 had ERRORS that needed CORRECTING AND REVISING ... so they took suggestions from advisors and "adopted a number of them." They CORRECTED and REVISED "a number" of the errors. Hmpf! Wouldn't you say by this that they purposely left some of the mistakes? One thing you

CAN I TRUST MY BIBLE'S INSPIRATION?

HAVE to agree on . . . they admit their 1973 new testament had errors. From their own mouths, we hear that CORRECTIONS and REVISIONS were necessary . . . and were MADE.

The NIV people themselves used the words "CORRECTIONS" and "REVISIONS." To be sure we are not misunderstanding these "godly" men, let us consult the dictionary . . .

correct: 1. to make right
2. to mark the errors of
3. to punish or discipline
4. to remove or counteract a defect

revise: 1. to read over carefully and correct, improve, or update
2. to change or amend

Under "correct," numbers one, two, and four apply. Under "revise," both definitions apply. The NIV committee readily admit that their 1973 new testament was WRONG, for it had to be "made right" . . . that it had ERRORS . . . that it had DEFECTS . . . that it needed to be CORRECTED, IMPROVED, and AMENDED. And they had the unmitigated gall to call the thing a NEW TESTAMENT!

In 1978, they came out with all sixty-six books. Look at what they say about their product on page 3 of the Preface: "Like all translations of the Bible, made as they are by imperfect man, this one undoubtedly FALLS SHORT." I take exception to their statement that ALL Bible translations fall short, but you can see the ALEXANDRIANISM dripping all over the place. Let me quote to you from the pages of the NIV.

> The law of the Lord is PERFECT, reviving the soul. The statutes of the Lord are TRUSTWORTHY, making wise the simple. The precepts of the Lord are RIGHT, giving joy to the heart (Psalm 19:7-8).

CAN I TRUST MY BIBLE?

By the statements, we read in the Preface of the NIV that its producers DO NOT BELIEVE IT IS THE PERFECT, TRUSTWORTHY, RIGHT Word of God!!! If THEY don't find it trustworthy, should YOU?

"Wait a minute, Lacy!" I hear someone shout. "I've read the Preface of the King James Bible! The translators never claimed that they were producing the one and only perfect, trustworthy, right Bible in the English language!"

Of course not. They very humbly said they knew they were handling the Word of God and translating it into English, but they did not know what God was doing through their efforts any more than John the Baptist knew that he was the reincarnation of Elijah. In John 1:21, John was asked if he was Elijah. He replied that he was not. Yet, Jesus flat said John WAS Elijah in Matthew 11:7-14 and 17:10- 13!

Did the Baptist LIE? Absolutely not. He didn't KNOW he was Elijah. The King James translators did not know what God was doing through their efforts, but that doesn't change a thing. The translation that they produced IS the PERFECT, INSPIRED, INERRANT Word of God in English! All the other English translations have errors.

So as to the first proposition that I tossed out a little while ago . . . no one has ever proven ONE error in the King James Bible. Now as to the second proposition . . . if the King James Bible is NOT fully the Word of God, but only contains PORTIONS of the Word of God, then we expect to find errors in those parts that are NOT the word of God.

Question: How are we to know WHICH portions are the Word of God and WHICH portions are not? Who is qualified to come forward and draw the line between the divine portions and the human portions? Will the Baptist Alexandrians play Catholic priest and act as interpreters of truth to us poor bewildered souls? Has God left us at the mercy of the great intelligent Alexandrians who stand

CAN I TRUST MY BIBLE'S INSPIRATION?

in their pulpits or their classrooms and "correct" the King James Bible, showing us its "errors" and "spurious passages" so that we will look to THEM for truth?

NO! NO! NO! God did a work in England early in the seventeenth century and gave us HIS Word in our language! Since God could only produce ONE Bible in any language without being the Author of confusion, He did His work at a time chosen by Himself . . . and the perfect, inspired, infallible Word of God was produced in English. Let me put it in the inspired words of Moses.

> *Give ear, O ye heavens, and I will speak; and hear, O earth, the words of my mouth . . . Because I will publish the name of the Lord: ascribe ye greatness unto our God. He is the Rock, HIS WORK IS PERFECT . . .* (Deut. 32:1, 3-4).

Yes . . . God's work is PERFECT! The Alexandrians have a panty-waist little god who couldn't inspire anything but some fibers in papyrus . . . but the great God of Heaven . . . His work is PERFECT! He did not inspire some parchments and ink that would dry up, crumble and disintegrate. He inspired His WORDS, breathed into them the breath of LIFE . . . and they are STILL inspired and STILL alive . . . even in our precious old King James Bible!!! STRIKE THREE! The Africans are out!

> *All scripture is given by inspiration of God, and is profitable for . . . CORRECTION . . .* (II Tim. 3:16).

Question: How could an *incorrect* Book be able to *correct* us? The answer is obvious. It couldn't. Only a perfect Book without error can correct my imperfections and my errors. Unless the Book is inspired, it is not perfect. If we are dealing with an imperfect Book we are in trouble. Where then is perfection to be found? The "originals" are long gone. Even the Masoretic Hebrew and Textus Receptus Greek manuscripts are only COPIES of a long string of copies. If the Almighty God has not done a "work" for us in our

CAN I TRUST MY BIBLE?

language, what hope do we have of knowing what to believe about life, death, and eternity? Is God so flippant about it that He doesn't care?

Let's face some facts here. Mere mortal, sinful human beings have areas of life that demand PERFECTION. Go into any courtroom when court is in session. You will see a court reporter sitting near the judge's bench punching the keys of a small machine. What is the reporter doing? He or she is keeping a record of EVERY word that is spoken. The record must be PERFECT because the WORDS that are spoken during that trial may make the difference in justice being done at a later time. Great care is taken to make sure the court record is PERFECT. To take a flippant attitude toward the record would be totally wrong and criminally inconsiderate.

Sit down with a mere mortal attorney. Watch him as he draws up any kind of a legal contract. He labors for hours on end, checking the legal language and the definition of words in an English dictionary with a single purpose in mind. The wording of the contract must be PERFECT. The careless use of ONE single word can make the contract null and void and cost his client dearly. It would be a profligate and irresponsible thing for that attorney to be anything but vigilant and prudent as he chooses the EXACT WORDS of the contract.

Watch your physician next time he writes you a prescription to be filled at your local pharmacy. He will very carefully choose his WORDS. When the pharmacist takes the written prescription in his hand, he will be very, very meticulous as he follows the directions of the physician, weighing every WORD to be dead sure he fills the prescription TO THE LETTER. To fail to do so could be disastrous or even FATAL for the patient.

Any Alexandrian that hasn't totally lost his marbles would agree on the absolute importance of EXACT and PERFECT wording of court records, contracts, and prescriptions. He would laud the

CAN I TRUST MY BIBLE'S INSPIRATION?

extreme care and effort of the reporters, attorneys, physicians, and pharmacists to make sure they hold to EVERY WORD in their work so that all goes well for the people who are affected by what they do. Yet that same Alexandrian will cast a doubt on the veracity, ability, and sincerity of the ALMIGHTY GOD when it comes to Him keeping EXACT and PERFECT wording in the most important RECORD, CONTRACT and PRESCRIPTION that exists . . . the WORD OF GOD!!!

God's Word is a RECORD, written perfectly and inspired so that we may know about Jesus Christ and believe on Him for salvation (I John 5:10-13). God's Word is a CONTRACT between Himself and mankind, which is perfect and cannot be broken (John 10:35). God's Word is a PRESCRIPTION, written perfectly and kept intact through time and translation to preserve the spiritual health of the souls of HIS people (Prov. 3:1, 8).

For the Alexandrians to say there is not NOW an inerrant, infallible, verbally inspired writing is to SLAP GOD IN THE FACE AND TO GIVE HIM CREDIT FOR HAVING LESS SENSE AND CARE THAN THAT SHOWN BY COURT RECORDERS, ATTORNEYS, PHYSICIANS, AND PHARMACISTS!!! It is a flat-out insult to my great and wonderful God, and I RESENT IT! Vengeance belongs to the Lord (Heb. 10:30), and I'll leave it to Him to handle the blasphemous Alexandrians, but I have to laugh at their utter foolishness. The Alexandrian preachers have NO BIBLE to preach! Their "bible" is a wispy phantom that they have never seen, that they cannot read nor hold in their hand . . . and therefore cannot PREACH. What I want to know is WHAT ARE THEY DOING IN THE MINISTRY?

God tells me to PREACH the Word (II Tim. 4:2). How could I obey His command IF I DID NOT HAVE THE WORD TO PREACH?

Well, bless God, I DO have the Word to preach! This precious

CAN I TRUST MY BIBLE?

old King James Bible is the INSPIRED, inerrant, infallible, LIVING Word of God! I can trust its INSPIRATION . . . and so can YOU!

V

CAN I TRUST MY BIBLE'S PRESERVATION?

A great deal of weight in Scripture is placed upon the Lord's WORDS. God always says precisely what He means . . . and He always means precisely what He SAYS. There is no way He can be thoroughly understood unless His hearers get each and every WORD He speaks.

In his thoroughly Alexandrian booklet on the King James Version controversy, John MacArthur says, "I'm sure you will agree that in this day and time we all need to be able to point to God's Word and say to the ungodly that it IS accurate and why. It is most important that we all know and be sure of what we are talking about in order to be witnesses of the TRUE Word of God. Keep in mind that the supporters of 'God wrote only one Bible' theology have mistakenly equated the 1611 King James Bible with the original manuscripts written in the first century. It is true that God wrote only one Bible, but it is also true that it was not the King James translation.

"Let me share with you my own conclusions after studying these issues. Bible versions such as the New International Version and the New American Standard Bible have been translated by godly men of demonstrated academic repute from the very best manuscript evidence that is available today. May I add, the manuscript evidence that is now available is far superior to that which was available to

CAN I TRUST MY BIBLE?

the King James translators in 1611. I would have no reservation in recommending these versions.

"There is a growing literature crusade which claims that 'God wrote only one Bible' . . . They conclude that the King James Version is the only English version which faithfully PRESERVES the original writings. They build their case upon such doctrines as the PRESERVATION of Scripture, the inerrancy of Scripture, and one's continued commitment to God. We do not have the originals of any of the books of the Bible. God never promised the perfect PRESERVATION of the originals, but He did promise PRESERVE their CONTENT."

My reader will immediately catch the Alexandrian odor that goes with such statements. I wholeheartedly agree with Mr. MacArthur that it is most important that we all know and be sure of what we are talking about in order to be witnesses of the TRUE Word of God. The only problem with such words coming from Mr. MacArthur is that he does not know what he is talking about.

Since Mr. MacArthur speaks (like J.H. Melton) as a typical Alexandrian, let me show you that he does NOT know what he is talking about.

1. The "God wrote only one Bible" supporters have NOT equated the 1611 King James Bible with the original manuscripts. WE KNOW THE DIFFERENCE BETWEEN HEBREW AND ENGLISH, AND GREEK AND ENGLISH! However, we DO believe that the Lord has PRESERVED the WORDS of the original Scriptures down through the centuries so that we have EVERY WORD in English as much as EVERY WORD was in Hebrew and Greek the original writings!

2. The original manuscripts were not written in the first century. Only the twenty-seven books of the NEW Testament were written in the first century. The thirty-nine books of the OLD Testament were written LONG before the first century!

CAN I TRUST MY BIBLE'S PRESERVATION?

3. When Mr. MacArthur says the translators of the NIV and the NASV had "far superior" manuscripts than the King James translators did, he means the ALEXANDRIAN manuscript. Pooey.

4. Johnny says it is true that God wrote only one Bible; then he recommends EITHER the NIV or the NASV. I didn't quote for you that he also pointed out that he "uses" the King James Version. I can still count . . . and that adds up to THREE. Since he says God DID write only ONE Bible . . . why doesn't he tell us which one of the three is GOD'S Bible? Psst! Hey reader! Come close, and I'll whisper it into your ear . . Johnny won't point out the REAL Bible because he is an Alexandrian! He doesn't believe that any of the three mentioned above is the REAL Bible. He's talking about the "original manuscripts," which as you know are long gone. Therefore, he can't point to ANYTHING that is "God's Word" and tell the ungodly (or anyone else) that it is accurate and why.

5. Mr. MacArthur is full of Mexican beans when he says God promised to preserve the CONTENT of the originals. Where in the name of Daffy Duck did he ever read THAT? Not in the King James Bible he "uses"! Nor did he find it in the NIV, the NASV, or even in his Alexandrian Hebrew and Greek texts. God never said any such thing. Let's see what He DID say on the subject.

> *The WORDS of the Lord are pure WORDS: as silver tried in a furnace of earth, purified seven times. Thou shalt KEEP THEM, O Lord, thou shalt PRESERVE THEM from this generation FOR EVER* (Psalm 12:6-7).

Anyone who is not self-blinded and prejudiced against the Word of God will see that according to this passage, the WORDS of the Lord (which make up His WORD) will be KEPT and PRESERVED by the Lord *HIMSELF* FOREVER!!! The WORDS, Mr. MacArthur . . . the WORDS! Not the *content*.

Maybe we should take a look at this passage in the New

CAN I TRUST MY BIBLE?

International perversion, which Mr. MacArthur has "no reservation" in recommending.

> And the words of the Lord are flawless, like silver refined in a furnace of clay, purified seven times. O Lord, you will keep us safe and protect us from such people forever (Psalm 12:6-7).

How's that for PERVERTING the Word of God in an attempt to cover up the truth that the Almighty God HIMSELF will *keep* and *preserve* His WORDS *forever???*

The Alexandrians vehemently insist that the only inspired WORDS were those INKED INTO the fibers of the "original parchments" . . . and even as Mr. MacArthur admits in his nefarious booklet, "We do not have the originals of any of the books of the Bible" . . . HE IS CALLING GOD'S STATEMENT IN PSALM 12:6-7 A LIE! Every Alexandrian believes the same thing . . . that the ONLY inerrant, inspired WORDS that ever existed were those of the "original manuscripts." Thus, when God says differently—that He, Himself will PRESERVE HIS WORDS FOREVER—every Alexandrian is bold-facedly calling God a LIAR!!!

Br-r-r-r-r-r-r-! That shivers my timbers! I would hate to be in their boots when they go into eternity and face Him!!!

We Antiochans believe God. We believe that He has PRESERVED His WORDS down to this very day . . . and that He will PRESERVE them FOREVER! When God made that statement in Psalm 12:6-7, He was fully aware that all peoples of the earth would not speak nor read Hebrew and Greek. He knew that He would have to KEEP AND PRESERVE HIS WORDS even through *translation*. Being God, He can handle it. Every ONE of the 810,697 WORDS in my ANTIOCHAN AV1611 King James Bible is GOD'S word!!!

Jesus told the devil, *"Man shall not live by bread alone,*

CAN I TRUST MY BIBLE'S PRESERVATION?

but by EVERY WORD that proceedeth out of the mouth of God" (Matt. 4:4). And ever since, the old serpent has been garnering his Alexandrian troops together in order to attack the truth of that statement. Sad, isn't it . . . that Satan should find so many willing recruits among "Fundamentalists"?

More than any court reporter . . . more than any attorney . . . more than any physician who writes a prescription . . . the Almighty God is very particular about His WORDS. Observe . . .

> *But I am the Lord thy God . . . And I have put MY WORDS in thy mouth, and I have covered thee in the shadow of mine hand . . .* (Isa. 51:15-16).
>
> *As for me, this is my covenant with them, saith the Lord; My spirit that is upon thee, and MY WORDS which I have put in thy mouth, shall not depart out of thy mouth, nor OUT OF THE MOUTH OF THY SEED, nor OUT OF THE MOUTH OF THY SEED'S SEED, saith the Lord, from henceforth and FOR EVER* (Isa. 59:21).
>
> *And Moses came and told the people all the WORDS of the Lord . . . and all the people answered with one voice, and said, All the WORDS which the Lord hath said will we do. And Moses WROTE all the WORDS of the Lord . . .* (Ex. 24:3-4).
>
> *And Samuel grew, and the Lord was with him, and did let none of his WORDS fall to the ground* (I Sam. 3:19).
>
> *EVERY WORD of God is pure: he is a shield unto them that put their trust in him. Add thou not unto his WORDS, lest he reprove thee, and thou be found a liar* (Prov. 30:5-6).
>
> *The Lord . . . will not call back his WORDS . . .* (Isa.

CAN I TRUST MY BIBLE?

31:1-2).

. . . Thou shalt be dumb, and not able to speak . . . because thou believest not MY WORDS . . . (Luke 1:20).

. . . Thou hast the WORDS of eternal life (John 6:68).

. . . Remember the WORDS of the Lord Jesus . . . (Acts 20:35).

And if any man hear MY WORDs, and believe not, I judge him not: for I came not to judge the world, but to save the world. He that rejecteth me, and receiveth not MY WORDS, hath one that judgeth him: the word that I have spoken, the same shall judge him in the last day (John 12:47-48).

Heaven and earth shall pass away, but MY WORDS shall NOT pass away (Matt. 24:35).

And he said unto me, Write: for these WORDS are true and faithful (Rev. 21:5).

For I testify unto every man that heareth the WORDS of the prophecy of this book, If any man shall add unto these things, God shall add unto him the plagues that are written in this book: And if any man shall take away from the WORDS of the book of this prophecy, God shall take away his part out of the book of life, and out of the holy city, and from the things which are written in this book (Rev. 22:18-19).

How foolish for the Alexandrians to believe that God cared so little about His WORDS that He let them die when the "original parchments" disintegrated! He flat said He would PRESERVE His WORDS forever, but they refuse to believe Him. He said His WORDS would NOT pass away, but still they refuse to believe Him.

CAN I TRUST MY BIBLE'S PRESERVATION?

They disdain the very words He uses to SAY that His WORDS are preserved forever and will never pass away! They DO NOT believe Him! They are like the chief priests, the scribes, and the elders who sent the Pharisees and the Herodians to "catch Him in His WORDS" (Mark 12:13).

I'll tell you who's going to get caught in His Words . . . it's the ALEXANDRIAN who speaks against God's pure, perfect, infallible, inerrant, inspired, PRESERVED Word in the English language! The ALEXANDRIAN who "corrects" the King James Bible, ADDING words and TAKING AWAY words, is going to be held responsible by its Author!

So then every one of us shall give ACCOUNT of himself to God (Rom. 14:12).

Part of that account will be WORDS that have been spoken.

But I say unto you, That EVERY IDLE WORD that men shall speak, they shall give ACCOUNT thereof in the day of judgment. For by thy WORDS thou shalt be justified, and by thy WORDS thou shalt be condemned (Matt. 12:36-37).

I cringe when I hear Alexandrians speaking harsh words against the King James Bible, saying it is NOT the Word of God, saying that it has spurious passages, and accusing it of having errors. They do it with no fear at all. In spite of the fact that God SAID He would PRESERVE EVERY WORD FOREVER, they say He has not done it. He has let the "originals" pass away, so His WORDS are no longer with us in Hebrew, Greek, OR English. To show their special dislike for the AV1611, they SPEAK HARSH WORDS AGAINST IT.

I wonder what you Alexandrians think of what the antichrist is going to do. Look at it.

And there was given unto him a mouth speaking

CAN I TRUST MY BIBLE?

> *great things and blasphemies . . . and he opened his mouth in blasphemy against God, to blaspheme his NAME . . . (Rev. 13:5-6).*

The antichrist is going to blaspheme God's NAME! What do you think of that? I'm sure most Alexandrians would say, "Oh, that's a terrible thing to do! It is a wicked and vile thing to speak in a derogatory way against the NAME of the Lord!"

I agree, but let me tell you boys something. What YOU do when you speak in a derogatory way against God's WORD is *worse*!!! God thinks very highly of His NAME, and it is a vile, devilish, and wicked thing to speak against it . . but there is something God thinks MORE of than He does His name! Take a good look.

> *I will worship toward thy holy temple, and praise thy name for thy lovingkindness and for thy truth: for thou hast magnified thy word ABOVE all thy name (Psalm 138:2).*

Do you see that? God has magnified His WORD *above* His name! It's bad enough to speak against the name of the Lord . . . but it's even WORSE to speak against His WORD!!!!

I can hear the Alexandrians cry, "Well, we don't believe the King James Bible is the Word of God!"

Most of you get behind your pulpits and CALL the King James Bible the Word of God. WHY DON'T YOU BE HONEST AND TELL YOUR PEOPLE THAT YOU ARE NOT PREACHING THE WORD OF GOD . . . THAT YOU DON'T BELIEVE THAT BOOK IN YOUR HAND IS THE WORD OF GOD? Others of you don't even "use" the King James Bible. You use the NIV or the NKJV or some other perversion. You who "use" the KJV and speak against it by "correcting" it are as guilty of blaspheming the Word of God as your Alexandrian brethren who use the perversions and speak out loudly against the KJV!

CAN I TRUST MY BIBLE'S PRESERVATION?

If you can imagine how God feels about those who by the spirit of antichrist (I John 4:3) blaspheme the NAME of God . . . try to imagine how He feels toward those who blaspheme His WORD, which He has magnified ABOVE His name!!!

I hear the Alexandrian cry repeated: "We don't believe the King James Bible is the Word of God!"

Well, boys, that's your privilege, but your unbelief doesn't change a thing. Just keep in mind what this ignorant preacher said . . . you will one day give an account to the Author of the Book for the WORDS you add to it, and the WORDS you take away from it, and the WORDS you "correct," and the WORDS you speak against it. You will also give account for believing that only the "originals" were the perfect, inspired Word of God when God flat SAID He would PRESERVE every word forever and that His Words would NEVER pass away.

You've been warned. The ball is in YOUR court, now.

Let's look at Psalm 12:6-7 again.

The WORDS of the Lord are pure WORDS: as silver tried in a furnace of earth, purified seven times. Thou shalt KEEP THEM, O Lord, thou shalt PRESERVE THEM from this generation FOR EVER (Psalm 12:6-7).

This is SCRIPTURE that we have just read. God has promised to KEEP and PRESERVE His Words FOREVER.

QUESTION: Will this Scripture be fulfilled? Will it be fulfilled in spite of the fact that the Alexandrians DO NOT BELIEVE it will be fulfilled? ABSOLUTELY!!!

The psalmist David is referred to as a prophet (Matt 13:35; 27:35). Keeping that in mind, let's see what the Author of the Bible has to say about the Scripture being fulfilled . . . EVEN the Psalms.

CAN I TRUST MY BIBLE?

> *Think not that I am come to destroy the law, or the prophets: I am not come to destroy, but to FULFILL. For verily I say unto you, Till heaven and earth pass, one jot or one tittle shall in no wise pass from the law, TILL ALL BE FULFILLED* (Matt. 5:17-18).

Actually, the entire Bible is God's "law," but I want you to be sure to understand what Jesus is saying here. As the Author of the Word of God, Jesus Christ will see to it that EVERY SCRIPTURE IS FULFILLED. I specifically pointed out that David was a prophet because it was David who wrote Psalm 12:6-7. Jesus said that He HIMSELF would fulfill the law and the prophets.

Do you understand? Jesus Christ HIMSELF will see to it that the pure WORDS of the Lord are KEPT pure, and HE will PRESERVE them FOREVER! He even said that HE would not allow one jot or tittle in His Word to pass away. This would be true of the WORDS given to the holy men who wrote the Scriptures in Hebrew and Greek in the FIRST place, and since Jesus also called a *translation* "Scripture" (Matt. 21:42; Mark 12:10; Luke 4:21; John 5:39; 10:35, etc.) . . . this would be true of His WORDS in pure translations . . . including ENGLISH!

Most of the Alexandrians claim to love and serve Jesus Christ. Why, then, don't they BELIEVE Him??? Jesus said that He would not allow one JOT or one TITTLE to pass from His WORD. Jots and tittles were the smallest marks used in the written Hebrew language. Since He was so careful about the jots and tittles, how can anyone think He would be careless or unconcerned about the WORDS? It is vastly important that EVERY PART AND PARTICLE of Scripture be preserved intact and kept pure.

I read a story once about an incident that took place back in the latter part of the nineteenth century. Telegraph was the best means of sending a message if speed was needed. A transatlantic cable had been laid between the United States and Europe in order

CAN I TRUST MY BIBLE'S PRESERVATION?

to expedite communications between people on the two continents.

A woman whose husband was well-off financially took a vacation to Europe alone. While there, she telegraphed her husband, asking permission to purchase a very expensive item.

You may recall that no punctuation was used in telegrams. The husband received the wire and promptly went to the telegraph office to send his wife a reply. He wrote it down thus: "NO. EXPENSE TOO GREAT."

Without punctuation, the message arrived in Europe looking like this: "NO EXPENSE TOO GREAT." The woman bought the item. When she returned home with it, her husband became very angry, and the telegraph company had their hands full with an irate customer. It was this incident that caused all telegraphers to use the word "STOP" between sentences . . . so that such a thing could not happen again.

This incident demonstrates how strategic and important it is that little things in a written message be carefully watched over to the most minute detail. How much MORE important is this principle when applied to the WORDS of Almighty God to His creatures on earth! The Alexandrians accuse the Author of the Bible of being careless and flippant about His holy, vital, and inerrant Word!

When Jesus walked this earth, all of the Old Testament "originals" had cracked, peeled, disintegrated, and gone back to the dust. The only Scriptures available in the old Hebrew were COPIES of COPIES of COPIES . . . or the Scriptures that had been TRANSLATED into Aramaic. Yet when He preached and taught, NEVER ONE TIME did He ever refer to the "original manuscripts!" NEVER ONE TIME did He ever say, "This passage is spurious. It is not found in the better manuscripts" . . . NEVER ONE TIME did He ever even intimate that the Scriptures had lost their inspiration or that EVERY WORD had not been KEPT pure and PRESERVED intact!

CAN I TRUST MY BIBLE?

For the Alexandrians to do such a wicked thing is to GO AGAINST the example set by the Author of the Book Himself. I repeat... Jesus Christ said that HE WOULD KEEP AND PRESERVE HIS WORDS FOREVER. I, for one, believe Him.

Let us take note RIGHT IN THE BIBLE as to how Jesus felt about the Scriptures being fulfilled.

And leaving Nazareth, he [Jesus] came and dwelt in Capernaum, which is upon the sea coast, in the borders of Zabulon and Nephthalim: THAT IT MIGHT BE FULFILLED which was spoken by Esaias the prophet... (Matt. 4:13-14).

And [Jesus] charged them that they should not make him known: THAT IT MIGHT BE FULFILLED which was spoken by Esaias the prophet... (Matt. 12:16-17).

All these things spake Jesus unto the multitude in parables; and without a parable spake he not unto them: THAT IT MIGHT BE FULFILLED which was spoken by the prophet... (Matt. 13:34-35).

Then said Jesus... how then shall the scriptures BE FULFILLED, that thus it MUST be? But all this was done, that the scriptures of the prophets MIGHT BE FULFILLED... (Matt. 26:54, 56).

... That all things which are written MAY BE FULFILLED (Luke 21:22).

While I was with them in the world, I kept them in thy name: those that thou gavest me I have kept, and none of them is lost, but the son of perdition; THAT THE SCRIPTURE MIGHT BE FULFILLED (John 17:12).

After this, Jesus knowing that all things were now

CAN I TRUST MY BIBLE'S PRESERVATION?

accomplished, THAT THE SCRIPTURE MIGHT BE FULFILLED, saith, I thirst (John 19:28).

One cannot read these Scriptures without being strongly impressed with the purpose and intent of the Lord Jesus to make sure that every word of Holy Writ is fulfilled. Who but a self-blinded fool would have the gall to say that Jesus did not care to KEEP and PRESERVE EVERY WORD of Scripture? And if they say He cared, but was NOT ABLE to KEEP and PRESERVE every word, they have just as much gall. Look what He said about the *written* Word and Himself, the *incarnate* Word.

> *Then he said unto them, O fools, and slow of heart to believe all that the prophets have spoken: Ought not Christ to have suffered these things, and to enter into his glory? And beginning at Moses and all the prophets, he expounded unto them in all the scriptures the things concerning HIMSELF* (Luke 24:25-27).

Jesus was very emphatic as He spoke to the Emmaus disciples concerning the Scriptures being TOTALLY ACCURATE when they spoke of HIM. Here's more.

> *And he said unto them, These are the words which I spake unto you, while I was yet with you, THAT ALL THINGS MUST BE FULFILLED, which were written in the law of Moses, and in the prophets, and in the psalms, concerning ME. Then opened he their understanding, that they might understand the scriptures* (Luke 24:44-45).

The Bible is the WRITTEN Word (Luke 24:44), and Jesus Christ is the INCARNATE WORD (John 1:1, 14). Do you see how important it is to Him that EVERYTHING said in the WRITTEN Word about the INCARNATE Word be perfectly accurate? Can you imagine Him being any LESS concerned with what is said in the WRITTEN Word about the *WRITTEN* Word? Only a slow-hearted

CAN I TRUST MY BIBLE?

FOOL would think so.

Only a slow-hearted ALEXANDRIAN FOOL could read in the written Word that Jesus said He, HIMSELF, WOULD see to it that ALL Scripture would be fulfilled . . . then have the purple, pink, polka-dotted audacity to claim that He FAILED on purpose, or that He was so weak and frail that He could not come through with His promise!

By the prophet David, the Lord flat SAID that He would KEEP AND PRESERVE EVERY WORD OF HIS BIBLE FOREVER (Psalm 12:6-7). Through Matthew's pen, the Lord said that heaven and earth would pass away, but His WORDS would not pass away (Matt. 24:35). Yet, in spite of these absolute guarantees made by the Lord Himself, the slow-hearted, self-blinded ALEXANDRIAN FOOLS will say the ONLY inspired, inerrant, infallible Scriptures that ever existed were the "original manuscripts"!

When the Lord Jesus appeared to the apostles in the latter part of Luke chapter 24, the Bible says, *"Then opened he their understanding, THAT THEY MIGHT UNDERSTAND THE SCRIPTURES"* (Luke 24:45). The apostles could only have their understanding opened IF THEY WERE WILLING to have their understanding opened. The Lord would not FORCE it on them. If you Alexandrians would quit being slow-hearted fools and allow the Lord to open your understanding of the Scriptures, then you would understand that when God said in Scripture that He would KEEP AND PRESERVE EVERY ONE OF HIS WORDS FOREVER, He meant it!

If you would take the blinds off your eyes that you put there yourselves, and let the Lord open your understanding to the Scriptures, then you would understand that when Jesus said in the Scriptures that heaven and earth will pass away, but HIS WORDS WILL NOT PASS AWAY, He meant what He said!

The *first* thing that you would understand is that when

CAN I TRUST MY BIBLE'S PRESERVATION?

COPIES were made of the "original autographs," the COPIES were just as perfect, just as inerrant, and just as inspired as the "original autographs." The reason is that the Lord HIMSELF preserved EVERY WORD, not allowing even ONE to pass away . . . and kept EVERY WORD perfect, inerrant, and inspired exactly as He said to Scripture He would do!

In chapter 2 of this book, I showed you how God made a copy of the Scripture that Jehoiakim shredded and burned . . . and KEPT it pure and inspired. Let's just take a look at some more Scripture about this subject of COPIES. In Deuteronomy chapter 17, God tells the people of Israel that after they come into the promised land, He will give them a king. He will want the king to obey His Word. The Levite priests have the written Word of God in their possession. Speaking of the new king, the Lord says,

> *And it shall be, when he sitteth upon the throne of his kingdom, that he shall write him a COPY of this LAW in a book out of that which is before the priests the Levites: And it shall be with him, and he shall read therein all the days of his life: that he may learn to fear the Lord his God, to keep ALL THE WORDS of this law and these statutes, to do them* (Deut. 17:18-19).

We have already learned that God's "law" and God's "precepts" are the same thing as His WORD. Please notice that Saul, the coming king, would obtain a COPY of the Word of God from the Levites . . . and that Saul (under God's command) was to keep ALL THE WORDS of the law and the statutes. It is quite apparent that God knew that even though Saul would only have a COPY of the "original manuscripts," Saul would STILL have ALL of God's Words!!! Certainly the Lord would not hold Saul responsible to keep ALL of His words unless Saul HAD all of God's Words!!!

We don't know that the Scripture the Levites had in their

CAN I TRUST MY BIBLE?

possession were the "original autographs" penned by Moses. They probably had COPIES themselves, but let's go so far as to say that the Levites actually had the inspired, preserved "originals" . . . most definitely what Saul was going to get was a COPY. The Scripture SAYS SO! Yet, in his COPY, Saul had "ALL THE WORDS" of God's law and statutes, and he was responsible to God for obeying them. Only a slow-hearted, self-blinded fool would say that the COPY Saul had was not as inspired, inerrant, and COMPLETE as the "originals."

Let's allow the Scripture to teach us further about COPIES of the Word of God . . . and how the Lord keeps EVERY WORD pure and PRESERVES every word when COPIES are made.

> *Then Joshua built an altar unto the Lord God of Israel in mount Ebal . . . an altar of whole stones . . . And he wrote there upon the stones a COPY of the law Moses, which he wrote in the presence of the children of Israel. And afterward he read ALL THE WORDS OF THE LAW, the blessings and cursings, according to ALL THAT IS WRITTEN in the book of the law. There has NOT A WORD of all that Moses commanded, which Joshua read not before all the congregation of Israel . . .* (Josh. 8:30-32, 34-35).

Isn't this interesting? Joshua took a hammer and chisel, and wrote a COPY of the law of Moses. When he had finished, he stood there before the whole congregation of Israel and read the words he had chipped in the rocks. Lo and behold . . . NOT A WORD was missing that had been written on the papyrus originally!

When will the Alexandrians open their eyes and let God give them understanding from the Scriptures? Joshua, who was just a mortal man, made a COPY of God's WORDS in stone, and NOT A WORD was left out! Yet the Alexandrians insist that ONLY the "originals" were perfect . . . and that NO COPY could be perfect. Ho

CAN I TRUST MY BIBLE'S PRESERVATION?

hum. They always sing the same old tune. It DOES get old, doesn't it?

Something else about COPIES of the Word of God . . . I have never met an Alexandrian who would deny that the book of Proverbs belongs in the canon. They all agree that Solomon wrote the book of Proverbs, and that the "originals" were inspired by the Holy Spirit. They would include Proverbs in the "all Scripture" of II Timothy 3:16.

There probably hasn't been one Alexandrian in ten thousand who has noticed that there are four chapters of Proverbs that were COPIES when they were inserted into the "original" canon. Take a look at it.

These are ALSO proverbs of Solomon, which the men of Hezekiah king of Judah COPIED out (Prov. 25:1).

The book of Proverbs opens up by saying in chapter 1, verse 1, *"The proverbs of Solomon, the son of David, king of Israel."* When you get to chapter 10, you are again reminded in verse 1 that you are reading the *proverbs of Solomon.* From chapter 1 through chapter 24, Solomon himself pens down his proverbs under the inspiration of the Holy Spirit. Then suddenly, chapter 25 opens up by telling us that we are now reading—NOT WHAT SOLOMON PENNED DOWN—but what King Hezekiah's men COPIED OUT from what Solomon had penned down at some earlier date. What they "COPIED OUT" goes through chapter 29.

Are the Alexandrians going to tell us that chapters 25-29 are NOT perfect, complete, and inspired because they are COPIES? Hmm? If they would only allow the Lord to open their eyes to the Scriptures, they would see that the Holy Spirit watches over COPIES of the true Scriptures EVERY BIT AS CAREFULLY as He watched over the ORIGINALS!!! Proverbs chapters 25 through 29 are included in the canon of Scripture, and they fall under the

CAN I TRUST MY BIBLE?

"all Scripture" that IS inspired by the Almighty God . . . yet those chapters ENTERED THE CANON—*not as originals*—BUT AS COPIES!!!

So as I said . . . if the Alexandrians would let the Lord open their blinded eyes, they would see *first* that when COPIES were made of the "original autographs," the COPIES were just as perfect, just as inerrant, and just as inspired as the "original autographs."

The *second* thing that the Alexandrians would see is that the Holy Spirit is JUST AS CAREFUL to preserve perfection, inerrancy, and inspiration when the Scriptures are TRANSLATED. I covered the subject of TRANSLATION thoroughly in chapter 3, so I won't dwell further on it here . . . except to say that the reason the Alexandrians think that NO translation can be inspired is that they stubbornly refuse to accept what the Scripture SHOWS us about inspired, perfect, preserved, inerrant COPIES from which inspired, perfect, preserved, inerrant TRANSLATIONS are produced.

Most Alexandrians claim to be saved, yet they say ONLY the "original manuscripts" were the inspired, perfect, incorruptible Word of God. Since the Bible says we can ONLY be saved by the inspired, perfect, and incorruptible Word of God (II Tim. 3:15-16; Psalm 19:7; I Pet. 1:23), these Alexandrians—by their own words—CANNOT POSSIBLY BE SAVED! Did they already KNOW the Hebrew and Greek languages in which the Bible was originally written when they made their profession of faith in Christ? And did they hear it or read it from the ORIGINAL MANUSCRIPTS? NO! Then according to their own Alexandrian teaching, THEY ARE NOT SAVED.

The *third* thing that the Alexandrians would learn if they would allow the Lord to open their eyes to the Scriptures would be that Egypt is a BAD place in the eyes of God . . . and that the city of ALEXANDRIA is known for its disputers against those who believe the word (Acts 6:9), its bad Bible teaching (Acts 18:24-26), and its

CAN I TRUST MY BIBLE'S PRESERVATION?

definite part in helping to transport the great Bible believer, Paul, to his execution (Acts 27:6; 28:11-16).

If the Alexandrians would face the facts, they would know that the Lord plainly teaches in His Word that a corrupt tree can only produce corrupt fruit (Matt. 7:17-18). Alexandria, Egypt is CORRUPT. Therefore, the manuscripts that were produced and collected there are CORRUPT. Therefore, ALL the English versions that were translated from Alexandrian manuscripts are CORRUPT. That leaves only ONE English Bible that is NOT corrupt . . . the AV1611, which was translated from manuscripts from Antioch, Syria . . . the location of the greatest New Testament church in the book of Acts.

If the Alexandrians would get their eyes open to the Scriptures, they would understand that I Corinthians 14:33 is solid proof from God that He could only produce ONE Bible in ANY language. They would then see the fact that GOD'S Bible to the English-speaking people is the precious, old Authorized Version of 1611 . . . the rough, tough, devil-kicking, Christ-exalting, sin-condemning, soul-saving, two-fisted, double-edged, God-honored, God-given, time-defying, PRESERVED, inspired, infallible, inerrant, incorruptible, uncorrectable, indestructible, powerful, living Word of God!

Let me speak to you Alexandrian preachers, professors, and laymen who "use" the King James Bible. Since you don't believe that it is the very PRESERVED Word of God . . . WHY DO YOU "USE" IT??? I will TELL you why. No doubt there are several reasons . . . but if the truth be known, it was the King James Bible that God employed to channel the Gospel to you. It was the King James Bible that enlightened you to your lost and Hell-bound condition before God. It was the King James Bible that convicted you of your sin. It was the King James Bible that brought you to the place where you saw that the only way of salvation was the Lamb of God . . . and pierced to the center of your sin-darkened soul, bringing light

CAN I TRUST MY BIBLE?

and deep conviction. You then bowed your heart before the Lord and asked Him to save you.

It is THAT tie with the King James Bible that keeps you "using" it, even though you don't BELIEVE it. Wake up! If you're saved . . . you didn't get saved by hearing or reading the "original manuscripts"! You got saved by hearing or reading the KING JAMES BIBLE! And I'll tell you what. The odds are that you believe in eternal security. You would stand and fight for that wonderful doctrine. You fully BELIEVE what Paul believed when he wrote,

The Lord . . . will PRESERVE me unto his heavenly kingdom: to whom be glory for ever and ever (II Tim. 4:18).

You really believe that it is the Lord's PRESERVING you from the evil works of the devil that will get you to Heaven, and not anything YOU can do to PRESERVE your own soul. Right? Right.

Yes sir . . . you believe the same thing Jude believed when he wrote:

Jude, the servant of Jesus Christ, and brother of James, to them that are sanctified by God the Father, and PRESERVED in Jesus Christ . . . (Jude 1).

Yep. You believe that you can't ever lose your salvation because you are PRESERVED in Christ Jesus by the Almighty God. You rest in this divine PRESERVATION.

I'll tell you something else. If I were a betting man, I'd bet that you would believe you are KEPT saved because Jesus prayed to His Father . . .

. . . Holy Father, KEEP through thine own name those whom thou hast given me . . . (John 17:11).

And what's more, you believe exactly what Peter believed when he wrote,

Blessed be the God and Father of our Lord Jesus

CAN I TRUST MY BIBLE'S PRESERVATION?

Christ, which according to his abundant mercy hath begotten us again unto a lively hope by the resurrection of Jesus Christ from the dead, To an inheritance incorruptible, and undefiled, and that fadeth not away, reserved in heaven for you, Who are KEPT by the power of God through faith unto salvation ready to be revealed in the last time (I Pet. 1:3-5).

Right? You believe you are KEPT saved by the power of God, but let me ask you something. How can you believe I Peter 1:3-5, John 17:11, Jude 1, and II Timothy 4:18 . . . and NOT BELIEVE Psalm 12:6-7???? By what stretch of your imagination can you conclude that the Almighty God can PRESERVE and KEEP your soul forever, if He cannot PRESERVE and KEEP His *words* pure, perfect, inerrant and inspired forever?

If the Lord can perfectly TRANSLATE you from the power of darkness into the Kingdom of His dear Son (Col. 1:13) . . . why can't He perfectly TRANSLATE His Word into any language He chooses? Even ENGLISH? You'd better face it. If the God of the universe cannot KEEP and PRESERVE His inspired words forever . . . you are hanging by a thin, burning rope over Hell because NEITHER CAN HE KEEP AND PRESERVE YOUR SOUL!!! Selah.

Just HOW do you know you are going to Heaven, Mr. Alexandrian? What PROOF do you have? Hmm? Did you play Oral Robert and Jimmy Swaggart and SEE A VISON? Hmm? I said HOW DO YOU KNOW YOU ARE GOING TO HEAVEN? If you are going to tell me that you know you are going to Heaven because the Word of God says so . . . I'm going to ask you to PRODUCE this "Word of God" you're talking about. CAN you? WHERE IS IT? Don't give me this "original manuscript" stuff. You have never laid eyes on the "original manuscripts," and you couldn't get your

CAN I TRUST MY BIBLE?

Alexandrian hands on them if your eternal destiny depended on it! In fact, if your salvation depends on the "original manuscripts," your eternal destiny DOES depend on it! Look what God said in His inspired Authorized English Bible.

> ... *Be ready always to give an answer to every man that asketh you a reason of the hope that is in you* ...
> (I Pet. 3:15)

Okay. Al Lacy would come under the category of "every man," so I am asking you for the reason of the hope that is in you. You say that you are saved and will never burn in Hell? You say that your sins have been forgiven, and you are going to Heaven? I now DEMAND that you obey God's command in I Peter 3:15! I'm asking you for the reason of the hope that is in you. SHOW ME THE "WORD OF GOD" UPON WHICH YOU BASE YOUR HOPE! If you cannot do this, you HAVE no hope!

Dear reader . . . it is my sincere hope that YOU can obey I Peter 3:15. Do YOU believe I Peter 1:3-5, John 17:11, Jude 1, II Timothy 4:18? . . . ONLY if you believe Psalm 12:6-7 and Matthew 24:35.

The question this chapter asks is "CAN I TRUST MY BIBLE'S PRESERVATION?" If your Bible is a good, old, God-blessed AV1611 King James Bible, you most certainly CAN trust your Bible's PRESERVATION!

> *Thy word is true from the beginning: and every one of thy righteous judgments ENDURETH FOR EVER*
> (Psalm 119:160).

VI

CAN I TRUST MY BIBLE'S AUTHORITY?

Every human being on the face of this earth was born with the innate knowledge that God exists and that the Creator is holy, and he will immediately or eventually exact punishment for wrongdoing.

I know this to be true because the Bible says so . . . and because I have seen it in human experience. The Bible calls Jesus Christ the "true Light" and says of Him,

> *That has the true Light, which lighteth EVERY MAN that cometh into the world* (John 1:9).

That's plain enough. EVERY person ever born into this world has been given light from the Lord. He has given them enough light about Himself to know He exists and to know He hates sin . . . and that He will punish the sinner. God has written His law on the "fleshy" tables of our hearts (Jer. 31:33, II Cor. 3:3) known as the *conscience* . . . and that law teaches us the truth of God's existence, His holiness, His wrath against mankind's unrighteousness, and our moral accountability to Him as our Creator, so that we are with out excuse before Him in our sins.

> *For the wrath of God is revealed from heaven against all ungodliness and unrighteousness of men, who hold the truth in unrighteousness; Because that*

CAN I TRUST MY BIBLE?

which may be known of God is manifest IN them; for God HATH SHEWED IT UNTO THEM. For the invisible things of him from the creation of the world are CLEARLY SEEN, being understood by the things that are made, even his eternal power and Godhead; so that they are WITHOUT EXCUSE (Rom. 1:18-20).

Thus we learn that there is no such thing as an atheist. When you hear a man or woman say, "I am an atheist. I do not believe God exists"...THEY ARE LYING! They KNOW God exists! GOD SAYS THEY KNOW HE EXISTS because He has manifested the truth of His existence to ALL men. They do not like to retain God in their knowledge (Rom. 1:28) because they love their sin (John 3:19) and do not like the idea of having to be responsible and accountable to God for it. Therefore, they play the fool (Psalm 14:1) by telling themselves that down in their hearts God does not exist.

But no matter what they tell themselves, GOD says they KNOW He exists. I believe GOD . . . not the lying atheists!

We just read that God has manifested the truth of His existence IN human beings and has shown it unto all of us. By the law, He has written IN us; we CLEARLY SEE that He exists and that we are accountable to Him for our wrongdoing. Therefore, the judge of the universe declares us without excuse before Him.

We are sinners by nature, and we are sinners by CHOICE, and we KNOW it. We also KNOW that our Almighty Creator will deal with us for our sins against Him.

I have traveled many parts of this world, preaching the Word of God. I have been amongst primitive, heathen people in the jungles of South America and have observed them in their pagan religions. Once I flew with some missionaries deep into the Amazon basin of Brazil and spent time with a heathen tribe who had yet to hear the Gospel because the missionaries were still attempting to learn their

CAN I TRUST MY BIBLE'S AUTHORITY?

language. Yet I saw with my own eyes that these people in their heathen darkness KNEW that God exists, KNEW that He is holy, KNEW that He had wrath against their sins, and KNEW that after death they would have to face Him.

These pagan, primitive people cut and mutilated their bodies, inflicting severe pain upon themselves in a sincere attempt to show their Creator they were sorry for doing Him wrong. The young mothers, when overwhelmed with guilt before their unseen Creator, will often feed their newborn babies to the crocodiles in the nearby streams in a show of contrition, so they will not have to face Him in His wrath after they die.

Such behavior is exactly in line with what we just read in Scripture. Therefore, I say to my reader . . . like me, you KNOW God exists. You KNOW He is a holy God who hates your sins. You KNOW you are responsible to Him for your unrighteousness. You KNOW there is punishment due to you from your Creator. Now, what are you to do in order to properly apply yourself so that your sins might be forgiven and washed away?

Your natural answer to me is "I must *learn* what God says I have to do to be forgiven and cleansed."

I agree, and just HOW and WHERE will you learn it? You say, "I must go to the proper AUTHORITY to learn this." Right, and just WHERE is the proper authority? Does God come and appear to men? Hmm? (I realize He appears to Charismatics, but the rest of us don't have that luxury!)

I repeat . . . WHERE is the proper authority? You say, "I must go to the written Word of God."

Ah, but if you listen to the "intelligent," "educated," "brilliant" Alexandrians, THERE IS NO WRITTEN WORD OF GOD FOR YOU TO FIND AND READ BECAUSE THE ONLY WORD OF GOD THERE EVER WAS OR EVER SHALL BE WAS

CAN I TRUST MY BIBLE?

THE "ORIGINAL MANUSCRIPTS," AND THEY ARE GONE! According to the Alexandrians, then YOU ARE IN A PICKLE! Neither YOU nor I nor the ALEXANDRIANS can know one blessed thing about life, death, punishment for sins, forgiveness, Heaven, Hell, or eternity because we HAVE no Word of God to read and study WITH AUTHORITY on these matters?

Now, let's face it. Either we have the perfect, infallible, inerrant, inspired Word of God, or we DON'T. If we DON'T . . . we are in a state of miserable confusion and despair. We have nowhere to turn for an AUTHORITATIVE answer to the questions that are innately inscribed on the tables of our hearts. In actuality, the ALEXANDRIANS want to be the AUTHORITY. Just ASK 'em! THEY can tell you which parts of our English Bible are inspired and which are not. They want you to believe that THEY are the AUTHORITY. Well, bless 'em. What in the name of Pope Pius XII are we going to do when these brilliant, gasbag Alexandrians DIE???

These wise-guy north African theologians must think God is some namby-pamby dope. Knowing that we find ourselves guilty before Him, He has written His law in our hearts, but He has cared so little about showing us the way of salvation and forgiveness that He once gave us a Book that would give us the answers, but we let that Book go back to the dust thousands of years ago.

The god of the Alexandrians is EXACTLY that kind of god . . . but the God of the Bible is NOT!!! As I have already demonstrated in previous chapters, we HAVE the inspired, inerrant, infallible Word of God in OUR language . . . the AV1611 King James Bible!!! This wonderful Book is our authority concerning life, death, Heaven, Hell, eternity, salvation, forgiveness . . . and how to know its Author personally. In our language, THERE IS NO OTHER AUTHORITY!

The Alexandrians want to have authority over the Book . . .

CAN I TRUST MY BIBLE'S AUTHORITY?

but in the end, they will find out that the Book has authority over THEM! They will be judged by God's ONE Bible!

I pointed out in the previous chapter that the Bible is the WRITTEN Word of God (Matt. 4:4, 7, 10; Luke 24:44; I John 5:13), and that Jesus Christ is the INCARNATE WORD of God (John 1:1, 14; Rev. 19:13). It is a fact that stands without controversy . . . both the WRITTEN Word and the INCARNATE Word point us to the WRITTEN Word as God's ONLY and FINAL authority on the matters of life, death, Heaven, Hell, eternity, salvation, and forgiveness for sin. I repeat . . . on this earth THERE IS NO OTHER AUTHORITY!

Men have written THEIR books on these subjects, but THEIR books have no divine authority. There is only ONE source of divine authority, and that is GOD'S Book! God's infallible Scripture is His witness of truth and authority to mankind.

If we receive the witness of men, the witness of God is GREATER . . . (I John 5:9).

The "witness of God" is His BOOK! God's Book is GREATER than anything men can write. When men write, they make errors . . . but when GOD writes, He writes infallible! When we look for authority concerning life, death, Heaven, Hell, eternity, salvation, and forgiveness for our sins, the Scripture ITSELF tells us to go to SCRIPTURE. Since Scripture is composed totally, and only, of God's WORDS, we understand that GOD HIMSELF tells us to go to Scripture for our ONLY and FINAL authority on these subjects.

Religious leaders dream up lies in their heads; then they preach these lies and write them in books. Neither these religious leaders NOR their books have any authority on these vital subjects at all. Look what God says about it.

I have heard what the prophets said, that prophesy

CAN I TRUST MY BIBLE?

LIES in my name, saying, I have dreamed, I have dreamed. How long shall this be in the heart of the prophets that prophesy LIES? yea, they are prophets of the DECEIT OF THEIR OWN HEART . . . The prophet that hath a dream, and HE THAT HATH MY WORD, let him speak my word faithfully . . . (Jer. 23:25-26, 28).

While wicked religious leaders endeavor to make THEMSELVES the only and final authority on eternal matters, God says there ARE men who have His Word. He wants those of us who have His Word to preach it FAITHFULLY, for His Word is the only and final authority. From the very beginning, God has had His Word WRITTEN DOWN and RECORDED so His Words would not be forgotten by men. The first five books of the Bible were written by Moses, and God had PRESERVED the words Moses had written down to the time that Jesus was on the earth, even though the "originals" were gone. He said to the religious leaders of Israel,

Do not think that I will accuse you to the Father: there is one that accuseth you, even Moses, in whom ye trust. For had ye believed Moses, ye would have believed me: for he WROTE of me. But if ye believe not his WRITINGS, how shall ye believe my words? (John 5:45-47).

In our King James Bible, we STILL have the words that Moses wrote as well as the words written by ALL the God-inspired prophets and apostles. The entire Bible is centered on Jesus Christ, as well as the books of Moses. God's infallible, inspired Book is His absolute AUTHORITY about *redemption* . . . which is His WRITTEN RECORD about His Son, the *Redeemer.*

If we receive the witness of men, the witness of God is GREATER: for this (Scripture) IS the witness of God which he hath testified of his Son . . . And this

CAN I TRUST MY BIBLE'S AUTHORITY?

(Scripture) IS the (written) record, that God hath given to us eternal life, and this life is in His Son, (I John 5:9, 11).

When it comes to life, death, Heaven, Hell, eternity, redemption, and ANYTHING else having to do with God, Scripture points us to Scripture for authority on these matters. Let me show you some examples.

And Joshua discomfited Amalek and his people with the edge of the sword. And the Lord said unto Moses, WRITE this for a memorial in a BOOK, and rehearse it in the ears of Joshua: for I will utterly put out the remembrance of Amalek from under heaven (Ex. 17:13-14).

Not only does God authorize the writing of this book, but the content of it is His own oath. It is the Word of God, His Word of absolute AUTHORITY. Because God has spoken it and had it WRITTEN down, it will surely come to pass. The same is true of His entire Bible.

A little later in Exodus, we began more about God's divine WRITING. In chapter 20, God speaks the Ten Commandments to the people of Israel. The people are terrified and shake in their boots. They ask Moses to act as mediator between God and them. From Exodus 20:22 through 23:33, God gives Moses MORE commandments which he is to convey to the people. In Exodus 24:4 we read that *"Moses WROTE all the words of the Lord."* Then he read all that he had written to the people and the people cried out, *"All that the Lord hath said will we do, and be obedient"* (Ex. 24:7).

The people of Israel accepted the WRITTEN Word as absolute AUTHORITY. They HAD the written Word to hold in their hands and read, and so do we. As the written Word held absolute AUTHORITY over the people of Israel, it holds absolute

CAN I TRUST MY BIBLE?

AUTHORITY over us today.

God is very, very particular about His WRITTEN Word! Now get a gander at this.

> And the Lord said unto Moses, Come up to me into the mount, and be there: and I will give thee tables of stone, and a law, and commandments WHICH I HAVE WRITTEN; that thou mayest teach them (Ex. 24:12).

Do you see it? God tells Moses to come up on the mountain where he will be given a divinely-written manuscript that God, HIMSELF had already written! Wow! God wrote this Scripture HIMSELF! Elsewhere too, we learn that God did the writing HIMSELF.

> And he gave unto Moses, when he had made an end of communing with him upon mount Sinai, two tables of testimony, tables of stone, WRITTEN WITH THE FINGER OF GOD (Ex. 31:18).

> And the tables WERE THE WORK OF GOD, and the writing WAS THE WRITING OF GOD, graven upon the tables (Ex. 32:16).

Here's something for you Alexandrians to think about. Later, Moses COPIED what God had written on the stones onto papyrus. It was what Moses COPIED onto the papyrus that was entered into the canon of Scripture.

QUESTION: Which was divinely inspired . . . the original writing done by the finger of God Himself or the COPY that Moses made when he COPIED it onto the parchment? Hmm? You birds hang so tight to the "originals" . . . saying that ONLY the "originals" were inspired . . . so c'mon. Tell me. How could what Moses COPIED be inspired and inerrant since GOD HIMSELF wrote the "originals"???

CAN I TRUST MY BIBLE'S AUTHORITY?

While the Alexandrians gnaw on it for a while, let me say to my reader that BOTH the "originals" written by God Himself AND the copy Moses wrote later are inspired . . . even as our King James Bible, which was translated from a COPY of a COPY, is inspired! Whether the words of God are engraved in stone, written on papyrus, or printed on the pages of my King James Bible, they are STILL the only and final authority from God!

Time and again, Scripture points us to Scripture as the ONLY authority on earth concerning life, death, Heaven, Hell, and redemption. We cannot be saved apart from the written Word of God. The Bible was written for the VERY PURPOSE of bringing us to Jesus Christ for salvation . . . and for guiding us through life after we get saved. God says,

These things have I WRITTEN . . . that ye may believe on the name of the Son of God (I John 5:13).

And many other signs truly did Jesus in the presence of his disciples, which are not written in this book: But THESE ARE WRITTEN, that ye might believe that Jesus is the Christ, the Son of God; and that believing YE MIGHT HAVE LIFE THROUGH HIS NAME (John 20:30-31).

For whatsoever things WERE WRITTEN aforetime WERE WRITTEN for our learning, that we through patience and comfort of the scriptures might HAVE hope (Rom. 15:4).

The Scriptures that were written and PRESERVED were not only written inerrantly and inspired so that we might be saved, but they were also written that we might HAVE hope concerning life, death, Heaven, and redemption. The ONLY authority on the face of this earth for our salvation and comforting hope is GOD'S WORD!!! You will note in Romans 15:4 that the Scriptures WERE written (past tense) that we might HAVE hope (present tense). God had the

CAN I TRUST MY BIBLE?

Scriptures written down in the PAST, but He has kept them perfect and inspired down to the PRESENT that we might be saved through them and that we might learn through them about the redemption that we have, and thus have hope.

If we listen to the Alexandrians, WE HAVE NO SCRIPTURES TO BRING US TO CHRIST, AND WE HAVE NO SCRIPTURES TO TEACH US AND GIVE US HOPE! But, thank God, we DO have the Scriptures in our good old King James Bible! It is here from the hand of God that brings us to Christ and that guides us through life till we go to Heaven.

> *We HAVE also a more sure word of prophecy; whereunto ye do well that ye take heed, as unto a light that shineth in a dark place, until the day dawn, and the day star arise in your hearts: Knowing this first, that no prophecy of the scripture is of any private interpretation. For the prophecy came not IN OLD TIME by the will of man: but holy men of God spake as they were moved by the Holy Ghost* (II Pet. 1:19-20).

God gave us His Word IN OLD TIME so that even today we might HAVE the SURE WORD. Scripture pervasively claims authority for itself in both the Old and New Testaments. Paul wrote of his writings,

> *. . . The things that I write unto you ARE THE COMMANDMENTS OF THE LORD (I Cor. 14:37).*

> *I charge you BY THE LORD that this epistle be read unto all the holy brethren (I Thess. 5:27).*

In II Peter 3:16, the Holy Spirit, through Peter classes, the epistles of Paul together with the "other Scriptures" . . . and Peter's writings identify themselves as "the Word" of the Lord that will endure forever (I Pet. 1:25).

CAN I TRUST MY BIBLE'S AUTHORITY?

We then conclude that the witness of Scripture to its own AUTHORITY is pervasive. The written Word always directs us to ITSELF for the ONLY and FINAL authority in the matters of life, death, Heaven, Hell, salvation, forgiveness, redemption . . . and the personal knowledge of our Creator.

The same is true of the INCARNATE Word. The entire earthly life of the Lord Jesus Christ was a witness to BIBLICAL AUTHORITY. I remind you again that when Jesus spoke of the Scripture, he NEVER ONCE mentioned the "original manuscripts." He pointed the people to an Aramaic TRANSLATION, and He NEVER ONCE corrected that TRANSLATION! The TRANSLATION He held in His hands was as much the inspired Word of God as were the "originals." Since what was written originally was written so that WE ALSO might be saved and learn from the Scripture, I say that we should take the same approach to the perfect, inspired Word of God in ENGLISH that our Lord took toward the perfect, inspired Word of God in Aramaic.

Jesus said, *"The scripture cannot be broken"* (John 10:35). He could not have possibly taken the attitude of the Alexandrians, who believe that the ONLY Scripture was the "original manuscripts." Certainly the "original manuscripts" were BROKEN. They were BROKEN by time and use . . . and finally crumbled to pieces and returned to dust. Jesus was making it plain that He would PRESERVE the WORDS of Scripture so that they would exist forever (even in TRANSLATIONS) and would hold AUTHORITY over us forever.

Scripture tells us that the Lord Jesus is our Example and that *"ye should follow his steps"* (I Pet. 2:21). Certainly, one way we should follow His steps is to have the same attitude toward the Word of God that He had while here on earth (and STILL HAS TODAY, for that matter!). If He never referred to the "original manuscripts" as the only inspired, inerrant, infallible Word of God . . . WHY SHOULD WE? If He could hold a pure translation in His hands and

CAN I TRUST MY BIBLE?

call it "Scripture" . . . WHY CAN'T WE? If HE never corrected that translation . . . WHY SHOULD WE ATTEMPT TO CORRECT THE TRUE TRANSLATION IN ENGLISH?

Satan started out in the very beginning by casting doubt on the Word of God (Gen. 3:1). The old devil has had his Alexandrian Jehoiakims slicing up the word of God down through the centuries . . . but in spite of them, the Lord has ALWAYS kept pure manuscript COPIES and TRANSLATIONS so that His WORDS are being kept and preserved FOREVER. While here on earth, the Lord Jesus never cast doubt on the COPIES of the original manuscripts nor the Aramaic TRANSLATION from which He taught and preached.

I cannot speak for my reader . . . but as for me and my house, we will follow the example set for us by the Lord Jesus Christ! We will totally submit to the Scripture as the ONE AND ONLY AUTHORITY from God on the face of this earth. We will always seek to encourage people to believe the Book they hold in their hands (IF it is an AV 1611!). We will NEVER cast a doubt on the COPIES of the original Masoretic Hebrew and Received Text Greek manuscripts nor the TRANSLATIONS that are done honestly and correctly from those manuscripts.

Let us now consider our Lord's attitude toward the absolute AUTHORITY of the Scriptures. We will learn how He feels about the AUTHORITY of the Scriptures IN TOTAL as we observe His attitude toward them *legally, historically,* and *doctrinally.* You will quickly see that it is impossible to take the Alexandrian view and have the same attitude toward the Scriptures that JESUS has, for—I repeat—when He was here on earth, He believed that He HAD the Scriptures, although the "original manuscripts" were long gone and although what He held in His hands was an Aramaic TRANSLATION.

Let me point out quickly that what Jesus preached and taught the people of His day was the WORD OF GOD. Mark 2:2 says, *"He*

CAN I TRUST MY BIBLE'S AUTHORITY?

preached THE WORD unto them." In John 6:63, Jesus said, *"The words that I speak unto you, they are spirit and they are LIFE."* Time and again, He said that the very WORDS He spoke were Scripture.

Heaven and earth shall pass away, but MY WORDS shall not pass away (Matt 24:35).

Whosoever therefore shall be ashamed of me and of MY WORDS in this adulterous and sinful generation; of him also shall the Son of man be ashamed, when he cometh in the glory of his Father with the holy angels (Mark 8:38).

Jesus Christ is God (John 1:1; Phil. 2:6, Heb. 1:8; Rev. 1:8). He said the WORD is made up of HIS WORDS. Therefore, He is the Author of the Bible. If we can imitate HIS attitude toward the Bible, we cannot possibly go wrong. If we do NOT have the same attitude toward the Book that He has, we are DEAD WRONG! When Jesus preached and taught, He did so with AUTHORITY. Listen to the people who heard Him . . .

And it came to pass, when Jesus had ended these sayings, the people were astonished at his doctrine: For he taught them as one having AUTHORITY, and not as the scribes (Matt. 7:28-29).

And they went into Capernaum; and straightway on the sabbath day he entered into the synagogue, and taught. And they were astonished at his doctrine: for he taught them as one that had AUTHORITY, and not as the scribes (Mark 1:21-22).

The scribes, like the Pharisees, leaned heavily on human tradition. Therefore, they could not speak with authority. The people recognized this; but when they heard the Lord Jesus speak, He gave them the Word of God. Thus they said He taught them as one having AUTHORITY and not as the scribes.

CAN I TRUST MY BIBLE?

Let us observe our Lord's attitude toward the Scriptures *legally*. The Lord's magnifying of the Scripture comes to the surface in an unusual discussion with the unbelieving Jews late in His earthly ministry. The manner in which He had been speaking of His relationship with the Father had convinced the Jews that He was blaspheming.

> *Then the Jews took up stones again to stone him. Jesus answered them, Many good works have I shewed you from my Father; for which of those works do you stone me? The Jews answered him, saying, For a good work we stone thee not; but for blasphemy; and because that thou, being a man, makest thyself God. Jesus answered them, Is it not written in your LAW, I said, ye are gods? If he called them gods, unto whom the word of God came, and THE SCRIPTURE CANNOT BE BROKEN; Say ye of him whom the Father hath sanctified, and sent into the world, Thou blasphemest; because I said I am the Son of God?* (John 10:31-36).

In reply to the Jews' charge of blasphemy, Jesus appealed to Scripture, calling it "law" even though the text he quoted is in the Psalms (82:6). This was because ALL SCRIPTURE POSSESSED BINDING *LEGAL* FORCE TO HIM! All Scripture is God's LAW, both OLD and NEW Testaments (Psalm 19:7; James 1:21-25).

Jesus called the Jews' attention to the word "gods" used by the psalmist in Psalm 82:6, referring to the judges of Israel as they exercised their God-given office. If these men could be called "gods" because they served as vehicles of God's Word, all the more does the One whom the Father consecrated and sent into the world deserve the title "God." By referring to the passage and calling it "law," Jesus is asserting its LEGAL AUTHORITY over the Jews Himself and all mankind. The Lord's statement that the Scripture cannot be broken is

CAN I TRUST MY BIBLE'S AUTHORITY?

His way of stating that all Scripture has LEGAL AUTHORITY over every man; and consequently, its statements, even in an assuming phrase such as is found in Psalm 82:6, is inviolable.

Jesus is making it clear that because all Scripture is God's LAW, we are bound to obey that LAW . . . and we will be judged by that LAW (John 12:48) because sin is the transgression of the LAW (I John 3:4). Even though Jesus never sinned, He still placed HIMSELF under the written LAW. It was LEGAL AND BINDING on Him to FULFILL THE LAW (Matt. 5:17)! This is why time and again He spoke of Himself fulfilling the PROPHECIES of Scripture (Matt. 26:56; Luke 4:21; 22:37, etc.).

Since Jesus is our Example, and He held this attitude toward the WRITTEN Word of God which was divinely preserved and inspired in the Aramaic language, most certainly it should be OUR attitude toward the WRITTEN Word of God in the ENGLISH language, the AUTHORIZED Version of 1611! It has LEGAL AUTHORITY over ALL English-speaking people whether they believe it or not.

Secondly, let us observe our Lord's attitude toward the Scriptures *historically*. Never ONCE did He ever cast doubt on the AUTHORITY of the Bible in regard to its historical narratives. He treated them as factually truthful accounts. In the course of His preaching and teaching, He made reference to the murder of Abel (Luke 11:49-51), the flood in Noah's day (Matt 24:38), Abraham's prophetic view into the future (John 8:56), the destruction of Sodom in Lot's day (Luke 17:29), the historical family relationship of Abraham, Isaac, and Jacob, (Matt. 8:11), Jonah's seventy-two-hour stay in the whale's belly and his preaching to the city of Nineveh (Matt. 12:40-41), the queen of Sheba visiting King Solomon (Matt. 12:42), David eating shewbread (Mark 2:25-26), and many other persons and events in Scripture.

Jesus confirmed to the people that the entire historical fabric

CAN I TRUST MY BIBLE?

of the Old Testament was absolutely true and reliable. Since He is the Author of the ENTIRE Bible (Rev. 22:18-19), He stands behind the historical AUTHORITY of all sixty-six books!

Since Jesus validated the historical truthfulness of Scripture using a perfect, preserved, inspired TRANSLATION, it behoves US to believe the historical truthfulness of God's ONE and ONLY perfect, preserved, inspired TRANSLATION in OUR language . . . the precious old AV1611 King James Bible!

Let us now observe thirdly, our Lord's attitude toward the authority of the Scriptures *doctrinally*. During His encounter with the devil in the wilderness, Jesus repudiated the three temptations by a slam-bang appeal to the DOCTRINES of Scripture (Matt. 4:1-11). Each time, He wielded the Sword of the Spirit (Eph. 6:17) against Satan by saying, *"IT IS WRITTEN"*!

My reader will note that at the time Jesus and ol' smuddy-face had their confrontation, the "original manuscripts" were long gone. All that was left of the Hebrew Scriptures were COPIES . . . and since Jesus SPOKE Aramaic in His day, the conversation between Satan and Him was no doubt in Aramaic. Yet, the Lord affirmed to the devil, "It IS written!" He did NOT say, "It WAS written" . . . He declared "It IS written"!!! Therefore, Jesus was stating that Scripture was STILL ALIVE AND WELL . . . was STILL INSPIRED, INERRANT, INFALLIBLE, and AUTHORITATIVE even though the "original manuscripts" were long gone! By "It IS written," Jesus is teaching us that the doctrinal authority of Scripture was STILL intact, even though there were only Hebrew COPIES and an Aramaic TRANSLATION!

The same holds true in His various debates with the religious leaders who constantly opposed Him. Often they brought up Scripture to Him in order to trap Him with it. He never criticized them for referring to the Scriptures, but He DID rebuke them for not BELIEVING the Scriptures and not studying them enough to

CAN I TRUST MY BIBLE'S AUTHORITY?

KNOW them. A good example is the incident in Matthew 22 where the Sadducees threw Deuteronomy 25:5 in His face with hopes of getting Him in a corner.

(Hee! Hee! I really have to chuckle at this! Just think of it . . . little pea-brain religious leaders attempting to "corner" the Author of the Book with His OWN WRITINGS!!! Hee! Hee!)

Anyway . . . the Master Debater put them to silence by quoting Scripture (Matt. 22:31-34); then He gave them a stunning karate chop by saying, *"Ye do err, NOT KNOWING THE SCRIPTURES . . ."* (Matt. 22:29)!

All religious people are off DOCTRINALLY, or they wouldn't BE religious. They do err, NOT KNOWING THE SCRIPTURES. Jesus scolded the Pharisees in Matthew 23:23 for their meticulous concern over the minutiae of the Law while neglecting the weightier matters of it. For their mishandling of the Scriptures, He called them "BLIND GUIDES WHICH STRAIN AT A GNAT AND SWALLOW A CAMEL." I love it!

The Lord Jesus was especially irritated at the scribes and Pharisees for the way they built DOCTRINES on human tradition rather than the Word of God. Listen to Him.

> *. . . Well hath Esaias prophesied of you HYPOCRITES (The Lord always called a spade a spade!), as it is written, This people honoureth me with their lips, but their heart is far from me. Howbeit in vain do they worship me, teaching for DOCTRINES the commandments of MEN. For laying aside the commandment of God, ye hold the TRADITION OF MEN . . . Full well ye reject the commandment of God, that ye may keep your OWN TRADITION . . . Making the word of God of none effect through your TRADITION . . .* (Mark 7:6-9, 13).

CAN I TRUST MY BIBLE?

The Lord Jesus Christ is not only the Author of the Bible, but He is also our Creator (John 1:1-3, 10; Col. 1:16; Heb. 1:2). He has a perfect right to be indignant when men invent religions by building their doctrines on human tradition rather than the Word of God. You will note that in Mark 7:13, Jesus said doctrines built on human tradition make the Word of God of NONE EFFECT. All religions . . . (DID YOU HEAR ME?) . . . ALL religions are built on human TRADITION. Therefore, ALL religious people are LOST! All religious people end up in HELL! The traditions they believe are anti-Bible, anti-truth, and anti-Christ. We can only be saved through the pure, inspired Word of God (Psalm 19:7; Rom. 10:17; James 1:18; I Pet. 1:23). Religious people, therefore, are LOST because their doctrines are human TRADITION, which make the saving Word of God of none effect.

Romans 1:16 says the GOSPEL OF CHRIST is the power of God unto salvation. Therefore, whatever comprises the Gospel is what saves us from Hell and the wrath of God when we believe and obey it (Mark 1:15; II Thess. 1:8-9). Let us look at GOD'S definition of the Gospel. Under the inspiration of the Holy Spirit, Paul wrote to the church at Corinth . . .

> *Moreover, brethren, I declare unto you the GOSPEL . . . By which also YE ARE SAVED . . . For I delivered unto you first of all that which I also received, how that Christ died for our sins according to the scriptures; And that he was buried, and that he rose again the third day according to the scriptures;* (I Cor. 15:1-4).

There it is. You have just read GOD'S definition of the Gospel. You will note that the Gospel is in three parts: (1) Christ died for our sins. (2) Christ was buried. (3) Christ rose again from the dead.

That's it. When Jesus went to the cross, He shed His precious blood and DIED. They BURIED His body. On the third day, He

CAN I TRUST MY BIBLE'S AUTHORITY?

ROSE FROM THE DEAD, and He is alive to save every sinner who will believe and obey the Gospel. This is the pure DOCTRINE of salvation, based upon the infallible, inerrant, inspired Word of God. When religious people ADD TO or TAKE AWAY FROM the Gospel, they are following human tradition, which makes the saving Word of God of NONE EFFECT. The Word of God cannot bring about salvation when people cling to religious tradition.

My reader will note that in the Gospel there is no BAPTISM, no CATECHISM, no COMMUNION, no CONFESSING TO A PRIEST, no CHURCH MEMBERSHIP, no CONFIRMATION, no ROSARY, no CRUCIFIX, no POPE, no MARY, no HOLDING OUT FAITHFUL TO THE END (a.k.a. Pentecostals, Campbellites, Nazarenes, Free Will "Baptists," etc.), no SPEAKING IN TONGUES, no "GOOD WORKS," no RELIGIOUS SINCERITY, and no BUYING SALVATION WITH MONEY. You add any of these things to the Gospel, and you nullify the Word of God. You will die and spend eternity in the Lake of Fire!

The only Person in the Gospel is JESUS CHRIST! He did EVERYTHING that had to be done to make the way of salvation open to ALL humanity. NOTHING ELSE CAN BE ADDED. When anyone adds any of the things I've listed (or ANYTHING ELSE) to procure salvation, they believe a LIE and will DIE IN THEIR SINS. In order to be saved, you must BELIEVE that Jesus paid the whole price, or you DO NOT believe the Gospel. You must OBEY the Gospel by repenting of your wicked sin of unbelief (Luke 13:3; John 16:9). Believing that Jesus does ALL the saving ALL by Himself from START TO FINISH, you CALL on Him (Rom. 10:9-13) and RECEIVE Him into your heart as your own personal Saviour (John 1:12; Eph. 3:17).

If my reader has never done this, I urge you to lay the book down right now and humble yourself before the Lord. Call on the Lord Jesus Christ, admitting your wicked sin of not believing on Him

CAN I TRUST MY BIBLE?

before now, and ask Him to cleanse your sins away in His blood and save your Hell-bound soul. I guarantee you upon the authority of the Word of God . . . He WILL save you if you mean business with Him! If you do this, please write me at the address in the front of the book. I want to guide you to a good King James Bible-believing Baptist church and help you get started right in your Christian life.

The Lord Jesus Christ is the Author of the Bible. He is also the one and only Saviour. While He was on this earth, He occupied Himself chiefly with the exposition of Scripture. He made it plain that the DOCTRINES of Scripture were the only and final AUTHORITY for truth concerning life, death, eternity, Heaven, Hell, forgiveness for sins, and salvation from the wrath of God.

When He referred to the Scripture, He ALWAYS referred to a Book that the people that He taught could HOLD IN THEIR HANDS. Once more I remind you that Jesus NEVER referred to the "original manuscripts," and He NEVER corrected the Aramaic TRANSLATION that He held in His hands. BEWARE OF MEN (and women) WHO CLAIM TO BE SENT FROM GOD WHO REFER YOU TO THE "ORIGINAL MANUSCRIPTS" WHICH THEY HAVE NEVER SEEN, AND WHO MAKE THEMSELVES THE AUTHORITY BY "CORRECTING" THE WONDERFUL OLD TIME-TESTED, GOD-BREATHED, HEAVEN-BLESSED, INERRANT, INFALLIBLE, INSPIRED AV1611 KING JAMES BIBLE!!!

Just as Jesus called the Aramaic TRANSLATION of His day "SCRIPTURE" . . . He has shown in many wondrous ways that He considers the KING JAMES ENGLISH TRANSLATION "SCRIPTURE." In English, the only and final AUTHORITY is the KING JAMES BIBLE!!!

You ask, "Can I Trust My Bible's Authority?" If your Bible is the Authorized version of 1611 known as the King James Bible, YOU MOST CERTAINLY CAN!!!

VII

CAN I TRUST MY BIBLE?

And now we come to the last chapter. So far we have seen that we can trust Satan to LIE, CHEAT, and DECEIVE. We can trust the dirty old devil to attack God's Word and lead his ministers to pervert it. We have learned that we cannot trust the modern day Jehoiakims (also known as Alexandrians) to have good sense nor to be truthful. Some of the "fundamental" ones that USE the King James Bible . . . even CALL it the Word of God . . . and APPEAR to believe it; then they attack it subtly by "correcting" it while preaching or teaching from it. LIARS.

We have learned that if we have an AV 1611 King James Bible, we can trust its TRANSLATION, INSPIRATION, PRESERVATION, and AUTHORITY. This fairly well sums up my purpose for writing the book . . . but in this final chapter, I want to spend just a short space of time in showing you why you CANNOT trust ANY English version BUT the AV1611.

Within the ranks of what is supposed to be true Christianity, we have spiritual leaders who purposely mislead the laymen in the pews regarding the Word of God. It is my duty and responsibility to warn God's people as best as I can about these sneaky Alexandrians. Not long ago, I preached a sermon in a church, naming many of the false prophets of our day who parade around in sheep's clothing. Many of those I labeled for what they are—"big name" television

CAN I TRUST MY BIBLE?

and radio "preachers." I put *preachers* in quotes because most of them can't preach their way out of a wet paper bag. They are "teachers." They don't PREACH. Paul warned us that this would be the case. After telling real, God-called PREACHERS to "PREACH THE WORD" (II Tim. 4:2), he said,

> *For the time will come when they (the people in the ranks of "true Christianity") will not endure sound doctrine; but after their own lusts shall they heap to themselves TEACHERS, having itching ears; And they shall TURN AWAY their ears FROM THE TRUTH, and shall be turned UNTO FABLES* (II Tim. 4:3-4).

Get a good look at what Paul said. We are living in the time he told us would come. Most "Christians" today do not want to hear PREACHING, so they turn from PREACHERS to *teachers*. They flock to churches where they will get the "deep stuff" . . . and they listen to television and radio *teachers* who give them the "deep stuff" but never offend them by stomping on their sins and their deviltry. Such men are NOT preachers of the Word (Isa. 58:1; Jer. 1:4-12; II Tim. 4:2).

Anyway, after this one service where I named a bunch of the sissy-britches, little television and radio *teachers,* a man came up to me and asked just what television and radio preachers he should listen to. I told him to FORGET IT and just to listen to his pastor. If there is a television or radio man left who really PREACHES THE KING JAMES BIBLE, I don't know of him. The man smiled, nodded, and said, "Okay. That's what I'll do."

I don't know of a time when there was a REAL Bible-believing, straight-forward, fearless BAPTIST preacher on regular national television. Any man who got on there and preached it STRAIGHT would be thrown off. If there is a man on national radio today (other than a couple of dead men whose tapes are still

CAN I TRUST MY BIBLE?

being played) who believes and preaches the King James Bible, I don't know of him. There might be one or two who USE the King James, but most of them such as James Dobson, Chuck Swindoll, and others have gone to the NIV. I have already shown you what John MacArthur is by his own mouth.

I can remember the old days when Dr. M.R. DeHann preached on his Radio Bible Class. He always preached the King James Bible, and I never heard him correct it or recommend another version. My . . . how things change. Dr. DeHann's son and grandson have "messed up." My reader is probably acquainted with the publication of the Radio Bible Class called *Our Daily Bread*. There was a time when Bible-believing Baptist pastors could order the publication for their people to use in daily devotions. NO MORE.

The publication has now gone with the "New" King James perversion! Let me give you an example of what is found in *Our Daily Bread* these days. For daily devotions on September 17, the page is headed "THE BEST BIBLE." Then they quote from the "New" King James perversion: " . . . desire the pure milk of the word, that you may grow thereby" (I Peter 2:2).

The first paragraph then says, "Sometimes we hear Christians argue about which Bible is the best. Some like the stately language of the King James Version. Others prefer the more up-to-date wording of one of the newer translations. To me, WHICH BIBLE YOU PREFER IS NOT AS IMPORTANT as whether or not you read it. The best Bible is a used Bible."

This is typical Alexandrian hokus-pokus. The present-day DeHanns seem to have the idea that ANYTHING that calls itself a "bible" is the Word of God. So you see, it is not important which "bible" you "prefer." The important thing is that you READ whichever "bible" you "prefer." If you "prefer" a perversion and want to poison your mind and your soul, that's okay . . . just so you are soaking it in. ANY PASTOR WITH GOOD SENSE IS NOT

CAN I TRUST MY BIBLE?

GOING TO ALLOW *OUR DAILY BREAD* TO GET INTO THE HANDS OF HIS PEOPLE!!!

Let me now show you why no born-again, blood-washed child of God should read, study, believe, or TRUST any of the so-called "up-to-date" perversions. They are POISON! The only REAL Bible in the English language is theAV1611 KING JAMES BIBLE!!! Avoid all others like the plague!

Since the "New" King James perversion and the New International perversion are by far the most popular perversions in the English-speaking world today, I will deal mostly with them. However, for those who still hold to the New American Standard perversion and Kenneth Taylor's Living (Ha! Ha!) Bible (Ha! Ha!), let me give you at least enough to see that they are indeed PERVERSIONS. Let's do a little comparing with the REAL Bible and the New American Standard perversion. I will identify the REAL Bible as KJV and the perversion here as NASV. Look at Luke 16:23.

KJV: *"And in hell he lift up his eyes, being in torments..."*

NASV: "And in HADES he lift up his eyes, being in torment..."

My reader will quickly notice the NASV changes "hell" to "HADES" and "torments" to "TORMENT." This is a blatant attempt to water down Hell and make it not seem so bad. By removing the "s" from "torments," it lessens the torture of Hell to a SINGLE torment. Not quite so bad as the naughty King James, eh?

Alexandrian "scholars" argue that it is all right for the NASV translators to replace "hell" with "HADES" since *hades* is the Greek word for "hell." Mm-hmm. Sure. You bet. The Lockman Foundation, which produced the NASV isn't kidding me! "Hades" just doesn't sound as bad as "hell," does it? They want to soften Hell ... make it not quite so offensive.

CAN I TRUST MY BIBLE?

I say it is rotten dishonesty and wicked inconsistency! If the NASV translators are going to leave in the Greek word for Hell, why don't they do the some thing with the Greek word for *Heaven*? Hmm? If they are going to be honest and consistent, they should translate Acts 1:11: "... Ye men of Galilee, why stand ye gazing up into OURANOS? this same Jesus, which is taken up from you into OURANOS, shall so come in like manner as ye have seen him go into OURANOS."

But then . . . how can we expect the NASV translators to be honest when they even have THE LORD JESUS CHRIST telling a lie?

Whenever Jesus spoke in the Gospels of His "time" or His "hour," He was referring to that time when He would relinquish Himself into the hands of His enemies to be crucified. Listen to Him in the KJV as He speaks to His earthly half-brothers (sons of Joseph and Mary).

Go ye up unto this feast: I go not UP YET unto this feast; for my time is not yet full come. When he had said these words unto them, he abode still in Galilee. But when his brethren were gone up, then went he also up unto the feast, NOT OPENLY, but as it were in secret (John 7:8-10).

In verse 8, Jesus says *"I go not up YET unto this feast."* The word "YET" tells us that He will go up later, which He DID, (though SECRETLY, so they would not take Him to crucify Him BEFORE it was time on GOD's clock). Now look at verse 8 in the NASV: "Go up to this feast yourselves. I do not go up to this feast because my time has not yet fully come."

Do you see that? The NASV has Jesus saying He will NOT go up to the feast. It leaves out the word "YET." However, in verse 10 of the NASV, they have Him go up to the feast! This makes Jesus a LIAR! The Bible says, "... *let GOD be true, but EVERY MAN A*

CAN I TRUST MY BIBLE?

LIAR" (Rom. 3:4). By their wicked translation of John 7:8-10, the NASV perverters make Jesus a LIAR, thus taking away His deity and making Him a mere sinful man!

But, of course, this should not surprise us. The NASV team of Bible perverters have attacked our Lord's deity in MANY other places. Let me show you a couple more. We read of Jesus in Luke 2:33.

KJV: *"And Joseph and his mother marvelled at those things which were spoken of him."*

NASV: "And His FATHER and mother were amazed at the things being said about Him."

If Joseph was the father of Mary's first-born Son, Jesus IS NOT DEITY! He is NOT the only begotten Son of GOD! He is a sinner just like the rest of us, and a LIAR like all men! BLASPHEMY!!!

In John 1:18, we have God's only begotten Son declaring the Father to the world.

KJV: "... *the only begotten SON* ... *hath declared him."*

NASV: "The only begotten GOD ... has explained him."

The NASV makes Jesus a begotten "God." This means He is not the ALMIGHTY, ETERNAL GOD ... He is begotten (born) as a God. He would be less than God the Father because He would be a CREATED God. This is EXACTLY what the Jehovah's Witnesses believe, and the NASV has translated it EXACTLY as the J.W.'s did in their vile New World Translation!!!

This is only the tip of the iceberg in the NASV, but it ought to be enough for any born-again child of God to see that it STINKS! It is an ALEXANDRIAN PERVERSION! It is plain to see that you cannot trust the NASV!

Now let's take a brief glance at Kenneth Taylor's Living (Ha! Ha!) Bible (Ha! Ha!). Even the cover is a LIE. It is NOT "living"

CAN I TRUST MY BIBLE?

because the Holy Spirit did NOT inspire it! It is NOT a "Bible" for the exact same reason! Look at I Timothy 3:16.

> KJV: *"And without controversy great is the mystery of godliness: GOD was manifest in the flesh . . ."*

> LB: "It is quite true that the matter to live a godly life is not an easy matter, but the answer lies in Christ who came to earth as a man."

What happened to "GOD was manifest in the flesh"? Taylor has just ripped the deity from Jesus Christ! To say "Christ came to earth as a man" means NOTHING. Kenneth Taylor came to earth as a man, AND HE IS NOT GOD! So did I . . . and I AM NOT GOD! If Christ is not deity, THERE IS NO SALVATION FOR LOST SINNERS BECAUSE HE IS ALSO A LOST SINNER! Look at Romans 10:9.

> KJV: *"That if thou shalt confess with thy mouth the Lord Jesus, and shalt believe in thine heart that God hath raised him from the dead, thou shalt be saved."*

> LB: "For IF YOU TELL OTHERS with your own mouth that Jesus Christ is your Lord and believe in you heart that God has raised him from the dead, you will be saved."

Well, there it is . . . salvation by HUMAN WORKS. Taylor wants you to believe that you can only be saved if you can find someone to talk to and tell them that Jesus is your Lord. DIRTY, SATANIC LIE! Romans 10:13 says, *"For whosoever shall call upon the NAME OF THE LORD shall be saved."* The "confession" in Romans 10:9 is NOT TO MEN . . . it is to THE LORD!!! What if some poor guy was stranded on a desert island and was starving to death, but he wanted to be saved? WHO could he TELL so that he could be saved? Ridiculous.

CAN I TRUST MY BIBLE?

We've barely scratched the surface here, but I believe my reader has seen enough to know you can't trust the so-called "Living Bible."

It should be quite evident to my reader by now that you cannot trust ANY Alexandrian "bible" . . . which leaves ONLY the King James Bible that you CAN trust . . . but let me show you WHY you can't trust the Alexandrian "bibles." Let us now take a look at the two most popular "bibles" in "Christianity" today. Let's take Jerry Falwell's "New" King James Version first. There is no question in my mind that it will fade out of existence within a few more years and that it will give way to the New INTERNATIONAL Version, which is fast becoming the ONE-WORLD "bible" for antichrist's ONE-WORLD religion. But since the NKJV is quite popular today, let's take a shot at it.

When I open my copy of the NKJV, the first thing I find is a foreword by Mr. Falwell, in which he brags on the NKJV committee for producing a "modernization of the present form of the King James Version." It is a modernization, all right . . . but as we shall see, its "form" is NOT like the REAL King James Version!

On page ii, I find that the NKJV has been COPYRIGHTED by Thomas Nelson, Inc., its publishers. Funny . . . I can't find a copyright in my REAL King James Bible. It has always been my understanding that when an author copyrights a book he writes, it is because it is HIS work, and he wants to protect it so that no one else can come along and write one like it. Right off the bat, we learn that the Thomas Nelson Company ADMITS that the content of their "New" King James bible is THEIR work . . . not GOD'S! If the words in the NKJV are GOD'S words, Thomas Nelson HAS NO RIGHT TO COPYRIGHT THEM!!!

On the same page we find these words: "All rights reserved. Written permission must be secured from the publisher to use or reproduce any part of this book, except for brief quotations in critical reviews and articles."

Strange, isn't it? For hundreds of years, publishers have been printing the REAL King James Bible, and they never had to be concerned about getting permission from GOD to do so, nor have they had to worry about GOD suing them. But friend of mine, if you were to print the "New" King James bible, Thomas Nelson would sue your socks off! What a shame . . to publish a "bible" which is supposed to be GOD'S Word, but when the publisher takes out a copyright, he admits it is not God's Word, but HIS OWN !!!!!

I guess since what I'm about to do here . . . make brief quotations in a critical review . . . I won't get sued.

I notice on page iv in the "Preface," we are told, "All participating scholars have signed a document of subscription to the plenary and verbal inspiration of the ORIGINAL AUTOGRAPHS of the Bible." Yup. Here we go again. The NKJV "scholars" are ALL Alexandrians! This will be even more evident as we progress. Remember that Jesus said, ". . . a corrupt tree bringeth forth evil fruit" (Matt. 7:17). The NKJV is loaded with evil fruit.

On page vii of the Preface, Nelson admits that the Alexandrian Text shows "signs of unreliability" and that the Text underlying the 1611 King James Bible is the Received Text; but as we shall see, the NKJV relies a whole lot on the Alexandrian Text. How utterly deceiving to call their nefarious book the NEW King James Bible. For shame.

On page iii of the Preface, we are told that the NKJV is "a continuation of the labors of the earlier translators, thus UNLOCKING for today's readers the SPIRITUAL TREASURES found especially in the Authorized (1611) Version of the Holy Scriptures."

Good grief, Charlie Brown! Are these clowns actually telling us that there are "spiritual treasures" that have been LOCKED UP for nearly four hundred years in the AVl611, and that NOW the

CAN I TRUST MY BIBLE?

"New" King James perversion is going to UNLOCK them for us? Oooooh! Somebody get me some Pepto Bismol! I think I'm going to be sick!

Between the covers of the NKJV, you cannot find the names of the "Translation Committee" nor of the "scholars" who slapped the thing together. I had to do a little searching to find a list of these "godly" men. I won't waste space here to list them; but if you will search them out as I have, you will find a mish-mash conglomeration of New Evangelicals, weak-kneed Southern Baptists, tongues-speaking, vision-seeking Charismatics (who believe they are working their way to Heaven), Calvinistic baby-sprinklers, and Bible-correcting "Baptists." Talk about a corrupt tree!

In an advertising brochure that was printed at the same time the "New" King James perversion was first published, the Alexandrian con-men stated that "after 371 years the Authorized Version has been carefully updated so that it will ONCE AGAIN speak God's eternal truths WITH CLARITY."

How did you like that? Reminds me of the advertisement in the *Sword of the Lord* back in 1973 when the New American Standard perversion came out . . . "AT LAST, A RELIABLE TRANSLATION!"

Ah, but I guess the Alexandrians found the NASV not quite so reliable; for now, the "NEW" King James is the one that speaks with "clarity." Several "spiritual" leaders allowed their names to be included in the brochure, including Truman Dollar, who at that time was pastor of Kansas City Baptist Temple; A.V. Henderson, who was then pastor of Temple Baptist Church in Detroit; Jerry Falwell, Ed Hindson, and Elmer Towns of Liberty University, Lynchburg, Virginia; Arthur Farstad and Walter Bodine of Presbyterian Dallas Theological Seminary; James Price of Tennessee Temple Schools, Chattanooga, Tennessee; Harold Ockenga (now deceased), father of the New Evangelical Sissy-britches Movement; and Curtis Hutson,

CAN I TRUST MY BIBLE?

Editor of the *Sword of the Lord*. To my knowledge, not one of these men has repented of having been associated with the "New" King James perversion, nor has he stepped forth and declared that he now believes that the AV1611 King James Bible is the inerrant, inspired, infallible Word of God.

Let's SEE if the NKJV speaks with "clarity." Let's SEE if it clears up passages that are muddled in the KJV. Let's SEE if it UNLOCKS spiritual treasures that we couldn't quite get out of the AV1611. How about starting right at the beginning? Genesis 1:1...

KJV: *"In the beginning God created the HEAVEN and the earth."*

NKJV: "In the beginning God created the HEAVENS and the earth."

There is a difference between the *heaven* and the *heavens*. By adding an "s" to "heaven" in Genesis 1:1, the NKJV Alexandrian translators are equating Genesis 1:1 with Genesis 2:1-2. "Finished" and "made" are NOT the same thing as "CREATED"! I defy ANYBODY to find anything CREATED in Genesis 1:3-31 except the SOULS of man and beast. The materials from which God made their BODIES was ALREADY in the earth or the sea (Gen. 1:20-21, 24-25; 2:7).

Instead of unlocking truth, the NKJV translators have COVERED UP the truth. God did not create the heaven and the earth without form and void. There isn't time nor space to go into it here, but a careful study of Scripture will reveal that Lucifer of old was the cause of a horrible, cataclysmic event that fell on the heavens and the earth, resulting in the earth being flooded and the lights of the heavens going out. Read II Peter 3:4-6, and you will see that the earth was flooded and the heavens were affected at the "beginning of the creation," LONG before Noah's flood.

Peter goes on in that passage to tell us that the heavens and

CAN I TRUST MY BIBLE?

the earth are going to be destroyed by fire . . . but you never read anywhere that the "heaven" is going to be destroyed. There is a difference between the "heaven" and the "heavens," even if the NKJV translators don't know it. This is why we read in Genesis 2:1-2 that God "finished" the heavens and the earth and rested on the seventh day from all His work which He had "made." "Created" and "made" are two different things. Note this in Genesis 2:3!

So we conclude that the "s" added to "heaven" in Genesis 1:1 is a typical Alexandrian boo-boo. Really clarifies the truth, eh?

> KJV: *"HELL is naked before him, and destruction hath no covering."*
>
> NKJV: "SHEOL is naked before Him, and destruction hath no covering."

Falwell, Nelson, and their buddies are just like the NASV dudes. They just GOTTA get rid of Hell! The reference is Job 26:6.

> KJV: *"The Lord gave the word: great was the company of those that PUBLISHED it"* (Psalm 68:11).
>
> NKJV: "The Lord gave the word: great was the company of those that PROCLAIMED it."

Check your dictionary. To "proclaim" is simply to announce. To "publish" is to proclaim, announce, and to WRITE BOOKS. To "proclaim" the Word is fine . . . but when the proclaimer dies, what he proclaims dies. Ah, but when the Word is PUBLISHED, it lives on, even after the publisher dies! Yes sir, the NJKV really unlocks great spiritual treasures. Here's a doozy in Ezra 8:36 . . .

> KJV: *"And they delivered the king's commissions unto the king's LIEUTENANTS, and to the governors on this side the river . . ."*
>
> NKJV: "And they delivered the king's orders unto the king's SATRAPS, and the governors in the region

294

beyond the River."

Satraps??? SATRAPS? *SATRAPS* ??? What in the name of Alexandria, Egypt is a SATRAP? Any seven-year-old child knows what a lieutenant is . . . but "satrap" will send you to the dictionary. It did me. And, lo and behold, here's the definition: "a petty tyrant." Yeah! That's what the dictionary says! Mm-hmm. The king's orders were delivered to his *petty tyrants*!!! And the NKJV bunch wants me to believe that their translators are great scholars! Yes sir, these "godly scholars" have really clarified that bad ol' AV1611 for us, haven't they? And, by the way . . . were the king's lieutenants and governors on THIS SIDE the river (KJV) or BEYOND the river (NKJV)? YOU figure it out.

Here's some REAL clarity for you.

KJV: *"Wine is a mocker, strong drink IS RAGING: and whosoever is deceived thereby is not wise"* (Prov. 20:1).

NKJV: "Wine is a mocker, intoxicating drink AROUSES BRAWLING and whoever is led astray by it is not wise."

"Arouses brawling" is a REAL improvement over "is raging," isn't it? The only thing is . . . they missed the point. God is not telling us here what strong drink DOES. He is telling us what it IS. Certainly when a person gets drunk they often brawl, but God says strong drink IS raging. Check your dictionary. To BE raging is to be forceful and violent, but it is ALSO "to be spreading unchecked like a disease"! Though alcoholism is NOT a disease, it spreads through a person's body LIKE a disease. It is RAGING. The NKJV boys didn't UNLOCK anything here. They LOCKED UP the truth! I believe my reader can readily see that you cannot trust the NKJV translators, nor can you trust their muddled-up book!

Look what they do to the deity of Christ in Matthew 20:20.

CAN I TRUST MY BIBLE?

KJV: *"Then came to him [Jesus] the mother of Zebedee's children with her sons, WORSHIPPING him, and desiring a certain thing of him."*

NKJV: "Then the mother of Zebedee's sons came to Him with her sons, KNEELING DOWN and asking something from Him."

BLASPHEMY! Just because she KNELT DOWN, does NOT mean she worshipped Him! People kneel before the queen of England, but they don't WORSHIP her! When I drop something from my desk, I kneel down to pick it up, but I am not WORSHIPPING the desk! The NKJV speaks with REAL CLARITY here. It is CLEAR that they purposely took a swipe at the DEITY of my Lord . . . and THAT MAKES ME ANGRY!!!

Ah, but this is not the only time these birds attack my Lord's deity. Look at Acts 4:27, 30 . . .

KJV: *". . . Against thy holy CHILD Jesus . . . the people of Israel, were gathered together . . . and that signs and wonders may be done by the name of thy holy CHILD Jesus."*

NKJV: "Against thy holy SERVANT Jesus . . . the people of Israel were gathered together . . . that signs and wonders may be done through the name of Your holy SERVANT Jesus."

What unmitigated gall! The NKJV translators have slapped Jesus in the face by lowering Him from God's CHILD to God's SERVANT! Anyone who would trust these underhanded culprits HAS ROCKS IN HIS HEAD!!! The word "servant" in Acts 4:27 and 30 in the NKJV is EXACTLY the same in the Communist-backed Revised Standard perversion!

The NKJV people want to stay "good buddies" with the religious crowd . . . so in MANY PLACES they have used the EXACT

SAME renderings as found in the Revised Standard perversion. Not only that . . . but they also want to keep a close kinship with Mother Rome, so they have "Catholicized" it, too. Watch this . . .

> KJV: *"Blessed ABOVE women shall Jael the wife of Heber the Kenite be, blessed shall she be ABOVE women in the tent."*
>
> NKJV: "Most blessed AMONG women is Jael, the wife of Heber the Kenite; blessed is she AMONG women in tents."

The text is Judges 5:24. We all know that in Luke 1:28, Mary of Nazareth is said to be blessed AMONG women, not ABOVE them. The Catholics don't like it, but it's there anyway. However . . . the NKJV compromisers (Who wouldn't DARE change Luke 1:28 to say Mary is blessed ABOVE women?) have stepped in to protect Mary and changed Judges 5:24 so that Jael, the wife of Heber the Kenite, is blessed AMONG women. Shades of Mariolatry! The NKJV "scholars" want to keep the pope happy! This is a wicked and purposeful twisting of the Scripture, for the Hebrew word meaning "among" is NOT the word meaning "above."

> Look at I Corinthians 15:55 . . .
>
> KJV: *"O death, where is thy sting? O GRAVE, where is thy victory?"*
>
> NKJV: "O death, where is thy sting? O HADES, where is your victory?"

The word should NOT be hades! It should be GRAVE! The NKJV boys are making Hell (which is the English Translation of *Hades*) the same as the grave . . . EXACTLY as the Jehovah's Witnesses teach it!!! Not only do the NKJV people want to be "buddies" with the rotten National Council of Churches and the old Roman Mother of Harlots . . . but they also want to "buddy" it up with the CULTS!!!

CAN I TRUST MY BIBLE?

Take a gander at I Thessalonians 4:16 . . .

KJV: *"For the Lord himself shall descend from heaven with a shout, with the voice of THE archangel, and with the trump of God: and the dead in Christ shall rise first:"*

NKJV: "For the Lord Himself will descend from heaven with a shout, with the voice of AN archangel, and with the trumpet of God. And the dead in Christ will rise first."

How many archangels are there? The REAL Bible says there is ONE, calling him THE archangel. In Jude 9, he is called Michael, THE archangel. The definite article "THE" means there is only ONE. The dictionary will tell you that the prefix "arch" means "CHIEF" or "PRINCIPLE." The police department only has ONE chief. The local school only has ONE principal. There is only ONE archangel . . . and strangely enough, the NKJV boys have Jude 9 calling Michael THE archangel. Seems they can't make up their minds. Can you trust these men? Is the pope a Baptist?

Check out I John 3:4 . . .

KJV: *"Whosoever committeth sin transgresseth also THE LAW: for sin is the transgression of THE LAW."*

NKJV: "Whoever commits sin also commits lawlessness, and sin is lawlessness."

I ask . . . sin is lawlessness against WHAT? GOD'S LAW, pal, that's what! The NKJV boys leave it a little vague, eh? REAL clarity!

KJV: *"For the wrath of God is revealed from heaven against all ungodliness and unrighteousness of men, who HOLD the truth in unrighteousness . . . Who CHANGED the truth of God INTO a lie . . ."* (Romans

1:18, 25).

NKJV: "For the wrath of God is revealed from heaven against all ungodliness and unrighteousness of men, who SUPPRESS the truth in unrighteousness . . . Who EXCHANGED the truth of God for the lie" (Romans 1:18, 25).

Thomas Nelson, Jerry Falwell, and their pals have once again joined hands with the modernist promoters of the Revised Stinking Version. The RSV also disagrees with God's REAL Bible and uses "suppress" instead of "HOLD" and "exchanged" for "CHANGED." There is a total difference between SUPPRESSING and HOLDING . . . and the NKJV boys (like their modernist pals) have taken the guilt from wicked men who CHANGED THE TRUTH OF GOD INTO A LIE . . . and made them innocent victims who were deceived by some outside force and merely EXCHANGED the truth of GOD for "the"(?) lie. Seems to me the words "suppress" and "exchanged" have been inserted to cover the wickedness of the RSV and the NKJV translators who actually DID change the truth and who actually DO hold the truth in unrighteousness!

Watch the NKJV "scholars" change John the Baptist's words to please the Charismatic crowd . . .

> KJV: *"I indeed baptize you with water unto repentance: but he that cometh after me is mightier than I, whose shoes I am not worthy to bear: he shall baptize you with the Holy Ghost, and WITH fire:"* (Matt. 3:11).

> NKJV: "I indeed baptize you with water unto repentance, but He who is coming after me is mightier than I, whose sandals I am not worthy to carry. He will baptize you with the Holy Ghost and fire." (Matt. 3:11)

CAN I TRUST MY BIBLE?

The Pentecostals and all other Charismatics love to preach from this text and "prove" by it that when they get "the baptism," they are also getting the FIRE OF GOD. If my reader will open your Bible and look at the verse JUST BEFORE John's statement, you will find "FIRE," which means "FIRE" . . . you know, *FLAME*. If you will note the verse that FOLLOWS John's statement, you find "FIRE" . . . unquenchable "FIRE" . . . you know, *HELL-FIRE*. There is no such thing as "the baptism of the Holy Ghost and fire."

John simply knew that some people in that crowd would get saved and be baptized with the Holy Ghost on the day of Pentecost. He knew that the rest of that crowd would NOT get saved. When they died, they would be baptized by Jesus Christ in HELL-FIRE.

Of course, I can hear the Charismatics holler, "Well, what about the cloven tongues of FIRE at Pentecost?" You misquoted it, dearie. Look at it.

And there appeared unto them cloven tongues LIKE AS of fire, and it SAT UPON each of them (Acts 2:3).

Notice TWO things. The cloven tongues were NOT fire . . . they were LIKE AS of fire, and they weren't BAPTIZED in the cloven tongues . . . the cloven tongues SAT UPON them!

The NKJV has pleased the Charismatics also, by making Eve "comparable" to Adam, rather than a help MEET for him. In the REAL Bible, we read, *"And the Lord God said, It is not good that the man should be alone; I will make an HELP MEET for him"* (Gen. 2:18). I touched on this back in chapter 1, but I want to go a little further here. The word "help" here is a noun. The word "meet" is an adjective. "Help," as a noun, means *"one who helps another."* "Meet," as an adjective, means *"suitable."* "Suitable" means *"that which fulfills or completes a given purpose."*

As I pointed out in chapter 1, man is not complete without a wife. God does a wonderful thing when He gives a man a good wife. However, the NKJV has covered this truth and made up a LIE by not translating the passage correctly. Look at it. "And the Lord God said, It is not good that man should be alone; I will make him a helper COMPARABLE to him."

"Comparable" means Eve was put on the SAME LEVEL with Adam, thus denying the Bible truth that the husband is the HEAD of the wife and that she is to be ruled by him (Eph. 5:23; Gen, 3:16). Anyone who is acquainted with the Pentecostal-Charismatic types knows that the WOMEN run the "show" in that movement. The women rule the homes, and they rule the churches. There are more women preachers in the Charismatic movement than there are in any other religious system. Those Pentecostal women are not about to submit to their husbands. They LOVE the "New" King James perversion. Notice Genesis 5:2 . . .

> KJV: *"Male and female created he them; and blessed them, and called THEIR name Adam."*

> NKJV: "He created them male and female, and blessed them and called them Mankind in the day they were created."

How do you like THAT? In the beginning, God established a form that He wanted followed on earth . . . that when a man and a woman married, the woman would take the MAN'S name for her own. Ah, but the "great, godly scholars" who slapped together the NKJV have flung such a practice back in God's face! But then, WHAT'S NEW? The Pentecostal-Charismatic women preachers have been throwing God's Word back in His face for nearly a hundred years.

> KJV: *". . . Jesus came . . . preaching . . . And saying, The time is fulfilled, and the kingdom of God is at hand: repent ye, and BELIEVE THE GOSPEL" (Mark 1:14-15).*

CAN I TRUST MY BIBLE?

NKJV: "Jesus came . . . preaching . . . and saying, The time is fulfilled, and the kingdom of God is at hand. Repent and believe IN the Gospel."

Nobody ever got saved believing IN the Gospel! Lots of people believe IN the Gospel, but they are as LOST as they can be. You must believe THE GOSPEL to be saved! Can you trust the translators and the backers of the NKJV? Yeah . . . about as much as you can trust a robber who takes your money at gunpoint to mail the money back to you.

And speaking of money . . . take a look at I Timothy 6:10 . . .

KJV: *"For the love of money is THE root of ALL EVIL . . ."*

NKJV: "For the love of money is A root of ALL KINDS of evil."

These NKJV guys are so smart; they know more than GOD does. Since they can't figure out how the love of money could possibly be THE root of ALL evil, they CORRECT GOD by making the love of money A root (one of MANY) of ALL KINDS of evil. There's a time of judgment coming. I wouldn't want to be in the shoes of the NKJV translators, backers, and lovers when they get REPROVED by God for tampering with His holy Word! At that time, He will label them for what they are . . . LIARS!

ADD thou not unto his WORDS, lest he reprove thee, and thou be found a LIAR (Prov. 30:6).

I could go on and on, showing you the wicked attack the NKJV makes on the TRUE Word of God . . . but we need to finish up with our unveiling of the rottenness of the NKJV so we can get to the rottenness of the NIV. Let me show you how Nelson, Falwell, and their bedfellows have tried to cover their tracks with this travesty that they have the nerve to call a Bible. II Corinthians 2:17 . . .

KJV: *"For we are not as many, which CORRUPT the word of God . . ."*

CAN I TRUST MY BIBLE?

NKJV: "For we are not, as many, PEDDLING the word of God."

The NKJV people KNOW they have CORRUPTED the Word of God, but since the MONEY from the sales of their nefarious book is so good, they must COVER their sin by kicking out the word "CORRUPT" and replacing it with "PEDDLING." However . . . in so doing, they have actually TOLD THE TRUTH. The dictionary says to peddle is to "SELL small articles." Certainly a book is a "small article." They are selling a book and CALLING it a Bible. But, bless their pea-pickin' hearts, they are RIGHT when they speak of themselves and say, "We are not as many, PEDDLING the Word of God." What they are selling is NOT the Word of God!

And by the way . . . the New World Translation of the so-called Jehovah's Witnesses ALSO corrupts the Word of God by sticking the word "peddling" in II Corinthians 2:17, EVEN AS THE NKJV CORRUPTERS HAVE DONE! But, then, what's to surprise us? Anyone who has read the rotten translation of the J.W.'S knows that they have kept the word "hell" out of it. I have counted twenty-three times where the NKJV has kicked the word "hell" out, and replaced it like the J.W.s as "hades." Birds of a feather DO flock together, don't they? There are many kinds of Alexandrians, but they ALL agree on ONE thing. They are ENEMIES of the blessed, old AV1611 King James Bible.

Can you trust the NKJV people? Yeah . . . about as much as you can trust the mobsters of gangland to tell you where they buried Jimmy Hoffa.

Now let us turn our attention to the perversion that is fastly gaining ground among "fundamentalists," so they can join together with the ecumenical hodge-podge of "Christians" INTERNATIONALLY (that's a Madison Avenue term for "ONE-WORLD" . . . you know, as in "antichrist" . . . Revelation 13:8). I speak of course, of the NEW INTERNATIONAL VERSION,

CAN I TRUST MY BIBLE?

published and copyrighted by the INTERNATIONAL Bible Society, otherwise known as the Zondervan Bible Publishers (Just drop into your local Zondervan bookstore and see how hard it is to get your hands on a King James Bible!).

Beneath their declaration of copyright (which, like the NKJV and ALL other Alexandrian bibles, is an admission that their words are NOT God's words), it says, "the NIV text may be quoted and/or reprinted up to and inclusive of 1,000 verses without express written permission of the publisher, providing the verses quoted do not amount to a complete book of the Bible nor do the verses quoted account for 50% of the total work in which they are quoted."

I'll be safe then. They won't be able to sue me because I won't be quoting a thousand verses. And if I had planned to, I would stop at 999 because of what comes next on the same page. If a person DOES quote over a thousand verses, he is told by Zondervan, "Notice of copyright must appear on the title or copyright page of the work as follows: Scripture taken from the HOLY BIBLE, NEW INTERNATIONAL VERSION, copyright 1973, 1978, 1984 International Bible Society. Used by permission Zondervan Bible Publishers."

I would stop at 999 because I ABSOLUTELY REFUSE to call the NIV the HOLY BIBLE!!!!!!! It is HOLEY (full of HOLES), but it is NOT holy, nor is it a BIBLE. It is a shameful counterfeit piece of shabby translating, and it needs to be labeled as such. Its cover calls it a "Holy Bible," and in the preface, it is called "Holy Scriptures," yet its Translation Committee says on page xi of the preface, "Like all translations of the Bible, made as they are by imperfect man, this one undoubtedly falls short of its goals."

Since the NIV admittedly "falls short" of perfection, it most certainly is NOT a Holy Bible, nor is it Holy Scriptures! These Alexandrians would agree that even though the original manuscripts" were penned down by "imperfect man" they were PERFECT . . .

CAN I TRUST MY BIBLE?

but true to their humanistic Alexandrian philosophy, they cannot believe that God could produce a PERFECT TRANSLATION by using imperfect men. As we shall see, the NIV is a LONG way from perfect. I have already shown you some of the NIV's imperfections, poor translating, and untruths. Let's look at some more. I said a month ago the NIV is HOLEY (full of HOLES). I want you to see some of the portions that they have ripped completely out of the New Testament alone.

There is a HOLE where Matthew 18:11 ought to be. They left out the entire verse which says, *"For the Son of man is come to save that which was lost."* Brazenly, the NIV "scholars" have cut out the VERY PURPOSE for which our Saviour came to this world.

There is a HOLE where Matthew 23:14 ought to be. The verse is not there. In the REAL Bible it says, *"Woe unto you, scribes and Pharisees, hypocrites! for ye devour widows' houses, and for a pretence make long prayer: therefore ye shall receive the greater damnation."* The crafty NIV translators have omitted the verse which condemns the sham of religious leaders and teaches that there will be degrees of torment in Hell where ALL religious leaders go when they depart this life.

There are HOLES in Mark chapter 9 where the NIV boys decided to soften Hell a bit by slicing out verses 44 and 46. In GOD's Bible they read, *"Where their worm dieth not, and the fire is not quenched."*

This makes the NIV more acceptable than that nasty, old AV1611. The television and radio audiences like it better. Ask Charles Stanley and Chuckie Swindoll if it ain't so.

There is a HOLE where Mark 15:28 ought to be, which is a slap in the face of the Lord Jesus because it refers to His fulfillment of Isaiah 53:12. In the REAL Bible, it says, *"And the scripture was fulfilled, which saith, And he was numbered with the transgressors."*

CAN I TRUST MY BIBLE?

But, so what? If you're brazen enough to chop out whole sections of His Word in spite of the solemn warning in Revelation 22:19 . . . what's a little ol' slap in the face?

There is a HOLE in Acts chapter 8 where verse 37 ought to be. The Ethiopian eunuch has been given the Gospel by evangelist Philip. When the eunuch spots water deep enough in which to be baptized, he says in verse 36, ". . . *See, here is water; what doth hinder me to be baptized?*" In the REAL Bible, we have verse 37, which says, ". . . *And he answered and said, I believe that Jesus Christ is the Son of God.*"

I can see why the NIV bunch cut this verse out. They have to make it fit the way THEY do it in their churches. All they want to do is add to their membership. Who cares whether they "believe with all their heart" and are genuinely saved? Just get 'em on the church roll. Don't bother them with personal questions . . . just DUNK 'EM and tell 'em now that they've "joined the church," they'd better plunk lots of moola in the plate!

Yep, the NIV is a HOLEY bible all right! It has plenty of HOLES where entire verses ought to be. I've only shown you a few. My reader will also find lots of HOLES where complete sentences and many words have been chopped out. We will also see that many phrases and words have been supplanted with poorly translated phrases and words to mutilate the truth.

In Genesis 1:1, the NIV has done the same thing that the NKJV did . . . adding an "s" to the proper "heaven," to obscure the truth of Satan's causing the earth to become without form and void and to become flooded with water after God had so beautifully CREATED the heaven and the earth. As I pointed out when discussing the NKJV, the ONLY things CREATED between Genesis 1:3-31 were the SOULS of man and animals. God had to MAKE their bodies from the sea and the earth, and God had to MAKE the earth over by bringing those things which had already been CREATED in Genesis

1:1 BACK TO USEFULNESS. The REAL Bible shows that God both CREATED and MADE during the six days from Genesis 1:3-31. The NIV LIES.

> KJV: *"And God blessed the seventh day, and sanctified it: because that in it he had rested from all his work which God created and MADE"* (Gen. 2:3).

> NIV: "And God blessed the seventh day and made it holy: because on it he rested from all the work of CREATING that he had done."

To create is to make something from nothing. To make is to build or form from existing materials. The NIV LIES.

Here's some Bible mutilation that weakens the work Jesus did on the cross.

> KJV: *". . . when he had BY HIMSELF purged OUR sins . . ."* (Heb. 1:3)

> NIV: "After he had provided purification for sins . . ."

What happened to "BY HIMSELF"? What happened to "OUR" sins? The NIV bunch seem unaware that the book of Hebrews is addressed to SAVED people. Jesus didn't simply PROVIDE purification for sins in general . . . He has ALREADY purged MY sins, and He did it BY HIMSELF on the cross!

The entire book of Galatians was written by Paul to negate the false doctrine that had been brought into the churches of Galatia by "troublesome bewitchers" (Gal. 1:7; 3:1) who were teaching that a person can stay saved only by doing human works . . . which is ridiculous when we are saved by GRACE. To be saved by GRACE and then to be persuaded by a false prophet that you have to follow the law in order to maintain your salvation is to make Christ of none effect to you . . . and to put you in a position where you are fallen from the doctrine of salvation by GRACE. Since grace IS grace, it is impossible to ever lose your salvation and return to the lost

CAN I TRUST MY BIBLE?

condition you were once in, but the NIV teaches that a saved person can be lost again.

> KJV: *"Christ is become of none effect unto you, whosoever of you are justified by the law; ye are fallen from grace"* (Gal. 5:4).

> NIV: "You who are trying to be justified by the law have been ALIENATED from Christ; you have fallen away from grace."

Hey! WAIT A MINUTE! When a person is ALIENATED from Christ, he is LOST! This is the condition of a person BEFORE he is saved . . . not AFTER he is saved and gets mixed up doctrinally! Writing to the Colossian Christians, Paul reminded them of their condition BEFORE they were saved. *"And you that were sometime ALIENATED and enemies in your mind by wicked works, yet NOW hath he reconciled"* (Col. 1:21).

Writing to the Ephesian Christians, Paul reminded them of their position BEFORE they were saved. *"That at that time ye were without Christ, being ALIENS"* (Eph. 2:12).

No saved person can EVER be ALIENATED from Christ (John 10:28; Rom. 8:35-39)! This is false doctrine! Of course, I expect this kind of stuff to show up in a "bible" that has men on its Translation Committee who believe they are working their way to Heaven . . . such as Pentecostals, Campbellites, Lutherans, Mennonites, Methodists, Anglicans, Nazarenes, and Wesleyans.

Can you trust the NIV? Hardly. It is the word of MEN . . . NOT the Word of God. In a wicked and vile manner, it waters down and denies the deity of Christ over and over again. Look at Luke 2:33, regarding the Lord Jesus . . .

> KJV: *"And Joseph and his mother marvelled at those things which were spoken of him."*

> NIV: "The child's FATHER and mother marveled at

what was said about him."

If Joseph was Jesus' father, Mary was immoral, the Bible is wrong when it says she was a virgin at His conception, and Jesus is a SINNER!

KJV: *"Great is the mystery of godliness: GOD was manifest in the flesh"* (I Tim. 3:16).

NIV: "The mystery of godliness is great: he appeared in a body."

QUESTION: WHO appeared in a body? The NIV doesn't say. The proponents of the NIV say it is obvious that it is God since the word "godliness" is used. BALONEY! The word "godliness" is used many times in Scripture in reference to Christians (I Tim. 2:2, 10; 4:7; II Peter 1:6, etc.). Christians are not God! The NIV translators even put a little footnote at the bottom of the page with reference to the word "he" in I Timothy 3:16 as follows: "Some manuscripts: *God.*"

Right here, these translators show their true colors. The "some manuscripts" they speak of are the ANTIOCHAN manuscripts of the Received Text! But these hoodlums are ALEXANDRIANS and ENEMIES of the Word of God. They will stick with their corrupt ALEXANDRIAN manuscripts and will RIP AWAY at the deity of my Saviour! If "some manuscripts" say "'God," why don't they put the word "God" in there? HUH? BECAUSE THEY ARE ALSO ENEMIES OF JESUS CHRIST, and they will purposely take their sly little swipes at His deity!

In Acts 13:28-34, Paul is preaching to the Jews about the resurrection of the Lord Jesus Christ. Look at Acts 13:33 . . .

KJV: *"God hath fulfilled the same unto us their children, in that he hath raised up Jesus again; as it is also written in the second psalm, Thou art my Son, this day have I begotten thee."*

CAN I TRUST MY BIBLE?

NIV: "What God promised our fathers he has fulfilled for us, their children, by raising up Jesus. As it is written in the second Psalm, You are my Son, today I HAVE BECOME YOUR FATHER."

When you read the NIV and compare Luke 2:33 with Acts 13:33, you will be led to believe that JOSEPH fathered Jesus through Mary; then God BECAME Jesus' Father on the day of the resurrection. Good grief! What kind of a mangled mess is this?

The wording of the KJV is correct: "This day have I begotten thee." In that the Father raised Jesus from the dead, He brought Him forth in resurrection glory from the WOMB OF THE GRAVE . . . but He did not BECOME Jesus' Father at the resurrection! The Father called Jesus His son THREE YEARS BEFORE THE RESURRECTION at the Jordan River when Jesus was baptized by the Baptist!

Now when all the people were baptized, it came to pass, that Jesus also being baptized, and praying, the heaven was opened, And the Holy Ghost descended in a bodily shape like a dove upon him, and a voice came from heaven, which said, THOU ART MY BELOVED SON, in thee I am well pleased (Luke 3:21-22).

The NIV crooks pull this same thing again in Hebrews 1:5 in a direct slam at the deity of the Lord Jesus. If God BECAME Jesus' Father at the resurrection, then He was NOT His Father before that moment. HERESY! The crooks ignore the fact that in the very next verse it says, *"When he BRINGETH IN THE FIRSTBEGOTTEN INTO THE WORLD, he saith, And let all the angels of God WORSHIP him"* (Heb. 1:6).

WHEN did God tell the angels to worship Jesus? WHEN HE BROUGHT HIM INTO THE WORLD THROUGH THE VIRGIN WOMB!!! The NIV is nothing but one-world, ecumenical, God-

CAN I TRUST MY BIBLE?

defying TRASH!

In Acts 16:31, the NIV took out "Christ," which is attacking His Messiahship. Messiah is GOD in human flesh. They took out "Christ" in Romans 1:16, making the Gospel only the Gospel, but NOT the Gospel of CHRIST! In Romans 9:5, they left "Christ" in the verse; then they put a footnote at the bottom of the page making "Christ" someone different than GOD! In the KJV, it equates Christ and God as being the same Person.

In comparing the KJV to the NIV, I lost count of how many times the NIV omitted the word "Christ" and the word "Lord" when it is attached to Jesus. Only a blind fool could miss what these wicked men are doing. Over and over and over again, they stab at the deity of my Saviour. Look what they've done with the most famous verse in all the Bible . . . John 3:16:

> KJV: *"For God so loved the world, that he gave his ONLY BEGOTTEN SON, that whosoever believeth in him should not perish, but have everlasting life."*

> NIV: "For God so loved the world that he gave his ONE AND ONLY SON, that whoever believes in him should not perish, but have eternal life."

There goes the DEITY of Jesus Christ, and there goes my SALVATION! "ONE AND ONLY SON" is not the same as "ONLY BEGOTTEN SON"!!! *Only begotten* is the VIRGIN BIRTH. I became a son of God the moment I received the Lord Jesus Christ as my own personal Saviour (John 1:12), but I am NOT virgin born. Jesus ALONE is God's ONLY BEGOTTEN Son! To call Him "ONE AND ONLY" Son is to take away His deity. Let me show you why . . .

John 1:12 TELLS me I am God's son. Let's say that there was a great, big, monstrous, gigantic nuclear explosion, and everybody in the world was killed except me (even all the truly born-again people). Then, on earth, I would be God's ONE AND ONLY son.

CAN I TRUST MY BIBLE?

Right? Right. DOES THAT MAKE ME DEITY? Absolutely not. Neither does the "ONE AND ONLY SON" in the NIV's abominable mangling of John 3:16 make Jesus Christ DEITY!

If the NIV's rendition of John 3:16 is right, I HAVE NO SALVATION, and neither do you, dear reader. If Jesus is God's ONE AND ONLY Son, then there is NO WAY you or I can be a son of God! If we are not God's children, WE ARE GOING TO HELL! Not only that, but the NIV's John 3:16 makes I John 3:1 a LIE! Look at it.

Behold, what manner of love the Father hath bestowed upon us, that we should be called the SONS OF GOD . . .

This would be an out-and-out FALSEHOOD if Jesus is God's ONE AND ONLY Son as the NIV perverters would have us believe. If Jesus is God's ONE AND ONLY Son, then I CAN'T be a son of God. There goes my salvation.

The REAL Bible calls Jesus God's ONLY BEGOTTEN Son in John 1:14, 18; 3:16, 18; and I John 4:9. The NIV changes it to "ONE AND ONLY" every time. At the bottom of the page each time, they have a foot note that says, "Or only begotten." My reader might ask, "Then, why don't they just put 'only begotten' in the passage and be done with it?"

The answer is obvious. They are willfully attacking the deity of the Lord Jesus Christ! I have heard NIV lovers say, "But the NIV doesn't take out ALL references to Christ's deity."

Of course not. The devil isn't dumb. If it did THAT, lots of people who DO believe in His deity would not buy it or use it. Too bad they can't see that if the NIV put only ONE question mark over His deity, it ought to be shunned.

Look what they've done to Christ's blood.

KJV: *"In whom [Christ] we have redemption*

CAN I TRUST MY BIBLE?

> *THROUGH HIS BLOOD, even the forgiveness of sins"* (Col. 1:14).
>
> NIV: "In whom we have redemption, the forgiveness of sins."

What happened to "THROUGH HIS BLOOD"??? Sneaky crooks. NIV lovers argue, "Well, they've left the blood in OTHER places!" Big deal. WHY DID THEY TAKE IT OUT, HERE?

Let me show you how they have mutilated one of the places where they left the blood in.

> KJV: *". . . Thou art worthy to take the book, and to open the seals thereof: for thou wast slain, and hast redeemed US TO GOD by the blood . . ."* (Rev. 5:9).
>
> NIV: "You are worthy to take the scroll and to open its seals because you were slain, and with your blood you purchased MEN FOR GOD."

They have taken away US being redeemed TO God! Jesus' blood did MORE than purchase men FOR God . . . it redeemed ME TO God ! !!

And John MacArthur has the gall to call these NIV translators "godly men of demonstrated academic repute"! Look what these "godly scholars" did to the very next verse in Revelation 5 . . .

> KJV: *"And hast made us unto our God KINGS and priests: and we shall reign on the earth"* (Rev. 5:10).
>
> NIV: "You have made them to be a KINGDOM and priests to serve our God, and they will reign on the earth."

REAL Scholarship, eh what? A KINGDOM does not reign. Priests do not reign. KINGS reign! Can you trust the NIV? . . . about as much as you can trust the Koran.

While we're in the book of Revelation, get a gander at how

CAN I TRUST MY BIBLE?

the NIV promotes the false idea of a UNIVERSAL SALVATION. Of the New Jerusalem, we read in Revelation 21:24 . . .

> KJV: *"And the nations of them WHICH ARE SAVED shall walk in the light of it: and the kings of the earth do bring their glory and honour into it."*
>
> NIV: "The nations will walk by its light, and the kings of the earth will bring their splendor into it."

Apparently the NIV boys took "WHICH ARE SAVED" out because they have the "international," "one-world," "universal" idea that EVERYBODY is going to Heaven. Boy, are they in for a shock! In fact, they are in for some more shocks. One of them is going to be shocked when they face the One who said, *". . . If ANY MAN* [including the NIV Translation Committee] *shall ADD unto these things, God shall ADD unto him the plagues that are written in this book: And if ANY MAN* [including the publishers of the NIV] *shall TAKE AWAY from the WORDS of the book of this prophecy, God shall TAKE AWAY his part out of the book of life, and out of the holy city, and from the things which are written in THIS BOOK"* (Rev. 22:18-19)!!!

Of course, the Alexandrian NIV boys have the mistaken idea that they are NOT ADDING TO or TAKING AWAY FROM the Word of God, because they believe that the ONLY Word of God that ever existed was the "original manuscripts." They don't believe that God said He would KEEP and PRESERVE His WORDS forever. Remember Psalm 12:6-7? Look at it again in the REAL Bible; then we'll look at it in the NIV.

> KJV: *"The WORDS of the Lord are pure WORDS: as silver tried in a furnace of earth, purified seven times. THOU shalt KEEP them, O Lord, THOU shalt PRESERVE them from this generation FOR EVER."*
>
> NIV: "And the words of the Lord are flawless, like

silver refined in a furnace of clay, purified seven times. O Lord, you will keep US safe and protect US from such people forever."

How's THAT for a sample of Alexandrian trash? Seems that since God is not going to KEEP nor PRESERVE His WORDS forever . . . and since His WORDS were lost when the "original manuscripts" disintegrated . . . they need not fear the consequences of Revelation 22:18-19. Fools.

Take one more look at the NIV mutilation of the book of Revelation . . .

> KJV: *"Behold, I come QUICKLY"* . . . *"behold, I come QUICKLY"* . . . *"Surely I come QUICKLY"* (Rev. 22:7, 12, 20).
>
> NIV: "Behold, I coming SOON" . . . "Behold, I coming SOON" . . . "Yes, I coming SOON" . . .

There is a BIG difference between coming QUICKLY and coming SOON. Jesus was not talking about how SOON He would come. He was talking about HOW FAST He would come when it was time. Think about it. The dictionary says *soon* means "promptly" or "in a short time." Now, a thousand years is as ONE day to the Lord (II Pet. 3:8), but it is not to us mortal earthlings. To say "I am coming SOON" to US, would be misleading; because to US, a thousand years is anything but SOON. Jesus would not mislead us. The Alexandrians would . . . but not the only begotten Son of God. He said three times on the last page of His Bible, "I come QUICKLY!"

This is in line with I Corinthians 15:51-52 . . .

> *. . . We shall not all sleep, but we shall all be changed, In a MOMENT, in the TWINKLING OF AN EYE, at the last trump: for the trumpet shall sound, and the dead shall be raised incorruptible, and we shall be*

changed.

A "moment" is QUICKLY. The "twinkling of an eye" is QUICKLY. Not long ago, the General Electric Company timed the TWINKLING OF AN EYE with their sophisticated electronic equipment. The "twinkling" of an eye is that little flash of light that someone sees on your eyeball when you move your eyes or turn your head and pick up the reflection of a nearby light. If memory serves me correctly, the General Electric Company said the "twinkling" of an eye is 1/30th of a second. Now THAT is quick! If they are correct, Jesus is coming SO FAST . . . He could come thirty times in one second!!!

Though I believe NOW Jesus is coming soon, His coming was NOT soon when John was on the isle of Patmos in A.D. 90. Ah, but when it is time . . . He is coming QUICKLY as He said in HIS Bible! Can you trust the NIV? . . . exactly as much as you can trust Mary of Nazareth to get you into Heaven.

Watch the "godly" NIV "scholars" blaspheme Jesus in Matthew 5:22 . . .

> KJV: *"But I [Jesus] say unto you, That whosoever is angry with his brother WITHOUT A CAUSE shall be in danger of the JUDGMENT . . ."*

> NIV: "But I tell you that anyone who is angry with his brother will be subject to JUDGMENT."

"Brother" is understood as ANYONE in the human race (a "brother" in humanity). The JUDGMENT is the WHITE THRONE Judgment where sinners are cast into the Lake of Fire. The verse goes on to speak of HELL fire. By taking out "WITHOUT A CAUSE," the NIV translators condemn JESUS to judgment and Hell because He was often angry (Matthew 21:12; 23:1-36; Mark 3:5). This is nothing short of BLASPHEMY!

Watch them once again rip the crown of deity from the

CAN I TRUST MY BIBLE?

precious head of the King of Kings. Look at Luke 23:42 . . .

KJV: *"And he [the dying repentant thief] said unto Jesus, LORD, remember me when thou comest into thy kingdom."*

NIV: *"Then he said, Jesus, remember me when you come unto your kingdom."*

One of the two books is LYING here. Either the thief called the Saviour "Lord," or he called Him "Jesus." You might ask, "What difference does it make?"

Plenty. WHICH did he say? If the thief said "Lord," we know he recognized His deity . . . but that is not necessarily so if he said "Jesus." There were other men named Jesus in those days (Col. 4:11), even as there are many Mexicans named Jesus today. Besides that, Scripture says the devil has a "Jesus" (II Cor. 11:3-4, 14-15). It also says there is only ONE Lord (Eph. 4:5).

So, you see, it is VERY important whether the thief called Him "Lord" or "Jesus"! Like I said, either the KJV is lying, or the NIV is lying. Does my reader have a problem deciding WHICH one is lying and WHICH one is telling the truth? Let me help you a little further. There was a wicked, satanic, humanistic philosophy that cropped up about a hundred years after our Lord was crucified known as *Doceticism*. Proponents of this vile cult taught that Jesus WAS the son of Joseph (even as the NIV says in Luke 2:33), but that He BECAME deity the moment He was baptized by John the Baptist. They said He REMAINED deity until the moment He was nailed to the cross. When the nails pierced His hands and feet, the deity left Him. He was just "Jesus" until His baptism; then He became "Lord Christ." When the Roman nails pierced His hands, the "Lord Christ" left Him, and He was just "Jesus" again.

When the NIV ripped the word "Lord" from the mouth of the dying thief, and replaced it with "Jesus," its translators showed

CAN I TRUST MY BIBLE?

that they are in agreement with the *Docetic* cult! The NIV LIES! The thief called the Saviour "LORD"! He also knew that the bleeding Man next to him was the KING! He wanted Him to remember him when He came into His KINGDOM! Can you trust the NIV? You can trust it to cast doubts on the deity of our Lord, but you CANNOT trust it to tell you the TRUTH!

Let me show you another BALD-FACED LIE in the NIV. Look at Mark 1:1-3...

> KJV: *"The beginning of the gospel of Jesus Christ, the Son of God; As it is written in the PROPHETS, Behold I send my messenger before thy face, which shall Prepare thy way before thee. The voice of one crying in the wilderness, Prepare ye the way of the Lord, make his paths straight."*

> NIV: "The beginning of the gospel about Jesus Christ, the Son of God. It is written in ISAIAH THE PROPHET: I will send my messenger ahead of you, who will prepare your way—a voice of one calling in the desert, Prepare the way for the Lord, make straight paths for him."

My reader, please note that in the REAL Bible it says, *"As it is written in the PROPHETS..."* In the counterfeit NIV it says, "It is written in ISAIAH THE PROPHET..." I double-ding-dong-dead-dog DARE the NIV translators, the International Bible Society, anyone in the Zondervan family, Charles Stanley, Chuckie Swindoll, OR ANY OTHER TWO-FACED ALEXANDRIAN to show me where it says in Isaiah, "I will send my messenger ahead of you, who will prepare your way"!!!!!!!!!!!!!!!!!!

Mark 1:2 is a DIRECT quotation from Malachi 3:1!!!!! The KING JAMES BIBLE is *correct* when it says the "prophets" because MALACHI wrote, *"Behold, I send my messenger before thy face, which shall prepare thy way before thee..."* ISAIAH wrote, *"The voice of him that crieth in the wilderness, Prepare ye the way of the Lord..." (Isa. 40:3)!!!*

Mark 1:2 is a quote from MALACHI. Mark 1:3 is a quote from ISAIAH. One and one equal TWO. That's plural. Yes sir, the REAL Bible says "PROPHETS"! When the rotten NIV quotes Isaiah as saying, "I will send my messenger ahead of you who will prepare your way..." It is an out-and-out BALD-FACED, DEVIL-INSPIRED LIE!!! That's how much Bible the NIV crowd knows! The devil is a deceiver (Rev. 12:9), and he is the FATHER of a LIE (John 8:44)! ALL Alexandrian "bibles" are chock-full of LIES! Therefore, we know WHO is behind them!

Satan HATES the TRUTH. The REAL Bible IS truth (John 17:17)! The devil DESPISES the King James Bible because there are NO lies in it... and it is the ONLY English Bible that could enter the New Jerusalem. Look what God says about His heavenly city,

And there shall in no wise enter into it anything that defileth, neither whatsoever worketh abomination, or MAKETH A LIE... (Rev. 21:27).

Do you SEE that? I have shown you LIES and UNTRUTH in the NASV the "Living(?) Bible(?)," the NKJV and the NIV. NONE of those books could ever pass through the gates of the New Jerusalem, but the precious old AV1611 KING JAMES BIBLE is God's TRUTH! It IS truth! It never MAKES a lie! It qualifies to enter the beautiful heavenly city! I ask my reader... WHY HANG ONTO A "BIBLE" THAT COULD NOT QUALIFY TO ENTER GOD'S HOLY CITY??? ALL Alexandrian "bibles" are corrupt because they come from corrupt manuscripts. If you've been an Alexandrian up till now, throw your rotten so-called bibles away; get yourself a good old AV1611 KING JAMES BIBLE... read it, study it, believe it, and live it! Stay with the ONE AND ONLY English Bible that is the perfect, infallible, inspired, inerrant Word of God!

CAN I TRUST MY BIBLE?

The KJV is not the "best" translation . . . it is the ONLY translation. When you say "best," that means that there are others that come close. NO! NO! All the others are Satan's counterfeits! They contain UNTRUTHS and LIES!

David of Old said emphatically to God, "I have STUCK unto thy testimonies" (Psalm 119:31). God's "testimonies" are His SCRIPTURES . . . all sixty-six books. So I say with David, "Lord, I have STUCK unto your King James Bible!" I'm sticking with it because it is the pure, perfect, inspired, infallible, inerrant Word of God! And the beauty of it all is that I can HOLD IT IN MY HAND! I can SEE it! I can READ it! I can STUDY IT! I can PREACH it! As I have shown throughout this book, the Alexandrians HAVE no Bible. They all agree that the only inspired, inerrant, infallible Word of God that ever existed was the papyrus and ink of the "original manuscripts." They cannot hold their Bible in their HANDS. They cannot SEE it. They cannot READ it. They cannot STUDY it. They cannot PREACH it.

Just as God calls His Word by other descriptions like His "testimonies," He also uses such words as His "statutes," His "precepts," His "commandments," His "way," His "judgments," and His "law." I want to show you something . . . then I will draw this book to a close. David wrote under the inspiration of the Holy Spirit,

I will Keep thy statutes . . . (Psalm 119:8).

I will DELIGHT MYSELF in thy statutes . . . (Psalm 119:16).

I have inclined mine heart to PERFORM thy statutes alway, even unto the end (Psalm 119:112).

The Alexandrians tell us that the only STATUTES of God that ever existed were the "ORIGINAL" statutes . . . that the ONLY inspired Word of God that ever existed was the fiber and ink in the

CAN I TRUST MY BIBLE?

papyrus of the "ORIGINAL MANUSCRIPTS." They say this in spite of the fact that Paul wrote under the inspiration of the Holy Spirit in Romans 15:4 and told us that *"For whatsoever things were written aforetime were written for OUR learning, that WE through patience and comfort of the SCRIPTURES might have hope."*

Let the Alexandrians remain in their stubborn and willful ignorance. I believe GOD. Therefore, I HAVE the SCRIPTURES in my possession AT THIS MOMENT! My inspired, inerrant, perfect, preserved-through-translation King James Bible has ALL of God's statutes from Genesis 1:1 through Malachi 4:6 and from Matthew 1:1 through Revelation 22:21!

How can I KEEP God's statutes, DELIGHT MYSELF in God's statutes, and PERFORM God's statutes always, even unto the end if I do not HAVE God's statutes? The Alexandrians are ignoramuses.

David also wrote under the inspiration of the Holy Spirit,

Thou hast commanded us to KEEP thy precepts diligently (Psalm 119:4).

. . . I will MEDIATE in thy precepts (Psalm 119:78).

Therefore I ESTEEM all thy precepts concerning all things to be right . . . (Psalm 119:128).

Now, pray tell . . . how can I KEEP God's precepts, MEDITATE in God's precepts, and ESTEEM all of God's precepts concerning all things to be right unless I HAVE God's precepts in my hands so I can SEE them, READ them, and STUDY them? How can I esteem them to be RIGHT concerning ALL things if I don't HAVE the PERFECT, INSPIRED, INERRANT, Word of God IN MY HANDS? The Alexandrians tell us there is no such thing as a perfect translation. THEN WHAT I HAVE IN MY HANDS IS NOT THE WORD OF GOD! It is NOT right concerning ALL things. Since my King James Bible is a translation, how can I ever come to

CAN I TRUST MY BIBLE?

the conclusion that God's precepts are right in ALL things?

I COULDN'T, if the Alexandrians were right. But since they are WRONG and the Bible is RIGHT in ALL things (even when it says that WE indeed have the Scriptures TODAY), I CAN keep God's precepts. I CAN meditate in God's precepts. I DO esteem ALL of God's precepts concerning ALL things to be RIGHT. No Alexandrian can say that! They don't HAVE God's precepts. Alexandrians are dipsticks.

David also wrote under the inspiration of the Holy Spirit,

I will RUN THE WAY of thy commandments . . . (Psalm 119:32).

. . . O let me NOT WANDER FROM thy commandments (Psalm 119:10).

. . . I do not FORGET thy commandments (Psalm 119:176).

How can I RUN THE WAY of God's commandments if I do not HAVE His commandments to READ so I can LEARN what the "way" of His commandments IS? It would be impossible for me to WANDER FROM God's commandments and FORGET God's commandments if I did not HAVE them in my possession! Alexandrians don't have the sense God gave a soda cracker!

David also wrote under the inspiration of the Holy Spirit,

I have CHOSEN the way of truth . . . (Psalm 119:30).

. . . QUICKEN thou men in thy way (Psalm 119:37).

How could I possibly CHOOSE the way of truth if I do not HAVE the way of truth in my hands to CHOOSE? How can God QUICKEN me in His way if His way is DEAD itself? Alexandrians are dorks.

David also wrote under the inspiration of the Holy Spirit,

CAN I TRUST MY BIBLE?

I will praise thee with uprightness of heart, when I shall have LEARNED thy righteous judgments (Psalm 119:7).

With my lips have I DECLARED all the judgments of thy mouth (Psalm 119:13).

Seven times a day do I PRAISE thee because of thy righteous judgments (Psalm 119:164).

I would like for these "intelligent," "educated," "godly" Alexandrians to tell me how I can LEARN God's righteous judgments if I do not HAVE His righteous judgments IN MY HANDS so I can READ them and STUDY them that I might LEARN them. How can I read, study, and learn something that DOES NOT EXIST? Moreover . . . how can I DECLARE *all* the judgments of God's mouth if I do not HAVE *all* the judgments of God's mouth? Jesus said man shall live by EVERY word that proceedeth out of the mouth of God (Matt. 4:4). I believe JESUS. He made it quite plain that I HAVE every word!

How can I join David and PRAISE the Lord seven times a day because of His righteous judgments if I have never SEEN OR HEARD His righteous judgments so I know what they say? Alexandrians are ninnies.

David also wrote under the inspiration of the Holy Spirit,

Blessed are the undefiled in the way, who WALK in the law of the Lord (Psalm 119:1).

Horror hath taken hold upon me because of the wicked that FORSAKE thy law (Psalm 119:53).

The law of thy mouth is BETTER unto me than thousands of gold and silver (Psalm 119:72).

Those who keep themselves undefiled as they live this earthly life and those who WALK in the law of the Lord are BLESSED. I

CAN I TRUST MY BIBLE?

want to be blessed of the Lord. How can I, if I have no law of the Lord in WHICH to walk? I would like for the Alexandrians to explain to me how they can walk in the law of the Lord, since according to them, the law of the Lord disintegrated thousands of years ago.

How can the wicked FORSAKE God's law if they have no idea what it says? Since the "original manuscripts" are long gone, and since according to the brilliant Alexandrians, the "original manuscripts" were the ONLY inspired law of God . . . why should David be horrified? The wicked have no law to read, hear, then forsake.

How can God's law be BETTER unto me than thousands of dollars in gold and silver IF NO SUCH LAW EXISTS? I can SEE gold. I can SEE silver. I can HOLD gold in my hands. I can HOLD silver in my hands. If I cannot HOLD God's law in my hands, how in the name of common sense can it be BETTER unto me than gold and silver? Alexandrians are loony.

David also wrote under the inspiration of the Holy Spirit,

. . . I HOPE in thy word (Psalm 119:81).

STABLISH thy word unto thy servant . . . (Psalm 119:38).

Thy word have I HID IN MINE HEART, that I might not sin against thee (Psalm 119:11).

According to Romans 15:4, what David wrote in the Psalms was for MY learning so that through comfort of the Scriptures I might have HOPE. How can I HOPE in God's Word if I do not HAVE God's Word to READ and STUDY? I cannot HOPE in something I have never SEEN or HEARD! How is God going to STABLISH His Word unto me? Is He going to come down from Heaven and TALK to me? Hardly. He doesn't NEED to. The Alexandrians are goofy. I HAVE God's Word to read and to study so that He CAN stablish it to me!

CAN I TRUST MY BIBLE?

How can I hide God's Word in my heart (which is to memorize it) if I do not HAVE His Word to HOLD IN MY HANDS and to read so that I can memorize it? Alexandrians are simpletons.

David also wrote under the inspiration of the Holy Spirit,

My zeal hath consumed me, because mine enemies have FORGOTTEN thy WORDS (Psalm 119:139).

How SWEET are thy WORDS unto my taste! yea, SWEETER THAN HONEY to my mouth! (Psalm 119:103).

The entrance of thy WORDS giveth LIGHT... (Psalm 119:130).

I have chosen some verses which refer to God's WORDS also. The Alexandrians say that God never said He would preserve and keep His WORDS . . . just the "message" or the "concepts" of His Word. Then they double-mouth by turning around and saying the ONLY inspired, inerrant Word of God that ever existed was in the fiber and ink of the "original manuscripts." Talk about being loony!

How could David's enemies FORGET God's WORDS if they had not first HAD God's WORDS to learn? How can WORDS be sweeter than honey to me unless I HAVE those WORDS? God says the entrance of His WORDS gives light. Since I HAVE those WORDS, I have light FROM those WORDS to teach me that I HAVE those WORDS! Since the Alexandrians DO NOT have those WORDS (by their own admission), it is evident that they are in DARKNESS! In fact, they give us MANY reasons to conclude that they are in DARKNESS. They can say of themselves, *". . . we wait for LIGHT, but behold OBSCURITY; for BRIGHTNESS, but we walk in DARKNESS"* (Isa. 59:9). As long as they believe that the only inspired Scriptures that ever existed were the "original manuscripts" and grope along with their NIVs and their NKJVs, and

CAN I TRUST MY BIBLE?

their NASVs, etc., and/or continue to "correct" the WORDS in the King James Bible, they will STAY in darkness!

Alexandrian preachers, teachers, and college professors who stand before their hearers "using" the King James Bible and "correcting" it by tampering with the WORDS are THIEVES AND PERVERTERS. They better pay heed to what God says about such wickedness.

> *Therefore, behold, I am against the prophets, saith the Lord, that STEAL MY WORDS every one from his neighbour. Behold, I am against the prophets, saith the Lord, that use their tongues, and say, HE [God] SAITH . . . and cause my people to err by their LIES . . . ye have PERVERTED the WORDS of the living God . . .* (Jer. 23:30-32, 36).

Go ahead, you Bible "correctors"! Stand behind your pulpits and in your classrooms, and LIE to your hearers, telling them that GOD SAYS something different than what you will find on the pages of the King James Bible! Go ahead. Assert YOUR authority over the Book. Have fun while it lasts, pals, because there's a day coming when you will stand eyeball-to-eyeball with the God who will charge you with, "YE HAVE PERVERTED THE WORDS OF THE LIVING GOD"!!!

In this same 23rd chapter of Jeremiah, God says, "He that HATH my word, let him speak my word *faithfully*" (Jer. 23:28).

Yes, Lord . . . we who HAVE Your Word and BELIEVE it will speak it faithfully! Thank You for giving it to us in 1611, and keeping it alive and well while the PERVERSIONS come and go. Thank You for commanding the New Testament church to teach our converts ALL things whatsoever You have commanded us; You made sure we HAVE the Book so that we can do it (Matt. 28:20)!

Thank You, Lord, for commanding us to PREACH THE

CAN I TRUST MY BIBLE?

WORD (II Tim. 4:2); You made sure we HAVE the Word so that we can preach it (inspite of what the "intelligent," "educated," "godly" Alexandrians tell us!).

Precious, wonderful Lord . . . You told us through John's pen that You want us to WALK IN TRUTH (II John 4; III John 4). The Alexandrians CANNOT walk in truth because they don't HAVE IT, but how I thank You that Your Word is truth (John 17:17) . . . and that You have given us Your perfect, inspired, infallible truth in the King James Bible! We who HAVE it and BELIEVE it can please You by walking in TRUTH.

Dear reader, you ask, "CAN I TRUST MY BIBLE?" IF you have an AV1611 KING JAMES BIBLE, you can! Yes! Yes! A thousand times, yes! In fact . . . 810,697 times, YES!!!

This book of the law shall not depart out of thy mouth; but thou shalt meditate therein day and night, that thou mayest observe to do according to all that is written therein: for then thou shalt make thy way prosperous, and then thou shalt have good success (Joshua 1:8).